FUNNY BOY

FUNNY BOY

THE RICHARD HUNT BIOGRAPHY

JESSICA MAX STEIN

RUTGERS UNIVERSITY PRESS

New Brunswick, Camden, and Newark, New Jersey
London and Oxford

Rutgers University Press is a department of Rutgers, The State University of New Jersey, one of the leading public research universities in the nation. By publishing worldwide, it furthers the University's mission of dedication to excellence in teaching, scholarship, research, and clinical care.

Library of Congress Cataloging-in-Publication Data

Names: Stein, Jessica Max, author.
Title: Funny boy : the Richard Hunt biography / Jessica Max Stein.
Description: New Brunswick : Rutgers University Press, 2024. | Includes index.
Identifiers: LCCN 2023034088 | ISBN 9781978836716 (hardback) |
    ISBN 9781978836723 (epub) | ISBN 9781978836730 (pdf)
Subjects: LCSH: Hunt, Richard, 1951–1992. | Puppeteers—United States—
    Biography. | Television producers and directors—United States—Biography. |
    Gay men—United States—Biography. | Muppet show (Television program)
Classification: LCC PN1982.H8366 S75 2024 | DDC 791.5/3092 [B]—dc23/20231003
LC record available at https://lccn.loc.gov/2023034088

A British Cataloging-in-Publication record for this book is available from the British Library.

References to internet websites (URLs) were accurate at the time of writing. Neither the author nor Rutgers University Press is responsible for URLs that may have expired or changed since the manuscript was prepared.

∞ The paper used in this publication meets the requirements of the American National Standard for Information Sciences—Permanence of Paper for Printed Library Materials, ANSI Z39.48-1992.

rutgersuniversitypress.org

For Andrée Cornelia, my Jersey girl

CONTENTS

PART V

FUNNY BOY

Spring, 1970

Richard Hunt was getting pretty desperate. He'd strung together a series of short-lived gigs in the year since graduating high school. Most of his close friends were off at college. The Beatles had broken up. The world was changing rapidly, but Hunt was stuck in suburban New Jersey, reading about it all in *The New York Times*. Though bucolic Closter lay just across the George Washington Bridge from the city, New York seemed increasingly unreachable, as did Hunt's dream of making it there as a performer.

But if Hunt couldn't find a performing outlet, he would make one. He was always "on." Aimlessly driving around with friends, he might break into a full-on imitation of a radio soap opera, improvising the music, the voiceover narration, six different characters in dramatic conversation. He acted in community theater and summer stock. He turned a two-week babysitting stint for a family of rowdy boys into a neighborhood archery tournament, swashbuckling like an Errol Flynn character, with dozens of children gleefully chasing him down the street, sailing arrows at his head. He put on puppet shows at children's birthday parties, and toured briefly with a marionette troupe—mocking that, too, for his friends, using his long limbs to pantomime a marionette's awkward shamble.

He had seemingly tried everything. He dropped by the CBS studios where his parents' friend Cosmo "Gus" Allegretti puppeteered at popular children's program *Captain Kangaroo*, starring Bob Keeshan as the grandfatherly title character. But when Hunt pitched the idea of working there, Allegretti heatedly warned him to steer clear of Keeshan, who as an employer was a far cry from the beloved Captain. "Gus went nuts," says Hunt's mother Jane. "He took Richard outside and said, 'Get out of here! Bob Keeshan is the nastiest man in the world, and I don't want you anywhere near him.'" So much for that idea. He dutifully applied at ABC, where his father clerked in the sports department, but nothing came of that either.

He half-heartedly prepared weather reports for disc jockey Bruce "Cousin Brucie" Morrow at Top 40 station WABC. "My qualifications were absolutely zilch," Hunt recalled. "I used to stick my hand out the window, feel what was going on out there, and write the report." He gave up about four months in. "I decided to make a career of resting," he said. "I quit, went home and watched Muppets."

Hunt watched a lot of television in those days. He would sprawl restlessly on the family room couch, staring at the screen, trying to ignore his mounting worries about where he might work—and by extension get out of the house, get out of Closter, explore a personal life in the city, make some real money, grow as a performer, reach a sizeable audience. One day, however, he realized he might be staring the solution right in the face.

"I had grown up watching the Muppets," Hunt said. Jim Henson's distinct, zany puppetry had caught his eye since elementary school. "I'd drop anything to watch them. I thought they were weird." When Hunt was a kid, in front of the family's black-and-white television, you really had to keep an eye out for the just-emerging Muppets. They made almost whack-a-mole appearances, popping up intermittently on variety and talk shows, from *The Today Show* to *The Tonight Show*, *Jimmy Dean* to *Ed Sullivan*, slowly building up their audience. Or you might glimpse the Muppets in a commercial; even there, the puppets had an electric, mirthful irreverence that made them mesmerizing. Hunt was also bowled over by the technical finesse behind the silly façade, as Henson brilliantly experimented with the tricks of television to make his puppets seem more *alive* than had ever been seen before. Like Hunt, the Muppets seemed to take very seriously the fine art of being very funny.

But now, the Muppets seemed on the verge of something bigger. They were finishing up their first year of *Sesame Street*, which drew in a surprisingly wide audience of all ages for a children's educational public television program with puppets. Hunt recognized in the Muppets a kindred sense of wild creativity, a place where his well-honed humor might be useful, especially as they found a more stable niche on television and seemed poised for further expansion. Why not hitch his wagon to that rising star? "I thought, oh, this might be a good way to do something," Hunt said. "I thought, 'The Muppets are nuts!'—*that* I could tell right away. I felt I would fit right into that."

So one afternoon in Manhattan, his confident, mischievous, gap-toothed grin disguising any nervousness he might have felt, Hunt strolled over to a pay phone, dropped in his dime, and cold-called the Muppets.

"Hello, Henson Associates," said the receptionist.

"Hi," Hunt said amiably. "I'm a puppeteer, can you use me?"

He was just eighteen years old.

Initially, Hunt figured the Muppets would be just another temporary gig, a side trip en route to a real career. "I thought—'cause I was going to be an *actor*—I thought, 'Well, I'll just do this for a couple of years, and it will be good, because, giving something to the children . . .' and twenty years later here I am."

PART I

Hunt in Closter, New Jersey, around 1960.

CHAPTER 1

Jersey Boy

T HE ENERGY DRIVING Hunt's phone call to the Muppets was born
of three things: personality, family, and urgent necessity.

Richard Henry Hunt—given his father's first name and his mother's
family name—was born in the Bronx, New York at Fitch Sanitarium on
August 17, 1951.

He was an entertainer from infancy. "He loved performing," recalls his
mother Jane. "From the time he was able to talk, he would just be himself, and put on a costume, and do a little act, and amuse us all." Though
barely old enough to toddle into the elevator of their Fordham Road
high-rise, in the hilly Bronx enclave of University Heights, Hunt stud-
ied all the people as they rode down the nine flights to the lobby. "He
loved to watch," she says. "He'd back up into a corner, and stand there
all the way down, just observing, not saying a word, just watching and
listening." She credits this sheer fascination with people as "the basis of
his talent."

"I came from a very ultra-liberal, supportive, loving family," said
Hunt. "We were very poor." His father Richard Bradshaw Hunt clerked
at CBS in the scenic design department, while his mother Jane Henry
Hunt took care of Hunt and his "Irish twin" Kathleen "Kate" Bradshaw
Hunt, sixteen months his senior. But in their hearts, his parents lived to
perform. A family friend got a typical first impression of them years
later in the New Jersey house: he opened the front door to find Richard

Bradshaw and Jane strolling arm in arm down the stairs, singing the title track from the movie musical *42nd Street*: "Come and meet those dancin' feet/On the avenue I'm taking you to." Hunt described his parents as "frustrated actors—I'm the only one who really made a living in it, as we all assumed I would."

Seeing his interest in their beloved field, Hunt's parents encouraged his talent from the very beginning, exposing him to the performing world—and he took to it like a plant to light. When he was about four, his parents took him and Kate to a Sunday matinee of *The Nutcracker* at the New York City Center of Music and Dance; afterward, star ballerina and family friend Diana Adams showed them around backstage. Hunt was "beside himself" looking at the costumes and the dressing rooms, becoming wide-eyed and silent as they walked to the subway with Adams and New York City Ballet founder George Balanchine. That night, after Hunt had been put to bed, his parents heard him sobbing in his room. His father went in to check on him. "He was reliving that thing from beginning to end," says his mother. "He just kept saying, 'It was so beautiful. It was so beautiful.'"

At around seven years old, Hunt made a gutsy attempt at a television debut, a prescient predecessor to cold-calling the Muppets. His parents scored "the hottest ticket in television": seats for Richard and Kate in the forty-seat children's audience, or Peanut Gallery, of *The Howdy Doody Show* at New York's NBC studios. It was every kid's dream. Hunt's baby boomer generation "wanted more than anything in the world to be in the Peanut Gallery," writes humorist Dave Barry. "The Peanut Gallery consisted of real live kids just like us." And these "real live kids" weren't just sitting passively in the audience, but singing the theme song and accompanying host Robert "Buffalo Bob" Smith on commercial jingles for the likes of Twinkies and Wonder Bread, their smiling faces beamed across the country.

This brief taste of the spotlight, however, only whetted Hunt's appetite. Just before the show ended, Hunt jumped out of his seat and ran over to the host. Jane, sitting with the adults, held her breath—"I was like, 'Oh my God, oh my God'"—as Hunt tugged on Smith's coat and said, lisping slightly from missing teeth, "I'm a magician. I want to do a magic thhrick." "I don't think we have time," Smith replied dismissively, but Hunt had already drawn the prop from his pocket—and finished his trick just as the show went black.

"He had that personality from the time he was born," says Kate. "He used to sit on the potty and sing: 'Take my hand, I'm a stranger in paradise.'"

By Hunt's eighth birthday, their two-bedroom Bronx apartment felt tight. Jane and Richard Bradshaw's family had expanded to five kids: Kate, Richard, Lyn (1955), Adam (1957), and Rachel (1960) on the way. The family found a house in the rapidly developing suburbs, moving to Closter, New Jersey in September 1959, just in time for Hunt to start third grade.

Though just fifteen miles from Manhattan, at first Closter seemed like a ghost town, its barely 8,000 residents a shock after the density of the Bronx. Here, the loudest sounds at night came from the crickets and distant freight trains. Closter got its name from being cloistered in the high cliffs of the Palisades above the Hudson River, which reminded its seventeenth-century Dutch settlers of a *klooster*, a place of sacred contemplation. Alternatively, local myth credits the name to early resident Frederick Closter. But the *klooster* concept applies more to Hunt's story: For the rest of his life, he would have a refuge at 52 Closter Dock Road.

The 1914 three-bedroom colonial, roughly 1,300 square feet, was a tight squeeze for the big family. "We had the two boys in one tiny little room, and three girls in the other room, and Daddy and me in the other one," Jane says. "And that was it!" The downstairs had a small living room, family room, and eat-in kitchen.

However, the house amply compensated for its size in sheer outdoor room and freedom. Their 1/3 acre lot was ringed with trees, with a playhouse for the kids and a barn that served as a garage. The property abutted a multiacre town park, Memorial Field, with ballfields and a playground, seemingly an extension of their own yard. The Hunt kids could run across Memorial Field to Tenakill Elementary just beyond it. They could always find someone to play with, and even commandeer the playground by claiming to own the field. ("That's our house right there!" Rachel would tell disbelieving kids.) Or they could wade and catch crawfish in Tenakill Brook, which ran through the woods on the other side of their house. "We just had all that space," says Kate. "And we were out all the time, till after dark." When dinnertime came, Jane would stand on the side porch and call the kids home in her melodious singsong: "Kath-lee-een! Kathleen Braaadshaw! Riii-chard! Richard Hennnry!"

Every weeknight at 7:30, after Richard Bradshaw came home from clerking at CBS, the family would squeeze in around the wooden kitchen table, often joined by friends. Dinner at the Hunt house was a production, with a British tinge as pleased their Anglophile father: tall candles, cloth napkins, and heated plates, and food that was often new to their friends such as artichokes, eggplant, and Hollandaise sauce, alongside meat from the Closter butcher. The kids had to finish their dinner before asking formal permission to leave the table, yet often sat with an empty plate to stay in the conversation.

After dinner, rather than watching television or going their own separate ways, the family often entertained each other. Performing was the family's shared game, their private language, instilled in the kids so early it was hard to tell whether it was nature or nurture. "We were always prepared, any of us, to get up and perform in some way," says Rachel. The family used the wide staircase landing as their stage, taking turns declaiming to an audience in the living room below, a perfect setup for a dramatic entrance, a scene, or a dance routine such as the young Hunt's flashy Fred Astaire impression. When the family visited friends, their parents would sometimes coach them in a show tune, practicing in the station wagon on the drive over; the friends would open the door to find the Hunt family singing on their front steps, in synchronized multipart harmony.

The family also harmonized strikingly on the hymns at St. Andrews Episcopalian Church in nearby Harrington Park. (Jane had been raised Lutheran, while Richard Bradshaw was Roman Catholic; Episcopalian was their happy medium.) They usually arrived late, but that just made for a better entrance, walking up the center aisle to sit in the front row, the girls in dresses, tights, and Mary Janes, and the boys dressed up like little Prince Charles in shorts and suspenders. Hunt served as an altar boy in middle school, showing an uncharacteristic solemnity and reverence for the role.

However, the Hunts were more likely to appear at church if they were between shows at the Elmwood Playhouse, a local community theater that was arguably the family's true spiritual home, housed in a former Lutheran church. The one-hundred-seat venue opened in nearby Nyack, New York shortly after the Hunts moved to Closter; Jane starred in the venue's first musical, *Finian's Rainbow*, in 1960. "I got the lead and been here ever since!" she told a local newspaper nearly a half century later.

At the Elmwood Playhouse, Hunt found fertile ground for his incipient talent. The actors' kids ran around in a pack; they played in the tiny front yard, their de facto domain, and roamed everywhere from the bird's-eye perch of the light loft to the dressing rooms down in the basement, even taking to the stage to imitate the adults. "We did our own drama," says Lyn. "We would say, 'Be happy. Be sad.'" Their parents recruited them to build and strike sets, fetch props, run errands. This is how you cultivate genius, like Albert Einstein hanging around his father's lab: learning first by observing, low-stakes, then participating, little by little. Play matures into work; yet the childlike, joyful element remains. Most importantly, says Lyn, Elmwood helped plant the seed of possibility: "Just seeing that you could go into that field—you could become an actor."

But Hunt could meet role models right in his living room. His parents' college friend Gus Allegretti, who performed on *Captain Kangaroo*, would put on puppet shows at the Hunt's birthday parties, hiding behind the piano as his puppet stage. Hunt's parents took him to the studio to watch Allegretti work, as well as to the set of *Kukla, Fran and Ollie*, where puppet mastermind Burr Tillstrom inspired Hunt to improvise scenes between his stuffed animals, holding up one in each hand. The kids might find Broadway tickets in their Christmas stockings; Hunt adored Julie Andrews in *Camelot*, a tale which became bound up in public memory with the halcyon Kennedy era.

And when his parents threw parties, they entertained their guests in both senses of the word. The Hunts became known in the neighborhood for their Memorial Day parties, where the whole family performed. The gatherings piggybacked off the town's annual festivities in Memorial Field, beside their house: a parade; a day of booths, food, and live music; and a dazzling fireworks display after dark. After dinner, the Hunts would put on a show, bringing out their living room routines for a larger crowd. Their yard filled with picnickers, friends from Closter, Elmwood, and the Bronx mixing pleasantly on the lawn, everyone keeping an eye on the children as they ran around.

In later years Hunt would find his childhood reflected in James Agee's idyllic prose poem "Knoxville: Summer 1915." The narrator, "successfully disguised to myself as a child," lives in a loving, lower-middle-class neighborhood of big families in turn-of-the-century houses with porches, yards, and trees, and longingly evokes summer evenings lying out with his family in the backyard, the air thick with the buzzing of locusts, the stars twinkling into view—a nostalgic portrait of an era just before it ended.

Shortly after Hunt began sixth grade at the Village School, CBS trimmed its staff, and his father was laid off. This exacerbated the family's money worries, as well as Richard Bradshaw's drinking. "He was a very sick alcoholic," says Kate. "It was around that time that things got really bad." Richard Bradshaw had long enjoyed his martinis at lunch, his glass of straight gin in the evenings. He would sometimes fall asleep on the bus home from work, and Jane would pick him up at the end of the line. Now he was out of work, and the family was out of money, afraid of losing their home. Jane joined the workforce after years of being a homemaker, selling curtains in a department store, using her acting skills to pretend she enjoyed the job. But even that wasn't enough. Reluctantly, Jane looked to her hometown for help.

Jane Henry (b. November 16, 1928) had never quite felt comfortable in small-town, class-conscious Marietta, Ohio. "My mother spent a lot of time making me presentable, doing things like straightening out my hair or pulling on my dress on the street when we would run into one of the grandes dames of Marietta," she recalls. "I never felt like I was good enough to be out there in front of people." The Appalachian town on the West Virginia border had its charms: the scenic confluence of two rivers; a lively, brick-lined downtown; a celebrated liberal arts college. Yet Jane's Scots-Irish family had been in Ohio for at least three generations, and she was glad to break with tradition. She went away to college for a year, but wound up back home, living with her parents Charles and Evelyn, and pursuing her acting dreams in the theater department of Marietta College. There she met Richard Bradshaw Hunt.

Richard Bradshaw Hunt (b. December 6, 1925) was from the exciting land of New York, where he had been raised in the Bronx by his mother and grandmother, Kathleen Bradshaw Hunt and Addie "Josephine" Bradshaw. He had been awarded a Purple Heart for his service in Germany in World War II, then gone to Marietta on the GI Bill. Certainly Richard Bradshaw had his worrisome, brooding moments. And he drank, like Jane's father did. But she found herself taken with this effusive actor, who shared her love of the stage. They would exchange quips and barbs, one-upping each other; they would study their lines together, dropping into dialogue or song at a moment's notice. With him, she *was* good enough. They had similar dreams of the future—and great chemistry. When at twenty-one she got pregnant with Kate, it was a simple decision: the couple moved to New York. She wouldn't have to parade her shame before the grandes dames, and he could look for work as an actor, or in the larger performance field. And the plan worked out for them, more or less—at least until the layoff.

Though Richard Bradshaw had lost his job, in 1962 the Hunts put on a big Christmas in Closter, carrying out all their favorite traditions: singing carols, decorating the tree with strings of cranberries and popcorn, reading Dylan Thomas's "A Child's Christmas in Wales." The kids woke up early Christmas morning and waited eagerly in their beds, having been instructed not to move until their parents were up, prevented from going downstairs by the row of bells their father had strung across the staircase, a makeshift kid burglar alarm. When their father was up and dressed in his robe and slippers, he shook the string, ringing the bells, cueing the kids to gleefully burst out of their rooms and thunder down the stairs to open their presents. Once the living room floor was fully strewn with wrapping, the family gathered in the kitchen for a cozy Christmas breakfast, capped off with the tangerines the kids found in their stockings.

But just after the new year, Jane sat the kids down and broke the news: the family had to split up, for an indeterminate amount of time. Less than a week later she grimly piled the kids into the station wagon and drove over 1,200 miles: first to Marietta, where she dropped off

Hunt and Kate on scholarship at a boarding school run by two of her former professors; then to Minnesota, to leave the three younger children with her sister Marilyn, who already had a baby and a toddler of her own. Hunt's siblings surmise that their father went into rehab during this time. Though the separation was rough for all the Hunt kids, Richard impressed Kate by making "tremendous friends" in Ohio, regaling his classmates with stories of the big city. "All these wealthy people thought he was fascinating, a New York boy in the Midwest." The kids rarely heard from their parents. None of them knew how long their exile from Closter would last.

Just after school let out for the summer in Minnesota, Hunt's little brother Adam came running to their sister Lyn with a new stuffed dinosaur, saying, "Lynnie, look, Mommy sent me this, and there's something for you on your bed." Lyn went into her room, and on her bed—was her mother! Lyn leapt into her mother's arms, exclaiming, "We made it! We endured this time!" Jane and the younger kids drove back across the Midwest, stopping in Marietta for Richard and Kate. "And then we drove back home, and were the Hunts again," Lyn recalls. Regardless of their family troubles, they *were* the Hunts, a tight-knit, idiosyncratic unit—and glad to be reunited. Richard Bradshaw had a new job at ABC as a program controller, working on the budget for new shows.

Hunt started seventh grade at the Village School as if he'd never been gone—but the threat of splitting up again lingered over the family, fueling his drive to provide. "He always knew he was going to be an entertainer," says Kate. "And he always knew he was going to have to take care of the family, from a very young age."

Eager to earn money, Hunt picked up a local paper route, delivering the *Bergen Record* on his bike. One day Hunt's principal called Jane to report seeing a group of local boys follow Hunt along his route, calling him names and dumping his papers into the mud. When his mother confronted him about the incident, she recalls, "He just shrugged it off. 'They're jerks.' He certainly didn't let it stop him from anything." That wasn't his style. Hunt was already an old hand at resilience. His friend Geni Sackson's father likened Hunt to a cork in the water: "You press him down, and he bounces right back up again."

Hunt's middle-school peers could be hard on him, he recounted years later: "To be blatant, my last name's Hunt, and they'd say, 'Hey, Cunt! You asshole, you faggot.' I'd go, 'Why do they do these things?'" He would develop a better understanding over time, especially once he found out that nearly all of the "Original Five" Muppet performers, as he called them—Jim Henson, Frank Oz, Jerry Nelson, Dave Goelz, and himself—had had similar experiences. "We all discovered, the Original Five, all but Jerry were outcasts as kids. We were all taunted and tormented by the rest of the children we grew up with." (Interestingly, Goelz disputes this impression of his childhood. "I was popular, never an outsider or ostracized," he says. But the salient point here is Hunt's perception of himself and his colleagues.)

Hunt believed his childhood peers were responding to a certain energy in him, a seemingly unwarranted exultation. "I was just so excited to be alive. And I thought everybody else would be too. So I was always *there*. And always present, and always at this high-level pitch. I think it's just too much for most people."

Most of the time in middle school, however, Hunt was simply too "excited to be alive" to pay his detractors much attention. "I just stuck to who I was, as dramatic as it may have been," Hunt concluded. "But I had a lot of fun. I laughed my head off as a kid."

Hunt spent his paper route proceeds generously, taking his friends and siblings out for Cokes at Closter's Varsity Diner, sharing his stash of snacks, comic books, and *Mad* magazines. And at Talbot's, the local fabric shop, he bought himself puppets for $5 apiece, one by one, amassing a collection: a king, a queen, a wolf, a devil. He earned a Boy Scout badge for building a puppet stage out of a cardboard refrigerator carton he and Jane rescued from the dumpster of the Closter appliance store and folded into the back of the station wagon. He practiced his craft wherever he could pull together a crowd—at school, after Scout meetings, backstage at Elmwood, at the family's Memorial Day picnics. Even without an audience, Hunt seemed to be always "on," audibly chattering away even after ostensibly going to bed. The family would hear him in the boys' room, improvising voices and punchlines, cracking himself up, his loud laughter ringing through the cozy house.

Hunt in his Northern Valley Regional High School yearbook with classmate Karen Langhorn, 1968.

CHAPTER 2

Making a Career

HUNT WAS BARELY fourteen when he began at Northern Valley Regional High School in fall 1965, but quickly sprang up to six feet tall alongside his classmates. He could be embarrassed about his unruly hair and the gap between his front teeth, but he soon discovered he could please people by making them laugh. "He was just finding himself," says high school friend Geni Sackson. "And he found he was funny. That's a good thing to be."

Hunt soon held court at the noisy center of a vibrant circle of friends, in an overall welcoming environment. Hunt's classmates recall Northern Valley as largely free of the divisions plaguing many U.S. high schools in the late 1960s, despite the school drawing from three adjoining towns—Closter, Haworth, and Demarest—with varying income levels. Hunt's classmate Sean O'Connor calls Northern Valley "a cauldron of classlessness and cultural comingling." Hunt was friendly to everyone, as he had been raised to be. "We're a family that was taught early on to appreciate other people and their stories, that everybody was of value," says his sister Lyn. Hunt's parents took the family into Manhattan for marches with the Congress of Racial Equality, as well as a peace march led by Martin Luther King Jr. in Hunt's sophomore year. Yet even beyond this upbringing and Northern Valley's warm atmosphere, Hunt seemed markedly immune to divisions and cliques, using his humor to connect widely.

In some ways Northern Valley remained firmly in the 1950s. Hunt and his fellow students tried to steer clear of assistant principal Anthony Colantoni, a strict disciplinarian who roamed the halls enforcing the dress code, making sure that girls wore skirts and boys kept their hair short—and who didn't mind yanking on a guy's long hair to make his point. But the school also had an eye for the future, growing rapidly to accommodate its "booming" population: setting up extra classrooms in temporary trailers; expanding its art, film, and music programs; hiring new—sometimes brand-new—teachers, who livened up the place.

One such liberating influence was music teacher and choir leader Gail Poch, a chain-smoking, coffee-swilling beatnik not much older than Hunt and the other self-described "choir geeks" who crammed into his office during free periods. The students never wanted the singing to end, despite rehearsing with Poch every weekday and on Saturdays in the All-County Chorus. ("My wife said I could never conduct a church choir, because I'd be gone every day," Poch jokes.)

Though many would later assume Hunt had advanced training, it was in fact Poch who provided most of his formal—and informal—music education. Hunt enjoyed experimenting with his voice, which Poch describes as an "unsettled" tenor, discovering what he could do with the instrument. Yet Poch taught Hunt not just how to foster his own talent, but how to work as part of an ensemble to elevate the whole group. Poch aimed to give everyone a chance, rotating solos so that no one student stood out. In this noncompetitive environment—a great incubator for Hunt's later collaborations—the students learned not just from Poch, but from each other. Among his peers Hunt was especially generous with his skills, helping his classmates learn harmony. This collaborative attitude was a boon in putting on the school's annual spring musical, again under Poch's direction.

Hunt quickly made a name for himself at Northern Valley by stealing the show in his freshman year musical, Cole Porter's *Kiss Me, Kate*. "Even in that first show, whenever he was onstage, the audience was on their toes," says Poch. "It didn't take him long to figure out who on stage they should be watching." Though first-years usually cut their teeth in the chorus, Hunt had the audience in stitches as one of three competing suitors in the song "Tom, Dick or Harry." There was something eminently watchable about his performing, classmates recall; you never quite knew what he was going to do.

Despite stealing the scene, in drama as in chorus Hunt was very consciously part of an ensemble. The drama club crew became "like a family" due to their constant proximity, recalls classmate Jon Nettinga. From tryouts in February to performances in May, they rehearsed nearly every day after school, adding all-day Saturday rehearsals as they approached opening night.

The artistic stakes for the musical were heightened in Hunt's sophomore year, when Poch brought in a Broadway choreographer to work on *The Pajama Game*. Poch had befriended Gerald "Buddy" Teijelo at a summer stock gig, impressed by Teijelo's work as the dance captain for the Broadway productions of *110 in the Shade* and *Subways Are for Sleeping*. Teijelo's presence at Northern Valley created a *Glee*-like atmosphere. Even the football and basketball players caught the dance craze, encouraged by their coaches and the administration. "We ended up with athletic dancers who could really move, and if they couldn't move he taught them how, and did choreography like you don't see in high school shows," Poch recalls. "That put the show on a whole new level, even though it was done in a gym." Hunt played Vernon Hines, the smooth-singing, knife-throwing second male lead, dancing a soft-shoe with his sister Kate that she recalls "brought down the house."

Northern Valley was a great place for Hunt to grow as a performer. As with his family and at Elmwood, a steady schedule of hard work seasoned with a sense of play, camaraderie, and creativity meant that Hunt was perpetually practicing his craft, amusing himself and whatever impromptu audience happened to be around—gaining skill and ability while having a great time.

Though Hunt thrived in Northern Valley's arts programs, he was a relatively slapdash, slipshod student, his restless temperament ill-suited to hitting the books. This could cause trouble for him at Northern Valley, a rigorous suburban school that required four years of English and math, three of science and history, and offered advanced electives from Shakespeare to speech; most of its students went on to prestigious colleges and universities. Hunt's junior year English teacher Vincent Fondacaro would tease him when he didn't complete his work. "Of course you didn't!" the teacher would exclaim. "It's your right! It's your civil liberty!" Hunt took the teasing good-naturedly, often riffing right back.

Though his grades weren't great, Hunt made himself so known in the classroom that his teachers never forgot him. "You think you're gonna be funny like your brother?" a teacher scolded Rachel a decade later. Hunt treated the classroom like a comedy venue, his classmates a captive audience, testing teachers to see just how far he could stretch them from the lesson. Yet Hunt could also be genuinely interested, his jokes a form of engagement with the material, often keeping the other students absorbed, or at least entertained. Most of Hunt's teachers had strong opinions about him one way or the other. "Those not on his side were either more conservative or more strictly academician," says Poch. "The other teachers were like, 'Well, he's not an A student, but I see he's got a lot of other stuff going for him, and I enjoy him in the class.'" Some teachers recognized Hunt's potential as an intellectual, hidden though it was behind his role as class jester. Hunt was truly eager to expand his mental model of the world, to make connections between ideas—in short, to learn. But that didn't necessarily translate to doing schoolwork.

It's hard to say which is the chicken or the egg: Hunt didn't succeed easily in school so he focused more on performing, or his performing detracted from his academics. He read for pleasure throughout his life, and in high school recommended books to friends such as Frank Herbert's *Dune*, the best-selling mythical science fiction epic. "Fear is the mind-killer," Hunt would quote. But by his junior year, in the competition between school and performing, performing was clearly winning out.

Hunt was by then a known local performer, getting paid for what he enjoyed doing. "When I was about sixteen I realized I could make ten bucks by taking a couple of puppets and making up a story at a birthday party," Hunt said. The neighborhood parents knew him through his babysitting gigs, and Jane spread the word. Hunt mostly improvised his performances, so the friends and siblings he recruited as assistants had to think fast on their feet. "Put Beelzebub on me!" he'd bark. "I need the wolf!" Local twins Matt and Damian Stoddart, three years younger than Hunt, made him a number of puppets: a hand-painted Punch and Judy; a mustachioed fop; a mischievous Scaramouche. (Matt credits

Hunt with kicking off his long career making puppets, which included a number of Muppet connections.)

One routine particularly entertained the kids. Hunt and his helper played one person; the helper stood in front, speaking, his arms hidden under a coat, while Hunt reached through from behind as the speaker's hands. When Nettinga played the narrator, dully demonstrating how to bake a pie, he didn't have to feign surprise and dismay at how "his" hands were behaving. "He starts feeding me. I'm getting plastered by all the food. I had food in my hair, food in my face. I was getting punched by spoons and pies and whipped cream." Hunt made his job easy. "It didn't matter what I did—the kids were hysterical."

As the local kids increasingly clamored for him, Hunt received $25 per party, a veritable fortune for a teenager when the minimum wage was $1.40, babysitting paid around fifty cents an hour, and a routine tip for a week of delivering papers was a mere dime. But for all Hunt's financial precocity, he felt like a kid riding with his mom to the gigs—since he still wasn't old enough to drive in New Jersey.

Hunt's vocal training with Poch accelerated in the elite upperclassman ensemble Modern Choir. He had a quick ear for music, and could sing back a piece after hearing it just once; he had little use for sheet music. Yet Hunt uncharacteristically lost his nerve while trying out for the prestigious upperclassman All-State Chorus; asked to sing back some tones from memory, he froze up, forgot them, and didn't make the cut, grousing about the incident for years afterward.

But forget New Jersey—Hunt's heart had already crossed the Hudson. Hunt and his music friends often took the bus into Manhattan, fueling his career dreams. Hunt, Sackson, Terry Minogue, Glenn Mure, Dale Pfeiffer and others would hang around the recently built cultural mecca of Lincoln Center, seeing shows, harmonizing for the crowds by the fountain, holding court at coffee shops. They'd check out new exhibits at the Museum of Modern Art, watch Bergman or Truffaut movies at the art-house theater. But the best times were open-ended. "We spent a lot of time just wandering around," says Pfeiffer. "Teenagers with no place to go but having a great time."

That spring, rumors circulated that talent scouts from New York were in the audience to see Hunt in Northern Valley's production of

How to Succeed in Business Without Really Trying. It didn't seem impossible: after all, Buddy Teijelo was back, coaching the students through Broadway-caliber choreography; Poch had even wangled costumes from the play's recent Broadway production. Though Poch had chosen the show with Hunt in mind as the rags-to-riches everyman lead character, Hunt was cast as the show's scheming antagonist. Still, Hunt had no problem capturing the audience's attention. "If he couldn't get the lead, he made the side the lead," says Sackson. "He made it hysterical." Minogue agrees: "When he was in the show, he stole the show."

One night a lackluster number, set in a men's washroom, was losing its audience. "Richard, to make up for that, was doing some very funny things," recalls Minogue. "He turned around and pretended to use the urinal on the back wall. He did shaving, he was doing his armpits, he was plucking his eyebrows—whatever it took to get a laugh." Yet Hunt resented the accusation that he was trying to hog the spotlight. "I wasn't trying to upstage," he said. "The scene just wasn't working." Despite his playful attitude, Hunt took even the most local production very seriously. "Other kids may have been doing the school show, but he had a vision for himself," says Sackson. "He was making a career."

The Hunt house was a center of neighborhood activity. "Richard's house was famous," says Sackson. "Everyone knew where it was and everyone went into it." Warm weekends found the front porch crowded with kids in sleeping bags. Hunt liked to hold court at the living room stereo, playing DJ, putting on everything from acapella to Frank Zappa. He knew his friends' tastes and had a knack for luring them outside their preferred genres, turning rock fans onto Broadway tunes and vice versa. He and his friends especially loved the Beatles' *Sgt. Pepper's Lonely Hearts Club Band*, released the summer before his junior year. A typical Sunday found everyone at the Closter house, listening to records, watching television, making fun of everything and laughing.

A big draw of 52 Closter Dock was Jane: barely forty, glamorous and gregarious as she bustled around the kitchen, trying to stretch food for seven people into dinner for ten. "This is where everyone wanted to be, in this silly little house," says Jane. "'Mother, can so-and-so stay over?' 'Yes dear, have her call.'" Hunt's friends loved his family's ceremonial dinners, with the candles and cultured conversation, as well as the ever-present humor. After dinner, Richard Bradshaw generally took up residence in his living room armchair, drink in hand, reading *The New York Times*. Sometimes he would turn on the charm when the teenagers came in late at night, a dramatic raconteur in his Brooks Brothers pajamas and robe, telling stories of his war days. Other times he could seem more distant. "Do I know you?" he would ask kids he had known for years. Often he was "too drunk to talk," says Jane, slumped drowsily in the armchair as the conversation played out around him.

Hunt and his friends tended to hang out in big groups, pairing off within the group rather than dating much one-on-one. He clowned around with girlfriend Joan Hueneman, turning their shared root beer float into a "hilarious" parody of 1950s romance, classmate Tana Reiff recalls: "He was doing this whole shtick like they were at an old-school soda fountain: leaning down to sip out of his straw, with his head right next to her head." While Hunt didn't frequent school dances—which students usually attended in groups rather than pairs—as a junior he attended the senior prom, alongside his sister and graduating friends.

The summer before his senior year, Hunt briefly dated classmate Alexa Munson. Interestingly, her family had lived at 52 Closter Dock decades before the Hunts; her mother had been born in the room he now shared with Adam. Friends remember the couple making out very publicly at a friend's graduation party, almost as if putting on a show. Hunt later made light of the relationship to O'Connor: "He implied that they only had one sexual experience, and he joked that while he was having the experience, he was thinking about some football player." Decades later, another Closter friend asked Hunt if he had been aware of his sexuality at Northern Valley. "Oh yeah, I was even back then," Hunt replied.

That summer Hunt discovered a landscape he would cherish for the rest of his life: the picturesque seashore of outer Cape Cod, Massachusetts. He traveled there that summer and the next as a mother's helper for a Closter family, and returned home driven to provide the Hunts a similar experience. "He loved it so much, he came back and said, 'I'm going to make sure my family one day gets to have a real vacation,'" Rachel recalls. The dream was one more reason to succeed as a performer.

Hunt's horizons expanded further that summer when at long last he turned seventeen and got his driver's license. He made fun of his mother's big blue station wagon, but loved to fill it with friends and go out for a spin. "We didn't even really go anywhere," says Nettinga. "We just drove around, because we could." It would become a lifelong pastime.

By Hunt's senior year—1968—the sixties had come to Closter. Northern Valley changed its dress code, allowing girls to wear pants and boys to grow their hair long; Hunt's cowlicky curls grew bushy and wild, and everybody started wearing blue jeans. Yet despite feeling freer at Northern Valley, Hunt was more than ready to move beyond it. Furthermore, with Poch having left to teach at Temple University, Hunt had lost much of his Northern Valley performing family, as well as his now-graduated friends like Sackson and Mure who had fanned out across the northeast.

Hunt turned his energy to directing the senior class play, a good-natured spoof of their teachers and fellow students, modeled after the comedy-variety show *Laugh-In*. He came up with most of the material, helping his classmates perfect their impressions. "He taught everybody in that group how to be funny," says Minogue. Hunt also widened his circles of friendship, playing basketball in Memorial Field with athletic classmates like John Potterton, whose father "Coach" Potterton led many school teams. He took O'Connor to the Closter Plaza strip mall to watch the "greasers" drag race in the parking lot. "Richard would stand up, pump his fist and go, 'Impressive! Very impressive,'" O'Connor recalls. "And he could get away with it. Richard could talk to anybody."

Hunt found a haven in senior film class with Rodney Sheratsky, a free-spirited mentor to many students. Sheratsky provided his students a yearlong crash course in classic movies—and wonderfully unfettered access to the school's Super 8 cameras. "Film—is *film*," Hunt parodied Sheratsky years later. "What, Bruce? You want to film a riot? Go right ahead!" Hunt had loved the movies since childhood, and was delighted to have free rein to experiment with the form. One afternoon Hunt's friend Ernie Capeci was hanging out in his front yard: "All of a sudden this car came by with this guy hanging off of it with a movie camera, going 'Faster! Faster!' at this little blond kid riding a bicycle—it was Richard shooting a movie of [his brother] Adam, riding a bicycle down the street."

But Poch's absence was painfully obvious when it came time for the spring musical, *Damn Yankees*. Poch had chosen the play specifically for Hunt to play the devil-in-disguise antagonist, a role for which his talents were wickedly suited. However, Hunt had never gotten along with Poch's replacement, George Strauser. "He hated Richard," says Hunt's sister Lyn. "He wanted to pick his favorites, and start his regime." The two particularly disagreed about how to produce the musical, for which each had a specific vision. To everyone's surprise, Strauser cast Nettinga as the devil, consigning Hunt to the chorus. Hunt and the teacher had heated arguments in rehearsal, as the other students sat hushed and wide-eyed. Hunt was particularly "livid" when Strauser advised Nettinga to play the devil more like Phil Silvers, who had just played him on TV. "Don't ever let a director tell you to play a role like another actor," Hunt told Nettinga. "It's your role—play it the way you think it should be played!"

Hunt felt an additional twinge of ambition whenever he visited Glenn Mure, now a Yale freshman starring in an undergraduate production of *The Fantasticks*. The two had long been competitive teammates in choruses and plays; Mure's senior yearbook had called him "best tenor in the state" and lauded his acting aspirations: "Self-pronounced destined to do Shakespeare." Hunt visited his old friend frequently, attending around fifteen rehearsals. He would crash on Mure's floor, coiled up like an S to avoid the heating vents. He seemed to have a bottomless appetite in the Morse Dining Hall, where he developed his lifelong taste for such fine fare as filet mignon and lobster tails. "Richard would sit at the table and look at us eating, and when we were done he would say, 'Do you want that? Do you want that?'" recalls Stuart Fischer, the Yale premed directing *The Fantasticks*. Fischer contrived to loan Hunt his school ID; Hunt would flash the ID with his finger over the picture, then sign in as Richard Nixon or General Westmoreland, and happily fill his plate.

But for all the time Hunt spent at Yale, it was clear that college was not in the cards, at least not presently. He interviewed at Antioch

College, which Pfeiffer now attended, stopping by her dorm room afterward, a downcast figure in his navy blazer. "He was really upset, like,
'I'm going to amount to nothing, my life is going nowhere, I don't know
what I'm going to do, I have to get into a college.'" And not just any college would do: he wanted a top-notch name, a place known for a strong
program. He also applied to Carnegie Mellon and Wesleyan, but was
not accepted anywhere. Even if he had gotten in somewhere, money
presented an additional obstacle, and his grades were hardly scholarship material. "So he said, 'To hell with you, I don't need college,'" says
Poch. "'I'll do something else.'"

PART II

Hunt in New Haven, Connecticut, 1969.

CHAPTER 3

Apprentice

W HEN RICHARD HUNT COLD-CALLED Henson Associates, he had uncannily good timing, in life as in comedy—for the Muppets needed him as much as he needed the Muppets.

In spring 1970, the Muppets were a relatively bare-bones operation. "I came when there were about eight people," Hunt said. "Real small." One secretary held down the 53rd Street office; the gleeful Jerry Juhl penned most of their material; Don Sahlin and Kermit Love designed and built the puppets; Diana Birkenfield produced; and just three puppeteers—Jim Henson, Frank Oz, and Jerry Nelson—did basically all the performing. Yet as Hunt suspected, this small company was about to have a big growth spurt. After fifteen years of handpicking a select few performers, Henson was preparing to fling open the doors of the Muppets and see who wanted to come in—in other words, he would hold his first major auditions. Hunt called at just the right moment.

Hunt bounded like a big puppy into his June 1970 audition, a voluble frenzy of restless energy, his eyes shining bright with exuberance. "Ask any of the originals what Richard was like at nineteen or twenty," Hunt recalled laughingly. "*Boing-boing-boing-boing.* People would just sit there, their mouths open—what *is* this?" He wore his usual uniform of jeans, a button-down shirt with rolled-up sleeves, and his ever-present sneakers, his chin-length curls cowlicking out in all directions despite his best intentions.

Hunt stood out from the hundreds of performers who traipsed through Kermit Love's Soho loft between June 1 and 3, walking past the colorful, fabric-strewn sewing area and office to the mirrored rehearsal studio in the back, where Henson and Oz tossed them a puppet to see who they were and what they could do. Hunt's talent and sheer raw vigor quickly caught the attention of Henson and Oz. "Richard stood out as an extraordinary uncontrolled spirit," says Oz. "Jim and I saw that out of all the hundreds of people, he had something there."

Hunt was pleased to discover that his private audition was essentially a creative play session. "They threw a puppet at me and said sit down," Hunt told his mother that evening. Henson's approach was to act as if you were already collaborators, out to have a good time together. "He created an atmosphere of fun and foolishness, intuiting that in order to create and feel free one had to feel 'safe,'" says performer Fran Brill of her own audition around the same time. The comfortable setting helped Hunt relax and show off his talents as he, Henson, and Oz put on puppets and brought them to life: reading and riffing off scripts, improvising voices, making their puppets breathe, move, and behave, all the while eyeing the mirror to see how it would look onscreen. In contrast to Hunt's boisterous energy, the lanky, bearded, thirty-three-year-old Henson spoke in a nearly inaudible voice, exuding a quiet, calm authority. "Jim and I were taking them through their paces," says Oz. "We pretty much knew, without talking, who was right."

What about Hunt was right? Ironically, being a puppeteer didn't necessarily work in his favor. Before the Muppets, most puppetry on television merely incorporated the puppet stage and the performer hiding behind it. Henson exploded what could be done visually with puppets on television by using the camera itself as the stage, framing the shot and simply hiding the performers outside the frame. Henson's other major innovation was to rig up monitors so the puppeteers could see and adjust their performance in real time. Yet many puppeteers who auditioned were too habituated to their existing methods to adapt to the new approach. "Most of the people who were winnowed were people who actually did puppets, because they were doing it the wrong way," says Oz, who with Henson saw that while Hunt needed some technical training, he was remarkably adaptable, happy to abandon his cardboard stage for the new medium of television and ferociously motivated to learn anything that might make for a better show.

Overall, it mattered that Hunt was a *performer*: by nature, by nurture, and by trade. And it mattered that he was a collaborator, practiced at being part of an ensemble, contributing with an eye to elevating the whole team. He knew how to complete a scene, to hold his place without overshadowing. He could deliver his own punchline, but he could also set up a colleague for the laugh and play off that laugh, building up the sketch together.

Most importantly, Hunt's comedic instincts were wonderfully compatible with the Muppets, as he had suspected back on the family room couch. "We knew right away we had the same sense of humor," he told his mother that evening. "I think they liked me!" It was particularly important to Henson to find people who harmonized with the group, to assemble a team that worked together smoothly. Hunt shared the Muppets' particular comic sensibility, which Oz describes as "affectionate anarchy": Nothing is out of bounds, from slapstick pratfalls to outright explosions, yet the humor never feels unkind.

But Hunt didn't just fit in with the Muppet humor; he took it even further, bringing an edgy young energy to the troupe. "Richie was the heart and soul of the irreverence," says Oz. "Jim created it, but Richie intensified it." Hunt's spirit not only complemented but *completed* the original core group of the Muppets, contributing just what they needed to launch themselves into success.

Years later, Hunt praised Henson's ability to put together the perfect troupe. "There are a couple of Jim's greatest talents," said Hunt. "He knew how to draw people to him. And once they came he knew how to pick the right ones. He would use their talents to his advantage. And to their own." Hunt's connection with the Muppets would be pivotal for the organization—and change his own life in ways he could hardly imagine.

Ironically, when Jim Henson (b. September 24, 1936) dreamed up the Muppets, he wasn't actually all that interested in puppets. To him, the medium was "a means to an end"—a way to get his foot in the door of the relatively new industry of television. He had shown little interest in puppetry in childhood, certainly nothing to indicate that he would

revolutionize the field. But when a local station put out a call for marionettists, the adolescent Henson gave himself a crash course out of
library books, building puppets in his living room with a friend. At
eighteen he began performing short live segments on the Washington,
D.C. local NBC affiliate, WRC-TV; the term "Muppet" first appeared
in print the following year. From their very beginnings, Jim Henson's
Muppets radiated their general essence: hilarious, unpredictable puppets who seemed amazingly alive due to innovative sleight of hand.

Henson's first major partner in puppetry was also his longtime major
partner in life: his wife and the mother of his five kids, Jane Nebel. The
couple met in a puppetry class at the University of Maryland, College
Park in Henson's early days at WRC-TV, and soon began performing
together. In 1955 they debuted the first Muppet television series, *Sam
and Friends*, putting on two live five-minute segments each weekday
evening. *Sam and Friends* introduces the format that Henson would
spend decades perfecting until it reached international stardom with
The Muppet Show: a comedy-variety format of sketches and songs performed by a handful of wacky, idiosyncratic characters. *Sam and Friends*
even featured an early version of Henson alter ego Kermit, at this point
more languorous lizard than frazzled frog. Jim and Jane also created the
iconic Wilkins Coffee commercials, with their merry puppet cruelty. By
the time *Sam and Friends* ended in 1961, the couple had two infant
daughters and a son on the way, leaving Jane little energy for puppeteering. Their U of M friend Bobby Payne pitched in, but Henson started
looking around for more puppeteers with whom he could deepen his
learning about the craft and continue to innovate the medium.

Of all the major Muppet performers, Frank Oz (b. May 25, 1944) is the
only one born to the field, a second-generation puppeteer who began
performing at age eleven. Yet Oz—legal name Frank Oznowicz—also
resisted the medium, claiming he worked at it throughout adolescence
only to save up for a trip to Europe: "I never wanted to be a puppeteer."
Though the seventeen-year-old had sworn off puppetry, he accompanied his parents two hours south of their Oakland home to the 1961
Puppeteers of America convention in Asilomar, California, where he
hit it off with Henson, sparking their iconic partnership. But Oz took
his time joining the Muppets, as he completed high school, contem-

plated pursuing journalism, and traveled in Europe. In his stead he recommended his friend Jerry Juhl, whose performing with the Muppets blossomed into writing their material.

In 1963, Oz flew to New York to start working with the Muppets, now occupying the second floor of a 53rd Street townhouse above a trendy gastropub, Chuck's Composite. Oz assisted Henson in his steady gig on *The Jimmy Dean Show*, where the genial host bantered with Rowlf the Dog, a puppet which required two performers to operate. But even as Henson's helper, the knowledgeable Oz helped Henson hone his own puppet manipulation. Already, Henson had a sharp eye for knowing what he needed and finding someone with the skills to make it happen.

Henson also roped Oz into his puppetry experiments with the LaChoy Dragon, an early prototype of a full-bodied, walkaround puppet like Big Bird, Sweetums, and Junior Gorg. Oz encountered the same problems Hunt and other performers would later find: it was impossible to see and not knock into things inside the oversized outfit. Exacerbating the hazard was the fact that builder Don Sahlin had rigged the dragon to breathe real fire. Oz was a very good sport.

When Oz was drafted into the U.S. military in early 1966, Henson hired bearded beatnik Jerry Nelson to pick up his duties. A veritable jukebox of character voices, Nelson fit right in with Henson's playful improvising. Joining the Muppets was another twist in the road for Nelson, who lived a storied, Forrest Gump–type life, blending seamlessly into various subcultures, resilient as the proverbial cat. Hunt and Nelson would become a Muppet comic duo akin to Henson and Oz, as well as a dynamic duo off the set, with Nelson being both Hunt's solemn mentor and irreverent partying pal.

Jerry Nelson (b. July 10, 1934) liked to say, "I'm from Oklahoma—*far* from Oklahoma." He was born in Tulsa and raised in the Washington, D.C. area. "My whole life was in preparation to do the kind of job I had with the Muppets," he says. "Of course, I didn't know it when I was ten years old driving my mother crazy, making funny noises, discovering and stretching my imagination, playing with my voice." Nelson first encountered Henson in 1956 while working as a page at WRC-TV, watching Jim and Jane rehearse *Sam and Friends*. Nelson had just returned from two years in the military, including a stint in Japan, and was working various jobs while attending college. Nelson was intrigued by Henson's innovative puppetry and whimsical humor, but puppetry wasn't for him—he was an *actor*, and soon moved to New York City to pursue his career.

For Nelson, as with Henson and Oz, puppetry was largely a means to an end. Nelson was determined to earn his living as a performer, but as money ran low he became more flexible about what that meant, especially once he had a family. He married Jacquie Gordon in 1960; their daughter Christine was born on August 14, 1961. "When Christine was born, Jerry and I were living the precarious, ever-hopeful lives of out-of-work actors in New York," Gordon writes. "Jerry's hero was Jack Kerouac, and my hero was Jerry, and we saw ourselves as part of the beat generation." Some months it seemed impossible to scrape together the $85 rent for their four-room walk-up on East 89th Street.

So, when Nelson saw a call for marionettists from puppet master Bil Baird (now best known for his puppet work in *The Sound of Music*), he showed up cold and did his best. Nelson liked to joke that his Oklahoma roots gave him a leg up with Baird, a fellow westerner. "Usually when people ask me how I got started in puppets, I say, 'I lied, and I wore cowboy boots,'" Nelson recalls. "He [Baird] said, 'Have you ever done puppets before?' and I said, 'Oh, sure.'" Bobby Payne connected Nelson to Henson after seeing him perform with Baird's company in the 1964 World's Fair. Nelson was grateful for any gigs—and elated when Henson chose him to fill in for Oz in early 1966.

"Wow, this is a great job, a great place to work," Nelson thought dreamily on his first day in the Muppets' comfortable 53rd Street office. He sat at the front desk with his feet up, watching models walk in and out of Chuck's Composite. He was exulting about his situation to a friend on the phone when Oz—supposedly off at army training—walked in, having failed his draft physical. Decades later, Oz still chuckled to recall how Nelson's face froze with surprise to see him. Nelson quickly wrapped up his call, got up from the desk, sat down heavily on the couch, and said, "Shit!"

Nelson's job was safe, however; Oz decided that since he had arranged to leave, giving up his job and apartment, he would travel to Europe, leaving Nelson to right-hand Rowlf on *The Jimmy Dean Show* through its March finale and summerlong cross-country tour. But once the gig ended and Oz returned, Henson had bad news for Nelson. "Jim said, 'Well, I don't have enough work for all of us, and you're the last one to have joined, so I'm going to have to let you go.'" That's how small the Muppets were then—little more than a partnership.

But that wasn't Nelson's worst news: Around the same time, five-year-old Christine was diagnosed with cystic fibrosis, a progressive lung condition. She had already exceeded the life expectancy for the disease. "Jerry and I can't believe it," Gordon wrote her mother. "He is almost catatonic and says her life is over." The news strained their already tenuous marriage, and a few months later the couple amicably separated. "There was too wide a gulf between my need for stability and order for Christine, and Jerry's anarchic approach to life," Gordon recalls. The peripatetic beatnik found refuge on the road.

Nelson characterizes the late '60s as "a strange time in my life." He spent the Summer of Love in San Francisco, with a front-row seat for Jefferson Airplane at the Fillmore. He hung out in L.A. at the Farm, a semi-communal Hollywood Hills retreat where anyone from Cass Elliot to Graham Nash to Emmylou Harris might drop by and sing on the roof. He worked intermittently with Henson and Oz, performing Muppet sketches and songs on the variety show circuit, building up their audience. The trio filmed the Muppets' first hour-long special *Hey, Cinderella,* which initially aired only in Canada. Nelson particularly appreciated being seen on camera in Henson's more experimental film work such as *The Cube,* since he still thought of himself not as a puppeteer but as an actor.

Yet at about the same moment that Hunt was restlessly sprawled in front of the television in New Jersey, Nelson decided it was time to go home. Not only wasn't he finding acting work in L.A., Christine's health was worsening—and she was his real priority. Back in New York, casting about for work, Nelson caught a glimpse of the nascent *Sesame Street* at a Christmas party and was "floored" by what Henson and Oz were up to. "When I saw it was the Muppets I went, 'Wow.'" He called up Henson and set up a meeting; Hunt made his own phone call a few months later.

Hunt cold-called the Muppets in spring 1970 almost out of desperation, restlessly tooling around Closter, needing to work. As seemed to play ubiquitously on the radio, "Freedom's just another word for nothing left to lose." The extroverted Hunt risked little by reaching out to someone who seemed like a comedic kindred spirit. As the company was so small in those days, Hunt likely got right through to Henson, an impossibility just a few years later.

Hunt made his life-changing call at just the right time: The Muppets were on their way up. Fifteen years of building a national audience were finally starting to pay off. Within the span of just a few weeks in April and May, the Muppets aired their first American full-length special, *Hey, Cinderella*, on ABC; finished *Sesame Street*'s pilot year to great fanfare; and racked up their twenty-fifth appearance on the *Ed Sullivan Show*. Now Sullivan was offering the Muppets a new opportunity: an entire episode of their own. Millions of Americans tuned in every Sunday night to watch Sullivan's legendary variety showcase, trusting him to curate their entertainment. The show had launched icons like Elvis Presley and the Beatles—from there, who knew where the Muppets could go? Regular specials? The silver screen? A variety series of their very own?

But to pull off any of this, Henson would need help. A *lot* of help. It was time to build a troupe, to expand his company beyond a few handpicked performers—so Henson took the unprecedented step of announcing the first major Muppet auditions. Some potential new hires, like Hunt, had already come knocking. Henson invited the promising contacts in his roster, but also took out a *Variety* ad, broadcasting his call for performers uncharacteristically far and wide.

Hundreds of performers showed up for the June 1970 auditions at Kermit Love's downtown loft. Henson and Oz winnowed those numbers down to just eighteen people; Hunt counted himself lucky to be among them.

But the test wasn't over yet: Hunt and the others had to attend training sessions which were really another round of tryouts. "After that first series of auditions, we go through a workshop period where we'll take two to three more times as many people as we want to end up with," Henson explained. Just one meeting wasn't enough to determine if a candidate might learn to develop the skills to work with the Muppets, let alone feel practiced and natural at it, so the trainings gave Henson more time to assess everyone. "At the end of that time, if we think they have an ability there that looks like it'll work out, we basically know whether or not the person will become a good puppeteer."

Whether or not he made the cut, Hunt was grateful for the workshop, which paid $75 a week, and where he found he hit it off with his fellow performers, especially Nelson. Fellow performer John Lovelady was impressed by the workshop's "seriousness," particularly from Oz, a striking contrast to the silliness they were creating. They worked a lot on lip-synch skills, all the better to make the character seem alive. Most importantly, the workshop seemed like a great career leap forward for everyone in it. "That was like the step into the big time," Lovelady recalls. "It began to sink in that if I got this job and stayed working with these people, not only was it going to be a great job and be fun, but it was part of a history, that meant something to a lot of people."

Eighteen participants the first week (June 15–19) became fourteen the next (June 22–26); then their numbers were nearly halved. Thankfully, Hunt was among the eight performers brought in to work on the *Ed Sullivan* special, a Christmas-themed story entitled *The Great Santa Claus Switch*.

But Hunt had to clear one more hurdle if he wanted to make a career as a performer: getting past the U.S. military draft. The family hardly had the money or the facility to pull strings; their connections were in performing, not politics. Hunt was a long shot for a student deferment, though he was reapplying to schools such as Wesleyan.

Just a few days after Hunt's Muppet workshop, the question was decided for him. All over America on the morning of July 1, men born in 1951 watched the government draft lottery and held their breath. The previous year's drawing had been an appalling spectacle: stone-faced officials playing bingo with birthdates, reaching into a clear bowl to pick out a plastic capsule like a prize in a gumball machine, literally playing the lottery with people's lives. And the lottery hadn't been so random, it came out; insufficiently shuffled, the later birthdates stayed closer to the top, making them more likely to get picked. At least this year the dates had been shuffled by computer, a salutary gesture toward randomness. If they drew your birthdate in the first one hundred numbers, you were in trouble; two hundred, you might start to let out your breath; two hundred fifty, you might breathe easy. But it turned out that Hunt didn't need to rush down to the family room for the 10 A.M. ABC broadcast; the lottery was nearly over by the time Hunt's birthdate, August 17, came up 343rd. Now he could take more risks in his career, not needing to siphon energy toward a backup plan for possible deferment.

Hunt turned nineteen during the first week of rehearsals for *The Great Santa Claus Switch*, the Muppets' most ambitious production yet. The special filmed intermittently from late August to early October at Toronto's CFTO-TV network studios.

Henson and writer Jerry Juhl had long kicked around the idea of a burglar who impersonates Santa Claus to sneak into people's homes. Hunt, a *Honeymooners* fan, appreciated that Jackie Gleason's comic sidekick Art Carney played both the burglar and the real Santa Claus, sometimes even onscreen at the same time. The special showcased the Muppets' puppetry trickery, seemingly designed to make viewers scratch their heads and say, "How did they do that?" Just a dozen puppeteers—primarily Henson, Oz, and Nelson, with Hunt and the other new hires, plus a marionettist borrowed from Bil Baird—embodied nearly three times as many characters, from full-body monsters taller than Carney to a range of hand puppets and marionettes.

Though Hunt would spend years apprenticing at the Muppets, in his first gig he was a full performer, supplying both the physical puppeteering and the voice for ensemble characters such as a chipper elf named Bing and a birdlike burglar's accomplice. He also did some puppeteering without vocalizing, as filming for television was far more fragmented than doing a straight-through puppet show, with each shot carefully planned to maximize the illusion. Many characters had both hand puppet and marionette versions, so Hunt might perform a character talking in close-up one minute while someone else made it walk in a wide shot the next. Despite his diverse performing experience, this gig was unlike any work he had ever done.

The Santa Claus Switch seemed promising as the Christmas season approached and the Muppets appeared with Ed Sullivan on the cover of *TV Guide*. Hunt packed the Closter family room with family and friends when the special aired on CBS on December 20. As his loved ones watched the screen, Hunt watched their rapt faces, bathed in the flickering lights of the TV and the Christmas tree, knowing that the same scene was playing in millions of living rooms across the country. Yet even as he savored the moment, another thought presumably nagged at him: How could he keep this up?

Hunt's career galloped out of the starting gate. The Muppets' episode-long appearance on *Ed Sullivan* rolled out the red carpet for them to appear more often on the show, as well as do more of their own independent television specials. And not only was there more work for the Muppets, but Hunt seemed promisingly on the ascent within the troupe.

Out of all the new hires, Hunt alone was chosen to join Henson, Oz, and Nelson for their next *Ed Sullivan* appearance, despite this being only his second Muppet gig. "The Wild String Quartet," a five-minute sketch which aired live on January 17, 1971, seems to leapfrog ahead to the Muppets' later work at their peak. The conceit is that Henson's feisty hipster character, a drummer, tries to shake up the other three staid musicians. Hunt plays a violinist (named Harrison in the script) who comes to life through Hunt's strong puppeteering, as the character tilts his head and determinedly saws away at his instrument. The sketch debuted the dynamic duo of Hunt and Nelson, whose characters harmonize charmingly together as if their performers had been doing so for decades. Indeed, Hunt's musicality likely contributed to his getting the part.

Hunt's role on the Muppets' *Ed Sullivan* appearance on February 21, "The Glutton," was more typical of his early years: he was an apprentice, helping Henson and Oz perform an enormous humanoid puppet as it gobbles up everything from a cookie to a chicken leg, ultimately consuming even itself. Henson performed the voice, mouth, and left hand; Oz puppeteered the right hand; and Hunt scrambled to manipulate the many props, presumably with a new respect for his childhood assistants. This was the Muppets' last appearance on *The Ed Sullivan Show*, canceled a few months later after nearly a quarter century on the air.

In March, Hunt was one of just three performers (along with Danny Seagren and John Lovelady) to join Henson, Oz, and Nelson in Toronto to film *The Frog Prince*, the second in the *Tales of Muppetland* fairy tale trio of TV specials (*Hey, Cinderella* having been the first). True to its name, *The Frog Prince* established Henson's Muppet alter ego, as Kermit was recognizably a frog as well as the zany crew's center of (in)sanity. The gig required Hunt to puppeteer his characters without voicing them, lip-synching to beeps that matched the dialogue which others would dub in later. This method required painstaking physical precision, leaving little room for interpretation, a challenge for a new performer like Hunt. By hiring local actors to do some of the voices, Henson could access local funding, as well as play to his performers' strengths. For example, while Nelson (already the king of voices) debuted his young frog character Robin, the challenging tiny puppet was manipulated by Oz. Similarly, while the full-body puppet of Sweetums—later one of Hunt's most celebrated roles—debuted here, Nelson wore the suit and a local actor supplied the voice. And while writer Juhl made a rare appearance voicing the witch Taminella's scratchy falsetto, Hunt was proud to physically bring her to life—and especially proud of the $1,900 ($12,000 today) he was paid for two weeks of work.

Hunt was riding high—at least on the surface. "A hell of a lot of things have happened to me (to say the least)," Hunt scribbled gleefully to Dale Pfeiffer in April, a stark contrast to his downcast appearance in her Antioch dorm room two years earlier. He recounted the *Ed Sullivan* appearances, the trips to Canada, even his *Frog Prince* salary ("believe it or not"). He reported that he had been accepted to Wesleyan—"A wise re-decision on their part if I do say so myself!" However, he never enrolled, choosing instead to cast his lot as a performer.

Yet despite this initial surge of work, in the apprentice stage of his career Hunt was acutely conscious that he was precariously stringing together gigs in lieu of steady employment. "There was very little work the first five years," Hunt recalled years later. "I don't know how I survived it. I don't know what I did. We did some *Ed Sullivan*s, we did a special a year, and that's what I basically lived on." After *The Frog Prince*, Hunt endured a nerve-wracking near year without Muppet work, back to feeling stuck in New Jersey, though with a car of his own and a little more change in his pocket.

Hunt lived in the Closter house, his decision to stay there motivated partly by money and inertia but mostly because it was *home*. "I'm still at 52 Old Closter Dock Rd. The in place to be!" he wrote Pfeiffer. As ever, the house was crowded: Hunt shared a room with Adam, while Lyn and Rachel had more breathing space in their room now that Kate had moved out. Hunt often brought friends home for dinner, still a formal production with candlesticks and recipes out of *The New York Times*.

Yet the dynamics of the house were changing. Hunt wasn't a kid anymore. As Hunt's career took off, he stepped up as the family provider, shouldering more responsibility and pressure. His family increasingly relied on him, especially as his father drank more and worked less. "Richard took over our father's role," says Kate. Hunt bought the family's first color television, installing it ceremoniously in the family room. He was particularly gratified to use his *Frog Prince* money to fulfill his dream of taking the family on a Cape Cod vacation, renting a week in a Truro cottage big enough for all the Hunts and even for each sibling to bring a friend. The trip would become an annual tradition.

Hunt found the Closter house a good base from which to travel, disappearing for days or even weeks at a time. The restless extrovert had his pick of places to housesit or couch-crash all over the northeast. He often stayed over in Manhattan, or took off on road trips to visit Mure and Fischer at Yale; Minogue, Sackson, and Poch at Temple University; or Kate, who now lived on Martha's Vineyard. In contrast to his loud personality, Hunt was an unobtrusive, considerate guest, generally leaving things better than he found them, not wanting to wear out his welcome. "We were all glad to have him," says Minogue.

But Hunt made sure to keep his hand in as a performer. Besides continuing to act at Elmwood, Hunt volunteered at his alma mater, helping head of humanities Rex Miller direct *Auntie Mame*. The position, though unpaid, was a flattering sign of hometown recognition. Miller and Hunt held rehearsals nearly every weekday from late September 1971 until Thanksgiving. Hunt's patient and respectful presence took some cues from Poch; Hunt took care to develop the cast as a collaborative ensemble, cracking jokes to relax everyone, wanting them to feel comfortable and enjoy themselves—not coincidentally the conditions that made for the best production. The effort paid off, recalls student Matt Stoddart: "He got great performances out of all of us."

Hunt also kept up his birthday party gigs around Jersey and in the city. He brought his independent shows to their greatest heights during these apprentice years when Bob Dylan hired him to perform at his son Jakob's birthday party, at the family's MacDougal Street apartment. Hunt used Dylan's piano as the puppet stage; Hunt's friend Ernie Capeci and brother Adam, assisting with the show, riffled furiously and furtively through the piano bench for handwritten music. While Dylan's wife Sara seemed to enjoy Hunt's performance, "Bob stood there, seeming very judgmental, and didn't say a word the whole time," Capeci recalls. The kids, of course, loved it. But once Hunt's television career started taking off, he largely curtailed his birthday party gigs.

Hunt hungered to do more with the Muppets. He wanted to stretch his potential, to learn on the job. He visited the site of his audition, Kermit Love's Soho puppet workshop, where Love held court as he designed and built big walkaround puppets such as Big Bird and Snuffleupagus. Love was a colorful figure who appeared on the cover of *New York* magazine as Santa Claus, hobnobbed with the likes of Barbra Streisand, and spoke in a vaguely British accent despite hailing, like Hunt, from New Jersey. Hunt soaked up Love's advice while watching the huge puppets take shape, helpful as some of his best-known characters would be similarly built and performed. Hunt also hung around the *Sesame Street* set to watch the Muppets at work—anything to get in the room.

So Hunt was pleased in February 1972 to fly back to Toronto for some more meticulous lip-synching on *The Muppet Musicians of Bremen*, the third and final *Tales of Muppetland* special. But he was even more elated to have to fly back and forth to Toronto three times that month, not just for *Bremen*, but because the Muppets needed him on both sides of the border—for Henson had finally hired him on at *Sesame Street*.

Hunt assists (or "does right hands") as Jim Henson performs Ernie on *Sesame Street*, with Frank Oz as Bert, mid-1970s.

CHAPTER 4

Sunny Days

H UNT WAS IN HIS ENERGETIC ELEMENT at *Sesame Street,* poking into every corner of the Reeves Teletape Studio at 81st and Broadway. He quickly became a popular figure, his loud laugh booming through the studio. As in high school, he seemed impervious to cliques, chatting as easily with the cameramen as with celebrity guests like Lena Horne or Johnny Cash.

Hunt had been astute to recognize *Sesame Street*'s rising star. As the first wave of baby boomers started having their own babies, a whole new audience was born that grew up with television—a demographic in need of their own programming. Just as the late 1960s reinvented American culture, the nonprofit startup Children's Television Workshop reinvented children's television with the novel idea of combining education with entertainment. Children already watched television, lots of it—and reacted to it. "We knew that young children ... liked cartoons, game shows, and situation comedies; that they responded to slapstick humor and music with a beat; and above all, that they were attracted by fast-paced, highly visual, oft-repeated commercials," said co-creator Joan Ganz Cooney. Why not harness that energy? What if instead of demonizing commercial tactics, a show used them toward loftier aims? What if you could get the alphabet stuck in your head as easily as the Doublemint jingle? A show like *Sesame Street* could level the educational playing field.

As luck would have it, Hunt got a taste of the *Captain Kangaroo* experience he wanted after all, as Cooney and co-creator Lloyd N. Morrisett poached much of the show's personnel—most notably former *Captain Kangaroo* writer and producer Jon Stone, an imaginative, mercurial Yale alum adept at thinking both in and out of the box. Stone wore so many hats around *Sesame Street*—producer, director, writer—that nowadays we would call him a showrunner. "In those days, Jon Stone was The Man," says *Sesame* writer Joe Bailey. "The whole show came out of Jon's head." Stone eagerly enlisted Henson from the very beginning; the two had worked together on a CBS pilot and found themselves very much in sync. Both had a working style that was at once tightly disciplined and whimsically playful, and both were intrigued by the creative possibilities of the medium of television. Stone had reputedly told the Children's Television Workshop that if they didn't hire Henson, they shouldn't bother having puppets.

True to Cooney's vision, each hourlong episode of *Sesame Street* looked much like what children were already watching on television—only tailored just for them. The Muppets made up the bulk of the hour, performing humorously educational songs and sketches but also expanding into their first regular appearances alongside a human cast in the storylines of the street scenes. These segments were broken up by commercial-like animation and short films, many also made by Henson.

By the time Hunt joined up in 1972, in the show's fourth season, *Sesame Street* was a hit. First of all, it really *worked*. Kids who watched it did better on cognitive tests and in first grade than those who didn't; and the more they watched, the better they did. And watch they did: by some estimates, over two-thirds of American kids tuned in. What's more, the show now aired in fifty countries, with additional co-productions in Spanish, Portuguese, and German airing across South America and Europe.

And yet to Hunt—as to anyone working on it—*Sesame Street* was just another gig. "You better come soon, because it won't last long," Hunt told his friend Stuart Fischer when he invited him to the set. After all, the show had made the rounds and been rejected by the mainstream networks before landing on public television, itself a relatively new medium, as obscure as the cable access channels that would emerge in the next decade. "Even those of us who believed in the show never imagined it would take on a life of its own," says Stone. "We assumed that like with every other job in TV, after a couple of years we'd be out on the street again." And since the show was initially opposed to commercializing itself and selling merchandise—wouldn't that be kind of hypocritical?—no one had a good sense of how long they could afford to keep it on the air.

Ironically, however, this uncertainty created a certain freedom—the perfect place for Hunt to learn. For in his early days he was very much an apprentice. This was par for the course with the Muppets, stresses Oz: "You don't audition and just get on. You audition to learn, and then eventually you start working." And yet the two processes were not so separate—especially when there was so much work to be done. The show was a great opportunity for the whole troupe to hone their artistry. "It was a blessing, almost like vaudeville, to do x number of shows a week and grow your characters and grow your craft," says Oz.

Just six puppeteers cranked out 130 episodes every season for most of the 1970s: Henson, Oz, and Nelson; versatile Caroll Spinney performing both the sunny, childlike Big Bird and the gruff, cynical Oscar the Grouch; lone female Fran Brill, who like Hunt had come through the *Santa Claus Switch* auditions; and Hunt. *Sesame Street* was a well-timed opportunity for Hunt, who leapt up the learning curve in his initial years on the show, allowing for a quick ascent within the Muppets.

Hunt was eager to learn—and even as he struggled vigorously to master the craft, he had a very good time, as was typical for a Henson work environment. "Jim would never teach, he would always just gently guide while we were playing," says Oz. "It was playing around and having a great deal of fun while working extraordinarily hard." The performers understood that enjoying themselves wasn't at odds with producing good work; indeed, the two went hand in hand. "When we worked puppets, we were trying to make each other laugh, or make Jim laugh," Nelson recalls. "Because we knew if we got them, it was funny." If a joke worked for them, it would work for the audience—if anything, *their* standards were higher.

No one took this humor to heart more than Henson, especially when he and Oz played Bert and Ernie, the Odd Couple of *Sesame Street*, with

Henson's impish Ernie aggravating Oz's uptight Bert. "It was hysterical," Hunt said. "Everybody would get into hysterics. They would laugh so much that we would end up *crying*. Frank was capable of reducing Jim to giggles, and vice versa." Hunt compared watching the pair work together to seeing the great comic duos. "You realized it was the closest thing you had to having watched Laurel and Hardy," Hunt said. "A team of that caliber."

Hunt had a front-row seat on the action when he was literally Henson's right-hand man. Hunt's first main job on *Sesame Street* was doing right hands on live-hand puppets such as Ernie. Live-hand puppets aren't just talking heads; they have an active pair of hands, making them seem more alive. Henson operated the head and the left hand, while Hunt crouched beside him with *his* hand in the puppet's right hand—a job which thus was called "doing right hands" or "right-handing."

"*Very* difficult job," Hunt said years later, by then having been on both sides. As Hunt quickly learned, right-handing exemplified how working with the Muppets required intense collaboration, as well as a laser-sharp focus. Hunt had to almost sense when Henson was going to move, and move seamlessly alongside him. "It's an instinctive chemistry thing," Hunt said. "If the person is instinctive to you, and the personality of the character you're doing, they can second-guess you—and so they'll be with you."

In his early days right-handing with Henson, Hunt didn't want to take any chances—so he physically held on so as not to miss a thing. "I would hold one of his belt loops with my left hand so that I was with him literally," Hunt recalled. "Then the minute he moves I'm feeling him move and I'm with the first spasm of the first twitch and I just immediately move with him." In later years, he passed on this advice to his own apprentices. "I tell the new kids when they do it, they're embarrassed, I say, no, grab his belt loop! Otherwise you're being dragged along."

Oz could also be challenging to right-hand with, but in a different way. Oz was a very particular technical performer, a bit of a perfectionist, the only one among them who would call for multiple takes. Oz was stern about the right-hand not drawing attention to itself; a right-hander must only blend in and complete the scene. "With the right hand, it's a subtle thing," Hunt explained. "I've seen hands look alive on their own.

It's wrong and it destroys the illusion." Oz taught his right-handers this lesson the hard way. If Oz thought his assistant was making the right hand too visible and distracting, he would simply grab it with the left hand, sometimes even physically holding it down. "You'd pull it out and Frank would grab it with the other hand and put it back in," Hunt recalled of right-handing with Oz on Cookie Monster. At one point Hunt decided to make it interesting. "I tricked him; it's a famous old story. I put it out and he'd reach over and pull it back in; he'd keep talking and I'd pull it out, he'd reach over and pull it back in. And then I reached out, and he went for me and he couldn't find it." As Oz groped around for the character's other hand, their colleagues exploded with mirth.

Hunt made a particularly strong connection with performer Jerry Nelson—which they needed when they performed the elephantine two-person puppet Snuffleupagus, Hunt's other major job in his early *Sesame Street* years. Both of them stood inside the gigantic costume, Nelson in front doing the voice, face, and front legs, and Hunt behind him in the back legs, the two very carefully walking in tandem.

While Hunt and Nelson had hit it off when they first met, working together on Snuffleupagus cemented their friendship. There was plenty of time to talk, crouched together inside the shaggy costume. Nelson mentored Hunt, teaching him the ropes, giving him direction and advice. "I took Richard under my wing when he first came in," Nelson recalls. Nelson was impressed by how quickly Hunt learned to read his movements almost before he made them, the pair communicating instinctually. "We got to the point where we would work—and play—really well together," says Nelson. "When one of us would start to go somewhere, the other would know what was happening." Nelson also appreciated Hunt's patience, as the costume could be sweltering under the lights. Nelson could at least get some air from the mouth opening, but Hunt was stuck in the back. "It wasn't much fun for Richard," Nelson says. "It was hot in there."

While Hunt was learning to work with Henson, Oz, and Nelson, he met the final member of the "Original Five," as he dubbed the core classic Muppet troupe: "Jim, Frank, Jerry, Dave Goelz, and me."

Dave Goelz (b. July 16, 1946) would perform characters that were weird even for the Muppets, such as Gonzo the Great, Bunsen Honeydew, and Boober Fraggle. Goelz initially approached puppets from a visual and mechanical perspective; he had worked as an industrial engineer, designing things like tractors and airplane interiors, and was captivated by what Henson could make puppets appear to do.

Goelz was visiting the *Sesame* set in September 1972 when he met Hunt—but their meeting didn't last long. "Richard suddenly got very upset and ran out of the studio and didn't come back," says Goelz. Eerily, on the same day Hunt met his future close friend and colleague, he lost an old New Jersey friend, Jeffrey Yagoda, in a tragic murder.

Hunt and Yagoda had enlivened many a statewide high school chorus rehearsal, as Yagoda nimbly played along with Hunt's impromptu routines. "Jeff was the only person I've ever met that could keep up with Richard in being funny and ad-libbing and doing impressions," recalls their mutual friend Terry Minogue. "You could sit there and watch those two and know they were destined for great things." The friends stayed in touch when, like Sackson and Minogue, Yagoda followed Gail Poch to Temple University to study music.

Yagoda, twenty-one, was mugged while walking home from a late campus screening of *Goodbye, Columbus*; he made it to his Spring Garden Street rowhouse, but was stabbed in his own backyard. He managed to crawl to the front door and ring the doorbell, but it was too late; horrified, his roommate opened the door just in time to witness Yagoda's last breaths. It was the third murder of a Temple student in six months, in addition to several stabbings and countless muggings in the neighborhood.

Yagoda's family held his burial within twenty-four hours, in keeping with the Jewish tradition, so everyone raced to converge in New Jersey. "Richard ran every single light from New York City," says Sackson. "He was frantic with pain and horror." Pulled over for speeding to the funeral, Hunt's reaction to the policeman was "the only time I've seen him lose his cool," Minogue recalls. While Hunt could usually talk his way out of a ticket, this time he got sent to traffic school.

Hunt was particularly shaken over Yagoda's death because the friends had fallen out the month before over "something trivial," says Minogue. "It was a shock to all of us, but it hit Richard the hardest, because they hadn't had a chance to take care of that business between them." Of the two friends "destined for great things," now just one was left. While Hunt had long believed in seizing the moment, wanting to advance quickly in his career, Yagoda's death only brought this home to him even more.

Hunt's feeling of urgency about his career meant that he was thrilled, in his second season on *Sesame Street*, to move up to playing his own character—though the role came with a big caveat.

The ironic story of Hunt's first major Muppet character has become legend, in large part because Hunt loved to tell it. Hunt couldn't wait to get a character of his own. Yet when he finally got a part, to his great disappointment the role of construction worker Sully was not a speaking part! "That was an amazing thing, to see Richard not talk," Hunt joked years later. "But it happened." Sully was designed to be silent because the show was hesitant to elevate Hunt to a speaking performer, as his change in status would necessitate a raise. "Initially the reason he didn't talk is because they wouldn't pay me," Hunt said. "They said, 'You can't talk cause it costs us extra money.' So I didn't."

Rather than being deterred, Hunt was determined to make the most of what he had been given, to find the silver lining of the limitation. What if the character's silence masked subtle hidden depths? "I developed this character who is quite sensitive," Hunt recalled. The puppet itself helped with that, expertly built by Don Sahlin to show feeling even without talking. "This puppet had a twist in its mouth and an ability just to look and say a thousand words," said Hunt, who decided to model his mute character after the silent film stars, maximizing facial and physical expression. "It was very Chaplinesque."

Nelson, playing Sully's fellow hard-hat Biff, also helped Hunt make the most of the role. In their first regular character pairing, Hunt and Nelson played off each other beautifully. Biff and Sully are a duo on a par with Bert and Ernie, another Odd Couple: Biff round and garrulous, Sully gangly and reserved. The running gag is that Biff never lets Sully get a word in. Yet as Biff prattles on, Sully subtly steals the audience's attention, revealing hidden character depths. For example, as Biff lectures Sully that he ought to express his anger, Biff doesn't notice as Sully nods, grimaces, shakes his fist, and bangs his (thankfully hard-hatted) head against the wall. Sully's nonverbal communication is so advanced, he even speaks American Sign Language with deaf *Sesame* resident Linda (Linda Bove)—no small feat given that the puppet can only move one arm and none of its fingers. This communication is all the more extraordinary as the puppet's bushy eyebrows cover his eyes, so they, too, can't be used for expression.

Hunt likened Biff and Sully to comedy couple George Burns and Gracie Allen: "It was based on Burns and Allen—'Yeah, hey, Sully, know what I mean? Huh, huh?'" But Hunt also found inspiration closer to home. "They were based on a couple of buddies of mine I grew up with," Hunt recalled. "Local bar in New Jersey where we would hang out. Charlie was Biff, always talking. And Harvey was this tall guy who never said a word. He'd just stand there, Biff going 'Yeah, me and Harvey were gonna didididdduh. Right, Harvey?' And Harvey wouldn't say anything, but there was a lot going on in his head."

As Hunt developed the character, he came to realize that Sully had the potential to show an "enormous sensitivity" that many kids might relate to—and which they didn't often see reflected on television. "That was a great character because there are lots of little kids like that, who don't talk, who are shy," said Hunt. "It was important for kids who didn't talk to have someone to identify with." Hunt was especially proud of one such sketch he came up with. "There's a bit that I once wrote where they were pushing in a piano and Biff forgot the receipt and he said, 'Sully, I'll go over and get it, you wait here.' He goes out and Sully plays a Chopin etude. Biff walks in saying, 'Whuddaya doing, playin' *Chopsticks*?' Just this enormous sensitivity that no one was aware of." Hunt emphasized, however, that this sensitivity was integral not just to him but all of the Muppets—and was in fact part of their appeal. "Frank certainly brought that through in Grover and Jim through Kermit," said Hunt. "There was this sensitivity that drew people, even unconsciously."

As *Sesame*'s fortunes rose, Sully's gag order was lifted. "The year after, they said, 'Okay, Sully can talk this year. We have more money.'" But by then, Hunt was pleased with the character as is. "I said, 'No, Sully doesn't talk.'"

Both onscreen and off, this sense of appreciating what people had to offer was par for the course in the early years of *Sesame Street*. Cast and crew felt united in the common purpose of using entertainment to do good. The more entertaining they could make it, the more entranced the viewers would be, and the more the kids would learn. It was a win-win. Hunt was thrilled not just to grow as a performer, but to do so in service of a higher mission.

Hunt proudly brought in friends to tour the studio, a grand old edifice originally built as a vaudeville theater. He led them under the broad marquee and through the lobby, showing them the majestic proscenium arch, taking them up to the balcony to watch the filming from there. In the center of everything was the Street—the *Sesame Street* set, that is: The Fix-It Shop, Mr. Hooper's Store, the 123 Sesame Street brownstone, Oscar's trash can, and Big Bird's nest. Anything else viewers saw was a painted backdrop. Hunt liked to smile mysteriously and point up to the ornate domed ceiling, where visitors were surprised to see the huge Mr. Snuffleupagus dangling from its storage perch. Surrounding the set were various rooms where the magic happened: makeup, carpentry, video, audio, and a props area where the wranglers looked after the puppets. Hunt would lead his friends up the narrow spiral staircase to the performers' tiny dressing rooms, where he might practice his puppet manipulation, read the newspaper, or adeptly imitate someone else's character. Or he would take his visitors around and introduce them to the cast and crew; as usual, Hunt wanted everyone to get acquainted.

Hunt's irresistible energy on the set drew in even more than just friends. Charles Gibson, a typist in the production department, had heard of Hunt—"the wonder boy from New Jersey"—well before meeting him while distributing the daily scripts. The two became "on-again, off-again" lovers, Gibson recalls; Hunt would call up Gibson in "the wee hours of the morning" and invite himself over with pot and orange juice, ready for a good time.

Gibson was one of a group of out gay men working at *Sesame* in its early years—also the early years of America's gay rights movement— but Hunt kept a lower profile. "Yeah, I fuck guys—but I'm not a homosexual," he would quip to his gay friends. Hunt didn't like those terms; if anything, the champion of comedy preferred the pun of calling himself a "funny boy." Hunt, usually so fearlessly provocative, was reluctant in this regard to jeopardize being universally liked on the job. Besides,

Hunt could be very private—ironically, his noisy extroversion could be a way of keeping people at arm's length.

Hunt's *Sesame Street* work buoyed his social life—and it also widened his travel frontiers. He took his first transatlantic trip in October 1973, flying to London for a week of work on *Julie on Sesame Street*, an ABC special starring Julie Andrews, whom he had admired since seeing her on Broadway in *Camelot*. Andrews still worked with her producer from her young vaudeville days, now a powerful media mogul: Lord Lew Grade.

The *Sesame* performers (minus Brill but plus Jane Henson) filmed the special at Grade's Elstree studios in Borehamwood, about a half hour northwest of London. Hunt right-handed with Henson and Oz; puppeteered some anonymous Anything Muppets; and did some fancy footwork with Nelson as Snuffleupagus alongside Andrews on *The King and I*'s "Shall We Dance?" The company covered his transportation, his lodging at the posh Royal Lancaster Hotel on Hyde Park, and a per diem of fifty dollars on top of his pay. But Hunt didn't know at the time that this gig would lead to much more for him—as well as for the whole Muppet team.

Hunt and Jerry Nelson's daughter Christine Nelson horse around on the *Saturday Night Live* set, 1975.

CHAPTER 5

Camaraderie

D ESPITE THE SUCCESS of *Sesame Street*, and his success on it, Hunt had his eyes fixed on a horizon beyond the children's program—and so did Henson. For Henson was not merely satisfied with the Muppets' popularity among young viewers; if anything, he was irritated that these accomplishments seemed to pigeonhole them, holding them back from reaching a wider audience. Henson was focused on a bigger prize: he was determined to get the Muppets their own regular show, starring a different guest each week. A weekly show wouldn't necessarily be that different from the Muppets' appearances on other people's shows, which had already proven popular with the viewing public. Hunt keenly followed their progress toward this goal, excited by what it might portend for his career. He and the rest of the troupe were delighted when ABC greenlit a pilot, which they filmed in December 1973 at the network's New York studios.

The Muppets Valentine Show, the first pilot for what would become *The Muppet Show*, is noteworthy as it was the first time that both Hunt and Dave Goelz, who had been building puppets in the workshop for about six months, stepped up to speaking roles. Thus, the pilot marks the debut of the "Original Five"—Henson, Oz, Nelson, Hunt, and Goelz—the core Muppet troupe that would propel the company to great heights.

It's no coincidence that the Muppets really started taking off when they hit upon this particular combination of performers. Together, the Original Five created something greater than the sum of their individual parts, something ineffable and unique that just *worked*. This special ensemble, in Hunt's opinion, ranked up there with some famous groups in terms of teamwork. "I don't know, maybe Monty Python fought their heads off, but *that* kind of camaraderie," Hunt reflected years later. "I think the Beatles were along the lines of us as well. They respected and liked each other and it was just later on, with their relationships with their wives, things came in." This magical combination would launch the Muppets to the height of their success.

The Original Five were joined by Jane Henson and John Lovelady for *The Muppets Valentine Show*, a loose collection of songs and sketches about love, guest-starring a doe-eyed and very pregnant Mia Farrow. The special is populated by oversized Muppet monsters as well as humanoid characters such as Henson's tepid host Wally and Hunt's Mildred, a quavery-voiced elderly woman who sings and plays piano. It aired to a warm reception on January 30, 1974, proving that the Muppets could indeed hold their own with audiences of all ages.

Yet the Muppets' all-ages aspirations did not mean that they were anything but elated in September when *Sesame Street's* six Muppet performers—Henson, Oz, Nelson, Hunt, Spinney, and Brill—won an Emmy for Outstanding Individual Achievement in Children's Programming. While the first three seasons had won Emmys for Best Children's Series, this was the first time the Muppets had been singled out, as well as Henson's first Emmy (besides a local one back in 1959 for *Sam and Friends*). The performers dressed up to receive their award at the ceremony—and Hunt received some ribbing along with it. "We just kidded the hell out of Richard," recalls *Sesame* writer Joe Bailey. "You're winning an Emmy for playing the back end of Snuffleupagus?"

Hunt took the teasing good-naturedly, not only because the consummate joker hardly objected to getting ribbed in return—but also because he *wasn't* just playing the back end of Snuffleupagus anymore. Hunt was moving beyond his status as assistant at the Muppets, stepping up in the troupe. As Hunt started his third season on *Sesame Street*, he got his own speaking roles there. His musical chops came in handy for Don Music, a dramatic pianist usually found in the frustrated throes of creativity. "Oh I'll never get it, never, never, never!" the character exclaims, banging his head on the keys.

What's more, besides stepping up on *Sesame Street*, Hunt was taking his place in the core Muppet troupe as they pursued a regular evening show. Henson was determined to trumpet the adult aspects of their work with the potential show's second pilot for ABC, mischievously titling it *The Muppet Show: Sex and Violence*.

Hunt appreciated having plenty to do on the new pilot, as the Original Five were again front and center as they filmed in New York from December 10 to 16, joined by John Lovelady and, unusually for the Muppets, four women (Jane Henson, Fran Brill, Caroly Wilcox, and Rollie Krewson, the last two doubling as puppet handlers). These ten performers played over seventy characters, many of whom are not just adults but explicitly elderly, as if to exaggerate the point that these puppets weren't just for kids. Writers Henson and *Sesame* denizens Jon Stone and Norman Stiles (along with Marshall Brickman, who later co-wrote *Annie Hall*) deliberately departed from their usual daytime fare. The pilot features the seven deadly sins, each embodied hilariously; Hunt plays Lust, a puppet who seems to be all hands and tongues, flirting with the secretary and making her squeal. Hunt also literally starts off the special with a bang as Crazy Harry, a character that Nelson would later run with, exploding a pack of dynamite with an impish cackle.

It is interesting to see the early "drafts" of Muppet characters, as the performers experimented with what worked best. While Statler and Waldorf debut here, they are not yet Henson and Hunt's quick-witted old men in the balcony; instead, played by Henson and Nelson, they are half-asleep (or half-dead), lying limply in an old-fashioned library, making the same quips day after day. The running joke seems to be how old and helpless they are. Notably, Statler and Waldorf didn't become fan favorites until they became lively and empowered. This is a repeated theme in the Muppets, often the difference between when the humor works and when it doesn't: viewers don't want to laugh *at* the characters—they want to laugh *with* them.

Despite flashes of great humor and boundless originality, *The Muppet Show: Sex and Violence* seems even more scattershot than the previous pilot, especially without a guest star to anchor it. The show aired on March 19, 1975 to mixed reviews, prompting ABC to nix a regular Muppet show—so Henson turned his sights elsewhere.

Hunt was particularly invested in the quest for an evening Muppet show because his family needed him more than ever. He was now the primary family breadwinner, as Richard Sr.'s alcohol-related health problems had progressed to the point where he could no longer work, though he was barely fifty years old. Normally a chatty entertainer, Hunt's father had become an echo of his former self, a quiet fixture in his living room chair, ever-present drink in hand. Still, the Hunt house remained a popular gathering place, with the kids bringing friends home. And Hunt started bringing someone home who was very special to him—even if he didn't specify exactly why.

Hunt had met Duncan Kenworthy, two years his senior, at *Sesame Street*, where Kenworthy coordinated the show's international co-productions. Kenworthy would later produce such blockbuster movies as *Notting Hill* and *Love Actually*. "Richard and I had a relationship," Kenworthy recalls. "Which was quite a big deal, for both of us." The two were polar opposites—Kenworthy a buttoned-down Brit who wore a jacket and tie to work, Hunt a larger-than-life extrovert with untamed hair and Adidas sneakers—but this contrast was part of what brought them together. "We were both attracted by the fact that we were each outside the other's experience," Kenworthy surmises.

Characteristically, Hunt wanted everyone to get acquainted; after staying over at Kenworthy's tiny Bank Street tenement, he often brought him out to Closter, where there was always room for one more at the table. Kenworthy appreciated the warm welcome, as he missed his own family back in England, yet these visits exacerbated an underlying tension between him and Hunt. "The one thing that we disagreed on was that I was out and trying to be outer, and he was definitely not in any way out," says Kenworthy, who felt uncomfortable having to pretend they were just friends, especially around Hunt's Jersey buddies. "We would debate this; he thought it would change the nature of his friendships." Again, Hunt's priority was being universally liked—even as it increasingly came at a cost.

Still, even if Hunt's need to be liked strained his most intimate relationship, it served him well as he collected friends all over the Eastern Seaboard. He developed a community on Cape Cod in Truro's cottage colony. In addition to the annual family vacation—now extended to two weeks—Hunt sped up to the Cape any chance he got, squeezing his sleeping bag into a friend's tiny screened-in porch or out on the beach. Everyone knew the tall, skinny extrovert with the wild hair and mischievous smile, the pied piper figure trailed by a pack of enamored kids. Hunt would deploy his Muppet impressions, doing a dead-on Kermit imitation, or charm the crowd with a cute Robin puppet, imitating the character's childlike voice.

From the Cape, Hunt often roared down to Martha's Vineyard on a BSA 500 motorcycle to visit his sister Kate and her husband Hollis Smith at their house in Menemsha, paying special attention to his infant niece Amanda, the first member of the next generation of Hunts. Hunt also got a kick out of his trips to the Vineyard because he was now a "brother-in-law" to famous folk singer James Taylor, as Smith's sister Jeanne was married to Taylor's brother Hugh. Hunt often stayed with Jeanne and Hugh in Aquinnah at their majestic cliffside house, where their raucous parties were populated by the likes of "Margaritaville" songster Jimmy Buffett. Hunt would have the Robin puppet make suggestive remarks to Buffett's wife Jane, sending her into gales of laughter. Though Hunt was generally unfazed by celebrity, he was awed to meet puppeteer Bil Baird, who summered on the island.

By the time the Original Five flew to L.A. in late July 1975 for a cluster of appearances, Hunt, like all the Muppet performers, keenly hoped for their own evening show. They were so close—and yet doors kept closing in their face. The troupe hoped that these appearances would show audiences, particularly the network brass at CBS, what a grown-up Muppet show could look like. But regardless of the outcome, Hunt was pleased to have more to do, both because he'd proven himself as an apprentice and because Henson needed to make the most of his whole team.

Hunt played a number of one-off characters—a snooty queen, a funny Whatnot, a singing chicken—in the Julie Andrews special *One to One*, a dismal infomercial for evangelical children's advocates World-Vision, and an oddly morose choice for a prototypical Muppet show. But Hunt shone in the Muppets' two appearances on the *Cher* show, debuting two of his most well-known characters. He used a falsetto in an early draft of his hippie character Janice, rather than the Valley Girl voice for which she would become known. And he made great use of his physical performing ability in his debut as the full-body monster character of Sweetums, dueting with Cher on "That Old Black Magic" and dancing disco inside the oversized suit.

Interestingly, it was Henson who first climbed inside the Sweetums suit on the *Cher* show—the only known instance of him doing so (besides one lip-synched line on *The Muppet Show*)—singing the Beatles' "Something" with the host. But when Muppet producer David Lazer spied Henson talking to Cher between takes, weary and perspiring from the heavy, furry outfit, Lazer decided, "No more. Jim is their equal, he shouldn't be getting hot and sweaty inside that costume." From then on, the role went to Hunt.

The more Hunt got to do, the more he showed what he could do—as with the troupe as a whole. These appearances played to the Muppets' strengths, including Kermit bawdily flirting with Cher and bantering charmingly with her young child. Unfortunately, despite Henson putting some of this great footage in his pitch to CBS for a regular Muppet show, the network turned him down, instead putting newsmagazine *60 Minutes* in the coveted Sunday evening time slot.

In their continued quest to prove their all-ages appeal, Hunt and the Muppets went to the ultimate opposite extreme. On the one hand, fall 1975 found them filming season seven of *Sesame Street*, where Hunt had a fun rapport with new cast member Buffy Sainte-Marie, a folk singer who shared his playful humor. But in stark contrast to the daytime children's show, Hunt and his colleagues started appearing on a show even more grown-up than the evening fare they envisioned: a daring new late-night program called *Saturday Night Live*.

Henson's agent Bernie Brillstein had made the connection. Brillstein also represented *Saturday Night Live* producer Lorne Michaels, a young Canadian who characterized his show as so risqué that even its Muppets were a new kind of "adult Muppets who can stay up late." Henson, Michael Frith, and the workshop designed and built all-new, decisively adult puppets for the show, including a big-breasted humanoid female. The gig was a coup for Hunt, as just six Muppet performers appeared on *Saturday Night Live*: Henson, Oz, Nelson, Hunt, Brill, and Alice Tweedie.

The Muppets debuted on *Saturday Night Live* on October 11, at the 30 Rock NBC studios at Manhattan's Rockefeller Center, having done a read-through three days earlier and partied late into the night the previous evening. "We were very friendly with [*SNL* actors] John [Belushi] and Chevy [Chase] and Danny [Aykroyd]," Oz recalls.

Yet despite the offscreen rapport between the Muppet performers and *Saturday Night Live* actors, the collaboration was awkward, to say the least. The *SNL* Muppet characters projected a meanness and vulgarity that contrasted jarringly with their usual good-natured sensitivity. Henson played the booming, bossy King Ploobis, who carps at his nagging wife Queen Peuta (Tweedie), fawns over his busty mistress Vazh (Brill), and slaps around his sidekick Scred (Nelson), as well as consulting unhelpful guru The Mighty Favog (Oz) for advice. Hunt played Ploobis and Peuta's son Wisss, a one-note "crater-head" (read: pothead). The crude jokes dripped with early *SNL's* trademark misogyny—and worst of all, they often just weren't funny.

Still, *Saturday Night Live* was a great opportunity for Hunt, and great fun. He shone in the October 25 episode centered around Wisss, a mossy-looking furball with bulgy eyes and a floppy trunk. The other characters worry about how Wisss is "smoking craters" and "acting like a crater-head"—especially funny to those who knew that Wisss's performer was a bit of a "crater-head" himself. Hunt as Wisss literally smokes in the sketch, pulling off the effect by puffing on a cigar through a rubber tube.

Hunt particularly enjoyed the social prospects afforded by the show. He took his family and friends on tours of the *SNL* set, gave them tickets to tapings, and brought them along to *SNL's* famously raucous afterparties, also frequented by Oz and Nelson.

Even when Hunt didn't perform on *Saturday Night Live*, he usually came to watch, often sitting with and looking after Nelson's daughter Christine, with whom he was close—and with whom it was especially fun to watch Nelson, *SNL's* Muppet standout. A consummate chameleon, Nelson fit right in with the show's edgy energy. He mimicked cast member Chevy Chase: "I'm Scred and you're not." He did a dead-on imitation of Gilda Radner's fluff-brained character Emily Litella, who gets worked up over misheard things, becoming outraged when a coffee shop patron ordered a "toasted English Muppet"; when corrected, he perfectly warbled Litella's trademark catchphrase: "Never mind."

Still, by the end of 1975, even Scred and Candice Bergen singing a charming version of "Have Yourself a Merry Little Christmas" (Hunt's favorite Christmas song) couldn't hide the fact that the collaboration wasn't working—so much so that the meta-sketch poked fun at it. Everyone has abandoned Ploobis's Christmas party for the one thrown by the bees (aka the *SNL* cast). Wisss (Hunt) and Vazh (Brill) come straight from the bees' party, banter humorously about what a great party it is, and then go right back.

By this point, *SNL* had found its own voice—and its vulgar comic sensibility just didn't fit with the Muppets' gentler affectionate anarchy. Muppet co-founder Jane Henson was particularly displeased with a sketch about a "marital aid" (or as Scred jokes, since cheating is involved, an "extramarital aid"). "Jane said, 'But that's not Muppets,'" Nelson recalls. "I said, 'This is a different show. This is real adult comedy. If kids are staying up and watching this, they're in trouble already.'"

The *SNL* performers and writers, too, were displeased with the collaboration. Belushi illustrated it best when he pulled a switchblade on Ploobis during one episode's end credits (though Radner and fellow cast member Jane Curtin did try to pry it from his hands). Belushi resented sharing precious screen time with the Muppets, famously calling them "the Mucking Fuppets." "He would have been just as happy if we had fallen in a big hole," says Nelson. And the writers had a hard time creating content for the Muppets, arguing over who would have to write that week's sketch. Henson penned the Muppet material for the April 24, 1976 episode, in which Ploobis and Scred join the rest of the puppets in a big trunk, with Wisss briefly popping up to look around. ("Hiya, Wisss, haven't seen you since November," Scred says in a shout-out to Hunt.) The trunk lid closes over them with a certain air of finality. In a sense, they were saying goodbye.

Ultimately, the Muppets appeared in just fifteen *Saturday Night Live* episodes (Hunt appeared in four)—an interesting if unsuccessful experiment in working together. "I felt the thing never really jelled," Henson mused a few years later. Oz offers a bit more explanation: "Eventually it was obvious that the styles didn't mesh," says Oz. "I really believe that was totally it, because we were on a very friendly basis with them personally, but it just fucking didn't work."

When the trunk lid closed over the *SNL* Muppets, they really *were* saying goodbye—for the Muppets were onto bigger and better things. They had finally achieved their dream: their own regular evening show, for an all-ages audience. To agent Bernie Brillstein, it was a miracle. "I was already busy trying to get out of there [*SNL*] and trying to convince Jim that this wasn't the place for him to be, and that's when Lew Grade came into the picture," says Brillstein. "Saved my life!" Though CBS had rejected a Muppet show, a CBS executive, Tom Miller, suggested that if Henson could film and fund the show elsewhere, perhaps the CBS affiliate stations could pick it up. Production mogul Lord Lew Grade, already familiar with the Muppets through their work with his client Julie Andrews, quickly saw the benefits in backing them.

Henson held a press conference on October 22, 1975 at Manhattan's posh 21 Club to formally announce *The Muppet Show*, at long last. Grade would produce the show at his ATV Studios in England and promote it through his vast distribution connections. Rather than being made for a specific network, *The Muppet Show* would air in first-run syndication, with stations paying to put it in their locally-controlled 7:30 Sunday time slot. As it turned out, what had originally looked like failure now worked marvelously in the Muppets' favor, as this arrangement had much more potential than merely signing with a single U.S. network: their work would be seen around the world.

Sesame Street, too, was spreading around the world. Hunt performed Bert, dressed up as Santa Claus, when the *Sesame* performers appeared on Germany's popular variety show *Peter Alexander Presents Specialities*, which its host flew over to film on the *Sesame* set. The Christmas special was the country's number one–ranked show for the year, drawing thirty-eight million German viewers when it aired in late November, plus millions more in Switzerland and Austria. Meanwhile, *Sesame Street*'s international co-productions were taking off: Germany's *Sesamstrasse* enjoyed great popularity; Mexico's *Plaza Sesamo* expanded and solidified; and Brazil's *Vila Sesamo* became nationalized. What's more, the original *Sesame Street* had dropped its initial misgivings on merchandising, quickly becoming a commercial juggernaut. Hunt was happy that both the show and his place on it were more of a sure thing—but like his colleagues, he was far more focused on the possibilities of their work for adults.

So Hunt was elated to fly out to England on January 17 for a two-week stint filming the first two episodes of *The Muppet Show*. "I'm having a really good time!" he wrote Kenworthy. A lot rode on these episodes, which Brillstein had basically begged '60s teen idol Connie Stevens and dancer Juliet Prowse to star in. While the material was experimental, the core members each already held their own. Henson and Oz manifested their strong dynamic, even borrowing Bert and Ernie from *Sesame Street*, but the newer players also delivered first-rate performances. Goelz debuted his endearing daredevil Gonzo and demonstrated his puppeteering skills as terse saxophonist Zoot. Hunt unveiled his young "gofer" character Scooter in a delightful song with Oz's Fozzie, "Simon Smith and His Amazing Dancing Bear," and shared the performing duties of Miss Piggy (at that point just a nameless pig). Jane Henson, John Lovelady, and new hire Erin Ozker also performed, while Nelson stayed in New York, a decision which would affect his position on the show.

Characteristically, Hunt quickly connected with people at Grade's Elstree studios, a half hour northwest of London. "I've made friends with a couple of blokes (ooh!) from the camera crew, nice, handsome, intelligent young guys who strangely enough (from American standards) care a good deal about the quality of their work!" he reported to Kenworthy. Yet he also struggled with the "tedious reality" of the "hard work schedule," as well as his accommodations. Hunt's room at London's Marble Arch–area Holiday Inn was just a ten-minute stroll from his previous fancy digs at the Royal Lancaster, but in his eyes, "this Holiday dump" was miles away. He did enjoy British television, which he found "absolutely hysterical, including the serious shows—a running Monty Python sketch."

Hunt's letter, scribbled on Henson Associates stationery, unwittingly reveals why Kenworthy might have been, as he says, starting to feel "overwhelmed" by their relationship. Hunt seemed almost dependent on Kenworthy to keep up his spirits, appreciating a few days they had managed to spend together before the trip: "Thank you very, very much for staying! It really brought me up so high." As usual, he wanted Kenworthy to connect with his friends—to take tai chi from one friend, and to become acquainted with another whose company he might not even enjoy: "I'd like you to meet him, but I guess you might not like him." Hunt also wanted—almost expected—Kenworthy to spend time with his family, even while he was out of town. "Have you seen Adam and the family, I hope so, I think you're good for Adam." And while he was suggesting Kenworthy see *his* family, he was getting in touch with Kenworthy's family. "I spoke to your parents tonight (your father didn't remember me at first). I'm going to try to get down there on Thursday. Your mum sounded nice!"

The letter rings with a clear, joyful affection. "I don't have to tell you I miss you terribly," Hunt wrote in closing. "But mostly I love you!" How was Kenworthy to reconcile all this with keeping their relationship a secret from family and friends? How could he be so much to this strong personality, while being such a reserved personality himself?

When Hunt returned to New York, it became clear that what had brought the couple together—their opposite temperaments—was now pulling them apart. Kenworthy had discovered that underneath Hunt's joyful façade lay indecision and even despair. While Hunt publicly radiated confidence, he felt pressured by work, the struggle to hide their involvement, and the responsibility of holding his family together. "The very private Richard was sad and lost—overwhelming to be with, and looking to me for answers that I simply didn't have," says Kenworthy. "I realized in the end that we weren't right for each other, or he wasn't right for me." While Kenworthy had initially been drawn to Hunt's voluminous energy, ultimately he found it "overbearing." In spring 1976, with Hunt about to go back to London for three months of work on *The Muppet Show*, Kenworthy suggested it was time to call it quits.

But Hunt's biggest loss, as he prepared to fly overseas, was saying goodbye to his father, who was so ill from cirrhosis that Hunt doubted he would ever see him again. Richard Bradshaw had started to resemble a spider, with a swollen abdomen and skinny appendages, sprawled in his armchair. Most eerily, he grew jaundiced—even the whites around his eyes took on a yellowish tinge. Hunt's father had also becomé uncharacteristically ill-tempered, which reverberated throughout the family. "As our dad got sicker there was a lot more yelling and screaming," Hunt's sister Rachel recalls. Jane agonized over the changes in her husband, frustrated with his seeming refusal to take care of himself; they fought dramatically.

So it was an emotional moment when Hunt boarded his British Air flight on May 10, 1976. He had worked hard to get here, making the most of his apprenticeship. He had joined the Muppets at exactly the right time: any earlier, and they wouldn't have had room for him; any later, and he wouldn't have had time to build his skills in close proximity to Henson, Oz, and Nelson. By the time they started the *Muppet Show* in earnest, Hunt had taken his place as one of the Original Five, the core troupe that would anchor the show for its entire duration, as other cast members came and went. He was still young, because he had started out so young, labored so unceasingly, and grown so much during these five short years.

He was surprised by what he had learned, he reflected years later. Ultimately, Hunt had to master the basic skills of bringing the puppets to life, making them breathe, move, and behave. The medium could be tricky to pick up, Hunt explained. "Technically it's the ability to control a piece of cloth and ping-pong balls or whatever to such a degree that it becomes completely lifelike. And in order to get that it takes years to perfect to whatever degree you're capable on that technical proficiency."

Yet unexpectedly, the most challenging part of the job wasn't puppeteering, nor was it developing performance skills. "We can be great actors, and that's enormously important," Hunt said. "And you can be a comedian and tell jokes and set up stuff well and that's important. But the silliness of Muppets, which is one of its trademarks, is a very scary jump into whimsy." The performers routinely struggled with this in their early days. "As all of us grew into it you would do too much and you would learn over that five-year period [of training] how to back off." This surrendering was arguably a performer's greatest challenge. "It's a letting go," said Hunt. "That's what's very hard to learn." It would be a challenge in his life outside the studio as well: letting go of desired outcomes, accepting and appreciating what came his way.

By the time he was off to England, Hunt was ready to assume his place in the troupe, to do some of his best work, to show off his talents to the world. "*Sesame Street*, he was still learning, in the beginning," says Oz. "But when he got to the *Muppet Show*, it wasn't a matter of learning anymore, it was just letting loose—letting him be Richie."

PART III

Hunt, mid-1970s.

CHAPTER 6

Affectionate Anarchy

A s SOON AS Hunt got word from the Royal Lancaster Hotel staff that he had an overseas phone call, he knew the worst had come. Hunt had been in London less than a week when his family called to tell him his father had died, on May 16, 1976. Hunt's father, Richard Bradshaw Hunt, was just fifty years old; Hunt was a few months shy of his twenty-fifth birthday.

Hunt agonized over whether to fly home for the funeral, speaking to each member of his family in turn. "We all told him, 'This is huge, the work you're doing. Dad would understand,'" says his sister Rachel.

Hunt even consulted psychic Betty Balcombe about the decision. The plainspoken, working-class woman, whose clients included rock royalty as well as actual royalty, served less as supernatural conduit than psychological sounding board. Hunt described Balcombe as "a friend who you reflected with on a spiritual level. And you could take relief." Hunt appreciated his sessions with Balcombe so much he recommended her to Henson, who saw Balcombe about a dozen times over as many years, like a cosmic checkup; Hunt sought her out more often, particularly when mulling over important choices. Balcombe, too, recommended that Hunt stay in London.

Hunt knew Henson would support whatever decision he made. Henson was very understanding, for example, when Nelson needed to prioritize caring for his daughter Christine as she struggled with cystic fibrosis. Yet Nelson's absences meant that he risked missing out on work opportunities such as doing characters. Hunt was well positioned in Henson Associates; he had hitched his wagon to a rising star, and now that star was rapidly on the ascent. Hunt not only wanted to be along for the ride, he needed to be. The death of his father only increased the pressure to provide for his family. What better way to honor his father, a performer himself, than to succeed at their shared craft? Ready or not, Hunt's apprenticeship phase was over. It was time to step up. *The Muppet Show* could be the career-making opportunity that Hunt had been waiting for all his life.

So Hunt didn't fly to New Jersey for his father's funeral, held at their church, St. Andrews Episcopalian in Harrington Park. Instead, the day after his father died, Hunt moved into the Portobello Hotel in Notting Hill; Nelson moved in down the hall a few days later. The bohemian mecca, suggested by a studio liaison, provided Hunt plenty of distraction from his grief. The Portobello catered to a colorful clientele of artists and musicians, with everyone from Patti Smith to Carly Simon parading through the lobby. This lively company compensated for the tiny rooms, barely larger than the beds they housed. Hunt also appreciated that the hotel overlooked the verdant Stanley Gardens.

In keeping with his usual practice of connecting with everyone, Hunt befriended the hotel staff. One day the concierge beckoned him behind the front desk, saying, "I want you to meet some people." In the lounge sat four skinny, sneering young men, their ripped clothes studded with safety pins: a new band called the Sex Pistols. Hunt loved to recount the incongruous encounter between the punks and the puppeteer. "Oh, what do you guys play?" Hunt asked amiably. "Hard-drivin', kick-ass, fuckin' punk rock and roll, like it or not," snarled a band member. There was a long pause. "Oh," Hunt replied. (This crossing of paths could have happened only in this slim window of time; soon the Sex Pistols would implode, while the Muppets would propel themselves well past the Portobello.)

Hunt, the irrepressible trickster, got up to his usual antics even on his commute. Producer Lord Lew Grade hired a minibus, *The Muppet Show* logo brightly painted on its sides, to wind through London picking up the performers and personnel for the fifteen-mile ride northwest to the ATV Elstree Studios in Borehamwood. Hunt could be impatient with the trip, a distance which took about a half hour directly but could eat up nearly two hours on the minibus's circuitous route. One day Hunt spied Grade's Rolls Royce on the road and quickly marshaled the driver and his co-workers into mischief. "The bus passed the limousine with a blare of its horns and a hearty, 'Hey, Lew!'" recalls Muppet writer Joe Bailey. "Every window on the left side of the bus flew open and a bare bottom instantly appeared in every one of them. Lew Grade was being magnificently mooned at 9:30 in the morning." Hunt was unafraid to prank even their vaunted producer.

But when Hunt and his colleagues arrived at Elstree's Eldon Avenue studios, it was time to get down to business. The *Muppet Show*'s first-season performers—the Original Five, John Lovelady, and new hire Eren Ozker—kicked things off in mid-May 1976 by packing thirteen episodes into three months of work. (Around the corner at Elstree's movie studios, an obscure science fiction fairy tale was underway: *Star Wars*.)

Hunt's talents were well suited to the format of *The Muppet Show*, a smart culmination of what the Muppets had been honing for years: a comedy-variety program of songs and sketches performed by a wacky, idiosyncratic ensemble of characters, each episode featuring a different guest star. The show had a fun metaconceit, in which the characters staged their own show in the Muppet theater, with plenty of backstage drama to boot. Hunt played a number of major characters, from a young intern to an old critic, a shaggy ogre to a mellow Valley Girl, a self-important crooner to an anxious lab assistant, plus nearly fifty minor characters and countless one-offs. By the second season his characters would both open and close the show.

Perhaps most importantly, Hunt's mischievous, no-holds-barred attitude was crucial to the *Muppet Show*'s offbeat comedic sensibility. While this was Hunt's role at the Muppets in general, his edgy comedy was particularly vital to the spirit and success of *The Muppet Show*, essential to conjuring up the "affectionate anarchy" that viewers adored.

The Muppet performers created a cast of characters who were a tightly interconnected tribe of weirdos. "It was a band of misfits that needed each other," says Goelz. "It was a metaphor for family." And behind the scenes, the performers mimicked some of these same family dynamics. Indeed, the characters themselves were often based on facets of their performers' essential natures. The performers would notice an element of themselves in the character as it was written, and build on or exaggerate that trait to make the character come alive. "All these characters, as I've said, are all of us. Very strongly," Hunt said. "Really, you can't make it up. You can't imitate anything."

The most well known *Muppet Show* alter ego is Henson's Kermit the Frog, who served as the show's host—a wise choice, as audiences already adored the skinny green amphibian from *Sesame Street* and Henson's earlier work. If the Muppet characters are a family, Kermit is unquestionably the dad. Kermit resembled Henson as the cheerfully overextended center of chaos, keeping many balls in the air, unflappably patient (for the most part) in the face of nuttiness. Yet it's misleading to cast Kermit, and by extension Henson, as the straight man in contrast to his wilder counterparts. "Me not crazy?" Kermit quips in a revealing line. "I hired the others!" Henson saw and appreciated his personnel for their full, unique selves, gratefully taking the good with the bad.

If Henson's Kermit is the dad in the Muppet family, Hunt also has an alter ego that represents his role in the dynamic: the young, eager apprentice of Scooter the gofer. Hunt openly identified with the character. "Scooter is very much me as a kid," Hunt said. "When I came I was eighteen, and I was really energetic. I'd say, 'Yeah, sure, anything you wanna do, boss, no problem.' I talked a lot like him, 'cause he's my voice."

Like Hunt, Scooter is a born performer. Scooter also resembles Hunt in his amiable disposition and his almost nonchalant acceptance of the other characters and their quirks. This acceptance stems from his own quiet confidence in himself—much like Hunt as a kid, happily amusing himself and the people around him. "Scooter is a perpetual kid and very comfortable with who he is," said Hunt. "It's certainly a part of me, and certainly who I am. I remember once getting a birthday card from Jim, '[to] the most sensational, perpetual teenager in the world.' So I play that out that way."

Just as Hunt had cold-called the Muppets, Scooter shows up of his own volition at the Muppet theater, cheerfully eager to work. Viewers met the character early on, in the Jim Nabors episode, the second to air in most U.S. markets. "I'm your new gofer," Scooter tells Kermit. "I'll gofer coffee, I'll gofer sandwiches, I'll gofer anything you need." Kermit initially writes him off as too young and inexperienced; only when Scooter casually mentions, "My uncle owns this theater," does Kermit hire him. The nepotism gag largely peters out after the first year, as Scooter—and by extension Hunt—earns his place.

Perhaps because Hunt identified so closely with this eager young kid, he had trouble playing a character who was the exact opposite: a jaded oldster, in a rare pairing with Henson. First-season head writer Jack Burns, along with writers Henson, Jerry Juhl, and Marc London, brilliantly retooled the two tired seniors from the pilot and turned them into the Muppet theater's resident hecklers. To this day, Statler and Waldorf—better known as the old guys in the balcony—remain among the most popular Muppet characters. (A handy mnemonic for who's who: Henson's Waldorf has a wide face, while Hunt's Statler has more of a slim face.) Statler provided Hunt plenty of screen time, as the pair in the peanut gallery appeared in every episode, judging acts as well as delivering the final punchline after the closing credits, getting in the very last word. This device cleverly allowed the show to make fun of itself—as well as its critics.

Despite how much fans loved Statler, Hunt never quite understood the character. "I never identified with Statler because he was too old for me," Hunt said. "I didn't know who he was." However, Hunt actually had much in common with the balcony heckler. A lifelong snarker, Hunt teased and criticized those he loved; it was how he showed affection, and the harder he was on you, the more he cared.

Hunt's pairing with Henson made the role particularly special; while the two had worked together on plenty of one-offs, a regular duo was unusual. Hunt and Henson shared a bone-deep irreverence, a sense that nothing was too sacred for a laugh. Other performers might be intimidated to play this critical role alongside their boss, essentially insulting their own work, but Hunt had no such qualms.

Indeed, Hunt didn't exempt Henson from his affectionate teasing. "He used to razz Jim something crazy," recalls Debi Spinney, wife of *Sesame Street* performer Caroll Spinney. "He would tease Jim the way no one else would tease Jim." Henson would pass by and Hunt would mutter, "Here comes this asshole. Look at this guy. He thinks he's so great." Henson would grin as he pointedly ignored Hunt. "I think he slipped my father into a father figure to him," says Henson's son Brian. "He was quite happy to be the naughty oldest son." This dynamic was especially meaningful to Hunt after he lost his own father.

Playing Statler and Waldorf gave Hunt and Henson an opportunity to get to know each other. "That was the time we would spend together," Hunt recalled. The duo would be squeezed into the tiny Statler and Waldorf set, an enclosed booth behind curtains, waiting in position between takes. It took so long to get in there that they just stayed in place, secluded from the frenzy of the studio. "We would spend two or three hours there," Hunt recalled. "And in between things, you know, 'So, what's going on.' That's when we would have these talks. We would talk about our families, and our hopes and desires, and politics." This pairing gave Hunt the opportunity to make a connection with Henson that, despite strains and twists and turns, would last in some form all their lives.

When *The Muppet Show* took a two-week break in early July, Henson invited Hunt along on a family trip sailing around the Aegean Sea. Hunt was happy to go, as he connected not just with Henson but with Henson's wife Jane and their five children. "This was the one time I spent a week with them all together," said Hunt. "I got along very well with the family and I love them all very much and I certainly felt comfortable." The family adored him in return. Jane Henson appreciated his wacky sense of humor, as well as the way that he honored her skill and experience as a puppeteer, rather than seeing her as just Jim's wife. The big Henson family reminded Hunt of his own; he easily fell into his big brother role. Lisa and Cheryl Henson were sixteen and fifteen, around the same age as Hunt's youngest sister. Hunt especially got along with Brian and John Henson, thirteen and eleven, who followed Hunt around like a cool older cousin. They appreciated his companionability, how he met them on their level. "He knew what kids thought was funny," says Brian. "He was happy to do things. 'Sure, I'll march around in the woods with you and you'll show me your swamp dwellings.'"

So while America celebrated its bicentennial, Hunt joined the Henson family, performer Peter Friedman, and secretary Caryl Starling on a charter boat sailing out of Athens. Fortunately they were flexible about their itinerary, as the captain had some ideas of his own. Hunt appreciated Henson's mild attitude as he tried to negotiate their route. "Every day this was the same thing," Hunt said. "This guy would say to Jim, 'We go anywhere you want to go! Anywhere at all!'" Henson would suggest a place, and the captain would say, "'No, we can't go there. We go here.' Everywhere we went was beautiful, but we were going to visit his friends. It was a joke between all of us."

While the group was good-natured about where they went, Hunt noticed that Henson was sterner about how their trip would affect the environment. The captain was dumping their garbage overboard, a common practice, which horrified Henson. "Jim couldn't cope with it," Hunt recalled. "'Look,' he said to the captain, 'I don't want you to dump the garbage over the boat. We're destroying ourselves as it is.'" Henson insisted that the captain bag up the garbage and dispose of it at ports. "I remember him very gently and very determinedly telling the captain, 'This is important to me.' 'Cause the guy looked at him like, 'You're nuts.'"

Hunt's most indelible memory from the trip was realizing just how much Henson truly resembled his alter ego. The group was swimming in a private cove when Hunt looked over at Henson in the water. "I'll never forget this image: there was Jim, swimming like Kermit, totally unconsciously." Henson lounged placidly on his back, treading water with his hands, totally in his element. "I said, 'You even swim like this frog! This is unbelievable!'" Years later, Hunt happily recalled the memory. "That was such a fun trip."

If Kermit is the dad of the *Muppet Show* characters, his on-again, off-again love interest Miss Piggy is the mom. The porcine prima donna remains one of the most controversial Muppet characters, equally beloved and despised, with rarely a fan who doesn't have a strong opinion. Though she is most associated with performer Frank Oz, Hunt performed Miss Piggy in eleven first-season episodes.

Piggy's transformation illustrates how characters often developed through sheer trial and error, especially in the early days. Originally just a nameless lady pig, Miss Piggy started taking shape during a "Muppet Glee Club" performance of Perry Como's hit "Temptation," where it became clear that Piggy would never settle for the chorus when she could be a showstopping soloist. Hunt and Oz split performing duties in the sketch, playing to their respective strengths. Oz did the initial dialogue and the overall puppeteering, exaggerating Piggy's lust for her beloved frog. "I made a big show of going for him," Oz recalls. "That was the bit that put Piggy in my head." Meanwhile, Hunt took the singing vocals truly over the top.

The character solidified in spring 1976 when the script called for Piggy to slap Kermit—and Oz instead delivered what would become her trademark karate chop. "That crystallized who Piggy was for me," says Oz. "The tough woman underneath the coyness. And the fact that she had to be coy to get things the way she wanted them, like most women at that time." Just a few weeks later, Piggy karate chopped not only Kermit but Nelson's hip alter ego Floyd Pepper and even guest star Florence Henderson herself. Realizing he was onto something, Oz approached Hunt in the rehearsal room. "Richard, I think something's starting to gel for Piggy," he said. "You're okay if I take her?" "Yeah, sure," Hunt replied. Hunt continued to pinch-hit Piggy, but soon even that was phased out.

Hunt was happy to surrender the character, as he wasn't particularly comfortable playing female roles. What's more, Miss Piggy posed a specific challenge as her furious ambition often went against the warm-hearted chaos of the overall Muppet sensibility. "Piggy is anger replete," Hunt said. "And on The Muppet Show, we don't like that kind of stuff. I'm sure Frank's uncomfortable with that."

Like Henson, Oz was a mentor to Hunt, though mostly by example. The tireless workhorse could be impatient if Hunt was late or fooling around, even as Oz, like Henson, appreciated both the pros and cons of Hunt's irrepressible temperament. "He's always been an extraordinary uncontrolled spirit to me, which is what I love about him," says Oz. Though less than a decade older than Hunt, their dynamic was as if Oz was much older, with Oz calling Hunt by the affectionate nickname "Richie."

Though Hunt was reeling from his father's death, he largely hid his grief from his colleagues, a master of compartmentalization. Yet in mid-August, he was sitting with Oz and guest star Candice Bergen when he started "sobbing uncontrollably," Oz recalls. Hunt's twenty-fifth birthday was just around the corner, his first without his father. Oz decided to organize a birthday party to cheer him up, taking pains to create a special surprise.

The party was in full swing when Bergen made a dramatic entrance holding aloft the surprise: a birthday cake that looked just like Hunt's trademark blue-and-white Adidas. Oz had "borrowed" the sneakers, made a mold from them, and baked a birthday cake that looked just like them, even carefully painting on blue-and-white frosting. Hunt's colleagues had long teased him about his sneakers, which he wore even with formal wear, symbols of his casual youthfulness; the cake was the perfect way for Oz and the rest of his colleagues to show that they appreciated him for exactly the energy he brought to the troupe. People started to laugh as they recognized Hunt's sneakers; but nobody roared with laughter louder than Hunt himself.

Hunt cut off his shoulder-length hair around this time, as if to mark the transition from hippie kid to serious careerist. As usual, Hunt rarely did things by halves; rather than a shorter bob or some such medium-length cut, Hunt lopped off all his long locks, leaving just a short wild frizz of dark curls. He would keep some variation of this simple haircut for the rest of his life.

Hunt turned twenty-five in New Jersey, home for a brief but eventful break. He and his colleagues squeezed in some work on *Sesame Street*. Hunt was assuming a more solid place at the show, filming its eighth season, as the show itself assumed a solid place on television. He and his colleagues had picked up another Emmy in May for Outstanding Children's Programming, and Hunt's stressed-out pianist, Don Music, was becoming a recurring character. Interestingly, as Hunt gladly relinquished the drag queen–like prima donna of Miss Piggy, he developed a similar character on *Sesame Street*.

Like Piggy, the dramatic diva Gladys the Cow began as a nameless barn animal. "She walks in, she was just supposed to do, 'Hi, I'm a cow,'" Hunt explained. But Hunt noticed an issue of *Variety* on Hooper's newsstand—and got an idea. "I thought, 'Oh, wouldn't it be funny if I turned Gladys into a theatrical cow?' So I started ad-libbing: 'Oh, the same old *cattle calls*. I'm so tired of playing *stock* every year.' It became this theatrical chanteuse kind of a thing." Hunt didn't have to look far for inspiration—just to the *Sesame* puppet workshop, where designer and builder Kermit Love held court. "I based the voice on Kermit Love," said Hunt. "He has a *veddy theatrical* voice. He's very flattered by it." (Love and Hunt's mother quarreled amiably at Hunt's parties over which of them had inspired the character, as it did also resemble the theatrical Jane.) As usual, Henson and Stone welcomed this sort of creative improvisation in the studio—especially when it was so funny.

Yet despite having created a hilarious character out of a generic cow, Hunt initially found it difficult to play female roles, particularly ones so flamboyant. "It's very hard for [lowers voice] *us men* to relax into the female characters we do," he said. "Yet we do some great female characters: Frank with Piggy, me with Gladys; that's the one I feel comfortable with, though I didn't at first." He resented the assumption that his sexuality meant that he favored such roles. "I never liked being identified with the women roles, because that's not what I am," he said. "I happen to be a man who likes guys, and loves everybody." (In the same 1990 interview, he also openly says, "I'm gay.")

Hunt grew more at ease with the role over time, delivering a strong performance a few years later with Gladys's gender-bending bovine anthem "Proud to Be a Cow" ("I'm proud to have an udder/like my father—no, my mother"). A consummate character actor, he could enjoy roles without necessarily relating to them. "It's not me!" he said of Gladys. "But it's a great character. I love to play it." Over time, he would become more comfortable playing female characters, but never at his happiest in those roles.

On September 18, Hunt and his cohorts made a triumphant return to *Saturday Night Live*. This time, they weren't pleading to return—they were promoting their own show. Hunt's character Wisss is smoking craters, of course, when the *SNL* Muppet characters wake up from a few months' nap in a file cabinet. Wisss is the one to tell host Lily Tomlin that their *SNL* characters are too adult for *The Muppet Show*. "They won't let us work on that," Wisss says. "That's family entertainment." Tomlin suggests they sing "Whistle a Happy Tune," but unfortunately the Muppets can't whistle, so the song trails off and they go back into their file drawers. "Let's get high," Wisss suggests during the fade-out.

Just two days after appearing on *Saturday Night Live*, Hunt eagerly tuned into New York's channel 2 at 7:30 P.M. for the American premiere of *The Muppet Show*. Most networks selected the Rita Moreno episode, a smart choice as this episode would net Moreno the Emmy that made her one of only eighteen performers (as of 2023) to have won an EGOT (an Emmy, Grammy, Tony, and Oscar). Hunt and his colleagues had little time to concern themselves with the show's reception, however, as less than a week later they were back in England for two months, finishing out the first season.

Hunt displayed his versatility with two more first-season debuts. The oversized ogre of Sweetums was the exact opposite of a lady diva like Gladys or Miss Piggy. "I, of course, being the biggest, hunkiest dude in the Muppets, I play Sweetums, who attracts a large percentage of the female audience," Hunt gleefully told the Canadian Broadcasting Corporation, assuming the character's macho growl. "*Sweetums, big butch monster, with shoulders out to here.*" Sweetums's exaggerated masculinity creates a great foil for female guest stars: he gobbles up Candice Bergen's camera, carries away Rita Moreno, woos Cloris Leachman, and dances masochistically with Ruth Buzzi, who breaks a chair over his head. ("My kinda woman!" he exclaims.) The huge monster also duets nicely with Nelson's tiny frog Robin, another strong pairing from the two pals. Sweetums required a whole different method of puppeteering from hand or rod puppets, as Hunt donned a full-body costume for the walkaround puppet, controlling the eyes and mouth from inside.

Despite being one of the show's most edgy performers, Hunt also played one of its most explicitly "normal" characters: the saccharine singer Wayne, half of the duo Wayne and Wanda. Eren Ozker, Wanda's portrayer, ably matched Hunt in singing and comedy skills, as the Turkish-born performer came to the Muppets from Off-Broadway theater. Modeled after 1930s movie crooners Nelson Eddy and Jeanette MacDonald, Wayne and Wanda radiate sincerity—but alas, wholesomeness is doomed on *The Muppet Show*. They sing "Trees" and a tree falls on Wayne, for instance; they sing "Autumn Leaves" and get buried in fallen foliage; they sing "Bewitched, Bothered and Bewildered" and Wanda is literally bewitched, turning into a hideous monster.

Wayne and Wanda's songs, like their single-season tenure on the show, are short-lived—especially as Ozker performed only in the show's first season. Ozker went on to advocate for puppeteers within the Screen Actors Guild, founding a Puppeteers Caucus and serving as its first chair before dying of cancer at only forty-four years old.

Hunt presumably tracked the progress of another performer who appeared only in *The Muppet Show*'s first season. John Lovelady had joined the Muppets at the same time as Hunt. Lovelady had originally thought he would be a math teacher while growing up in Grenada, Mississippi, so close to Henson's hometown of Leland that they attended the same elementary school. Lovelady entered the Muppets primarily as a puppet designer and builder, but pinch-hit a scattering of parts in *The Muppet Show*'s first season, primarily when Nelson wasn't available. Yet as the season drew to a close, Henson decided that Lovelady's talents were better suited back in the workshop. Just as Nelson had had to make way for Oz, in a way now Lovelady made way for Nelson—and, arguably, for Hunt.

Hunt finished filming the first season of *The Muppet Show* just in time to fly home for his first Thanksgiving without his father. Had it been worth missing the funeral? He had done good work, and critics seemed positive, but American audiences seemed largely underappreciative. While the show's ratings inched up each week, they remained unremarkable. Viewers weren't used to tuning in to the relatively new prime time slot of local programming. The show had limited rivals in California, but in Chicago and New York it competed with the popular game show *Hollywood Squares*, where viewers could see a bevy of celebrities instead of just one (who, in *The Muppet Show*'s first season, wasn't even necessarily a big star). Still, an optimistic mood reigned at the company Christmas party at 30 Rock's Rainbow Room, as Hunt and his colleagues toasted a job well done.

Regardless of what happened with *The Muppet Show*, Hunt had certainly grown as a performer over the past year: pairing with Henson and Oz as a colleague rather than as an assistant; developing a wide variety of his own characters; rising within the company as the company rose in the public eye; and truly taking his place as one of the Original Five, an essential co-creator of their long-dreamed-of all-ages evening program. He had gotten himself to a good place, whether or not the Muppets kept ascending. Besides, if this puppet thing didn't pan out, he could always pursue on-camera acting—still his underlying dream.

It's the Royal Muppets

By appointment : : : head and shoulders above other stars

By David Wigg

SHOWBIZ kept a big beady eye on the Queen last night.

From Her Majesty's point of view, the eye-catcher was a monster from the Muppet Show—one of children's TV favourites.

The Queen and the Monster Muppet, Sweetums, exchanged glances at the London Palladium's Royal Variety Show line-up.

Bing

For Kathy Crosby—at the show with her son Harry—the show was a sad occasion, Husband Bing should have been top of the bill. He made the appointment before his death.

Instead, compering the show was Bing's oldest buddy, Bob Hope.

Before the curtain went up Bob spoke of "the great loss" of Bing Crosby.

"I did not feel like work-ing again after his death, but I realised we all had to go on," he said.

Kathy Crosby, he said, had been "a marvellous example. She was so brave when she spoke on television soon after he died."

Bing's death was an even greater sadness, he said, because they had so much more planned together.

"We were talking about shows with each other, new films, the possibility of a record together and a new 'Road' film."

But the show must go on . . . and Bob had a wealth of royal jokes when the curtain went up.

Looking at the Queen's box he said : "You know, I'm starting a nappy company and I wanted to start at the top.

"I want to congratulate Her Majesty on becoming a grandmother.

"She now has another title—the royal baby-sitter."

● The draw raised a record £1 million for the Queen's Silver Jubilee charities.

PICTURE BY BARRY GOMER
Peek-a-boo Ma'am . . . Muppet Sweetums looks on as the Queen meets Royal Variety performers

Left to right: Dave Goelz, Hunt, and Jerry Nelson meet Queen Elizabeth II, November 21, 1977. From the UK's *Daily Express* the following day.

CHAPTER 7

Muppetmania

I F HUNT WONDERED how the Muppets were doing in spring 1977, he merely had to look around him on the Queen Elizabeth 2, a majestic British ocean liner which was practically a city on the sea. Henson had decided to kick off the *Muppet Show*'s second season in style, booking passage on the QE2 for most of the show's major personnel: performers Henson, Oz, Nelson, and Hunt (Goelz flew over); agent Bernie Brillstein; newly promoted head writer Jerry Juhl; and writers Don Hinkley and Joe Bailey. They left New York on May 8 for the weeklong voyage across the Atlantic.

A thousand feet long, the QE2 boasted ten decks housing nearly two thousand passengers and a thousand crew members. Hunt and his fellow passengers could avail themselves of two swimming pools (outdoor and indoor), a library, a theater, even a spa; Hunt liked to lounge on the sun deck. Yet despite all these amenities, the Muppet gang found themselves with idle time on their hands—which they naturally filled up with impish shenanigans.

The ship's formal dinners were a production in themselves, requiring the men to dress up in tuxedos to avail themselves of the sumptuous entrées and rich desserts. Henson and Bailey jokingly lorded their active metabolisms over the others. "We can have some deep dish apple pie with double Devon cream sent to our rooms later," Henson said loudly to Bailey at one meal. Hunt didn't miss a beat: "You know, you need a prescription to get that in the States."

After dinner, Hunt and his colleagues decamped to one of the ship's numerous watering holes, still in formal dress. "We'd stand around and look elegant with a glass of scotch," Nelson recalls. On rough evenings at sea, Oz and Bailey liked to visit the bar on the highest deck, where the ship was most unstable, watching drunk patrons try to dance as the room pitched and pivoted. They slipped five-dollar bills to the bandleader to play tangos, cha-chas, and even the Mexican hat dance, holding fast to their barstools—nailed to the floor—as the dancers listed and reeled.

The makeup of the ship lent itself to these sorts of pranks. During a cocktail party in his cabin, Hunt noticed how easily passengers got disoriented while walking down the long windowless corridor crisscrossed by intersecting halls. Hunt stationed his friends where they could observe the main hallway without being seen. When three intoxicated couples in tuxedos and evening gowns came walking unsteadily up the hallway, seemingly unsure about which way to go, Hunt casually crossed in front of them—*backward*. His unwitting victims were utterly befuddled, scurrying back and forth like rats in a maze, as the Muppet guys held their stomachs in silent mirth.

Characteristically, Hunt not only hung out with his friends, but befriended other passengers as well as crew members. "Richard got to know everybody on the ship," says Nelson. Hunt went barhopping with the waiters among the crew-only establishments, including a gay bar, reporting back to his friends about the "parallel universe of neon and linoleum instead of paneling and carpet," Bailey recalls. Hunt explored practically every inch of the ocean liner, making himself welcome wherever he went. "He went down below decks, back into the bowels of the ship, where no passenger has probably ever been before," says Nelson. "That's just how Richard was—so open and magnanimous, people were just drawn to him." It was also like Hunt to make the most of every moment, to tour the ship so thoroughly, because who knew if he'd experience an opportunity like this again? He tried not to take anything for granted.

Docking in Southampton on the morning of May 14, Hunt and his colleagues found themselves smack in the middle of a longshoremen's strike—which meant they had to carry all their own baggage off the dock. This would have been a rough schlep with their suitcases alone, but the Muppet gang had made good use of the ship's generous unlimited luggage policy, bringing over all the puppets, props, costumes, and so forth needed for the season. Hunt and his workmates gamely and good-naturedly loaded everything onto carts and dollies, lugging it all through customs.

Once they were cleared to enter the country, however, they were quickly relieved of dockworker duty. The studio had sent a fleet of Daimler Princess limousines, whose drivers rushed obsequiously to grab all their baggage and load it into the cars. This royal treatment, like their swanky setting on the boat, seemed to symbolize the change in status that awaited them in England.

While Hunt and his colleagues had been across the pond, British audiences had fallen in love with *The Muppet Show*. Viewers held fast to the show even as local networks tinkered with its time slots, finally settling on Sunday evenings at 7 P.M. What's more, the brand-new *Muppet Show* album was rocketing up the British charts, propelled by Nelson's young frog Robin's "Halfway Down the Stairs," a musical rendition of an A. A. Milne poem. By the time the Muppet gang arrived back in England, 15 million British viewers tuned in each week. The *Muppet Show* minibus, with its prominent logo across the sides, was mobbed by fans at a traffic light. Muppetmania had officially begun.

Goelz quickly noticed the difference. He frequented a bakery in the country village of Harpenden, where the maternal ladies behind the counter had taken him under their wing. They knew he worked for the Muppets, but hadn't really known what that meant. When Goelz stepped into the bakery at the beginning of the second season, however, the women started whispering amongst themselves; when he went up to place his order, they asked for his autograph. He was polite and obliging, humoring them as he drank his coffee and munched his toast—and then he never went back. Unlike Hunt and Nelson, who identified as actors and longed for the fame that accompanied on-camera performing, Goelz cherished his anonymity, wanting a hangout where he could be "off-duty," not representing the brand.

The Muppets' success led to some corresponding upticks in Hunt's quality of life. He left his tiny room at the Portobello Hotel for a one-bedroom at 6 Westmoreland Place in Pimlico, a Central London neighborhood a few blocks north of the Thames. Henson helped him secure the apartment, surveying the performers about their preferred living situations and having the company set it up. Hunt's new place boasted a good-sized sitting room, a kitchenette, even a backyard garden where he could sun himself when the weather allowed. Hunt also bought himself a battered, boxy Ford Cortina, piloting himself and his friends around the city with the knowledge and ease of a cabdriver.

Now Hunt had about a half-hour drive to Elstree, where there was plenty of work to be done, and at first only the Original Five to do it. By now the performers had a set schedule which they generally followed for the rest of the show. They filmed an episode every week—sometimes more if needed.

Sunday

While many Brits attended church, the Muppet personnel began their workweek with a Sunday morning read-through of their own temporary bible: that week's script. Hunt hustled up to Elstree for the 10 A.M. meeting, curious to see what was in store for the week, joining the guest star, his fellow performers, the writers, floor manager, and other personnel in Rehearsal Room 7/8 on the fourth floor of ATV's main building Neptune House. The cold reading could be nerve-racking, as Hunt and his fellow performers were seeing the script for the first time.

Hunt's laughter rang out over the others as they read—and the laughter in the room affected the script, not yet set in stone. Head writer Jerry Juhl appreciated ad-libs and often wrote them in. Juhl resembled the Muppet character Ernie with his mischievous spirit and infectious grin; Hunt described him as "a gentle man who had enormous respect for Jim." Juhl had written for the Muppets since their days on *The Jimmy Dean Show*, penning all their major specials, and liked to incorporate the performers into his writing process. Hunt described Juhl's philosophy as, "Make the character come to life for me and then I can write for that character." Juhl added more character-based humor to the show's variety format, bringing a sitcom-like aspect and loose plotlines to many episodes, greatly strengthening the show.

Under Juhl's leadership, a number of beloved Muppet characters came to life. Meanwhile, the performers grew even more at ease in working together, in both new and familiar combinations. The Muppet family was coming together, both on and off set. *The Muppet Show* house band, the Electric Mayhem, embodied this shift in dynamic. Led by Henson's robust vocalist Dr. Teeth, with Oz's id-personified Animal on drums and Goelz's drowsy Zoot playing saxophone, the band shone in the second season once Nelson was around to develop hipster bassist Floyd Pepper and Hunt took over lead guitarist Janice.

Fan favorite Janice is a rare female humanoid Muppet, a recognizable bohemian chick with sleepy eyes and a ready smile. (Interestingly, Janice was originally designed by Michael Frith as an androgynous, Mick Jagger–type male.) Hunt jettisoned the sultry tones Ozker had used and substituted a Valley Girl voice he had done since high school. "It's a California surfer girl," Hunt said, speaking in the character's voice. "Her name is Janice, y'know, and she's got long blond hair, and she's really fer sure kinda together lady. I don't surf anymore, because, like, there are no waves here in England, I don't know why!"

Janice exemplifies how Hunt's humor pushed the envelope on *The Muppet Show*, bringing a needed edge to the mild-mannered comedy. Janice contributes some of the show's most adult content, dropping the word "hell" into a song and delivering some of Hunt's naughtiest ad-libs. When Janice sings, "I get high with a little help from my friends," one can easily imagine her lighting up backstage with her buddies.

What's more, Janice is a hot item with bandmate Floyd Pepper, the closest Jerry Nelson came to a *Muppet Show* alter ego. If Kermit is the dad, and Piggy is the mom, Floyd is the beloved hip uncle, quick to emit a wheezy laugh or groovy riff. Janice and Floyd were Hunt and Nelson's first regular *Muppet Show* duo, building on their *Sesame Street* experience, a combination which strengthened both characters.

Yet despite his facility with the role, and the license he had to liven her up, Hunt couldn't quite relate to Janice, as with his other female characters. "Janice never clicked with me," he said. "Though people from California and Florida adored her, because they knew her sideways tilt, I never identified with her at all. She's just a caricature of herself." Hunt's ability to flesh out a character that didn't really resonate with him, to make her a fan favorite, testifies to his talent.

The Original Five were often in their Electric Mayhem personae on late Sunday mornings after the read-through, when they gathered around music associate Derek Scott at the piano in the far end of Rehearsal Room 7/8, learning and practicing that week's songs. Hunt could quickly pick up a tune by ear, though lyrics took longer.

After lunch, Hunt and his workmates rehearsed and blocked that week's songs and sketches with the guest star. The performers were fascinated by how each guest worked differently, particularly noticeable one Sunday in August 1977 when John Cleese and Dom DeLuise came in back to back. Cleese loved ad-libs, incorporating moments that got a laugh into the script; while DeLuise just wanted to know when he would need to react, trying out new reactions each time. "There are many ways to be funny," Goelz observes, reflecting on this. "You just have to find your own."

Sundays lasted until around 5 P.M.—their earliest-ending day of the week—when Hunt jumped into his rusty Cortina and sped back to London.

Monday

Hunt could sleep in on Mondays, which the performers called "Band Day," devoted to recording the music for that week's episode. The *Muppet Show* musicians recorded their instrumental parts in the morning, as well as making individual tracks for performers whose characters were "playing" an instrument. Sometimes Hunt's colleagues drew themselves symbolic sheet music to practice with, though Hunt preferred to play things more by ear.

The performers and guest star arrived around 2:30 to record their vocal tracks. Songs were recorded ahead of time, given the impossibility of nailing the vocals and the puppeteering simultaneously. Hunt prided himself on doing a quick, efficient job, not holding up the tight schedule; Henson appreciated this about him as well.

"Let's start with Richard's number," Henson said during one typical recording session. "That shouldn't take too long."

"Good old 'One Take' Hunt," Hunt bantered back. "You can always rely on him."

Even in a recording session, the material on the page was still open to interpretation. Henson trusted his colleagues and welcomed their input. In this particular session, Hunt played a high-strung man singing the Carpenters' hit "Close to You." "I'm a wimp," Hunt said, getting into character. He ran through the tune in a fearful, wobbly voice, then stopped. "I'd like to do this a completely different way," he said to Henson. "I can't buy the idea of this timid little guy not noticing all the stuff that's going on around him. This guy's *very* nervous. He would jump out of his skin if a leaf fell behind him, yet we've got him ignoring the fact that stars are falling around his girl's head. That doesn't make sense."

Henson responded with typical openness. "What do you have in mind?"

"I see this as being sung by a real pompous guy, real conceited," Hunt replied. "He cares more about the fact that he has a trained voice than he does about his girl. He's so full of himself that he doesn't notice what's happening to her. Someone who thinks he's Howard Keel," Hunt said, reaching into his endless roster of allusions for a 1950s MGM star with a rich bass-baritone. Hunt ran through the song again in showy, grandiose tones.

While Henson was open to suggestion, ultimately he had the final say. "I think I like that," Henson said. "Let's go with it." And they did.

Hunt never knew exactly when he would get home on Mondays, as recording sessions could run anywhere from an hour to a few hours— but he did his best to be as efficient as he could.

Tuesday

On Tuesdays the performers were called to the studio at 9:30 A.M., though not needed on the floor until 10:35; Hunt usually came skidding in just in time for a morning of blocking and rehearsing with the guest star and his colleagues.

The studio, nicely tailored to the performers' needs, facilitated Hunt's job. Studio D was an enormous, windowless room of about

10,000 square feet, with bright overhead lighting. As always on a Henson production, the studio had monitors throughout so the puppeteers could see and adjust their performances in real time. Best of all, the studio had customized sets, one of the show's biggest budget allowances. Most sets were built on platforms up on stilts about 38–42 inches high, with entrances for puppets cut into them. The sets had to be exactly the right height for the puppets and the guest stars, who often needed their own platforms, too, to stand at the same level as the puppets and make it all look natural and to scale.

Hunt enjoyed when they had visitors watching from the 350-person capacity risers along one wall. Though the set was closed to the public, friends and family visited, and school groups came in for tours. Potential visitors didn't necessarily understand how much work and different shots and editing went into the show, how many takes were often needed for tricky shots, nor how long and tedious the shoots could be. "If we have a half hour free, we'd love to come see the show," friends would say to Goelz, who would think, "You have no idea." The bleachers were more crowded when they landed well-known guest stars—which was starting to happen more often. "When we had Raquel Welch in the studio, we had a good 150 guys from neighboring studios," said Henson. While agent Bernie Brillstein had previously struggled to land big names, now agents were calling *him* to try to get their clients on the show.

Hunt strongly connected with the guest stars. "The fact is, when we had guests, they went away remembering Jim and Frank, and the only one else was Richard," recalls Goelz. Hunt often made a memorable impression before the guest even arrived, pulling his car up alongside them in the limo en route to the studio, yelling and gesturing wildly. The limo driver, Stefan—another friend of Hunt's—would remark mildly, "That's Richard Hunt, you'll meet him in a few minutes." Guest star Linda Lavin typified how guests appreciated the warm welcome. "He waved and winked, so I felt comfortable with him before I even met him," she recalls.

Fittingly, in the second season, Hunt's alter ego Scooter became the character to reveal the guest to the audience (which had previously happened during the theme song). Scooter opened each episode by poking his head into the star's dressing room to deliver a friendly warning, calling them by name: "Fifteen seconds to curtain!" (Since Statler and Waldorf generally delivered each episode's final quip, Hunt now both prominently opened and closed each show.)

And yet Hunt didn't single out the guest stars for special treatment; he welcomed people equally, rather than being drawn by someone's fame or accolades. "I think it's just, did he like them as people, that's all," says Oz. More than any other performer, Hunt connected not just with the guests but with the crew, knowing everyone's names, asking after their families, and even visiting them at their homes. What mattered most to Hunt was making a connection, and making everyone who stepped onto the set feel at ease.

Indeed, Hunt was the unofficial tour guide of *The Muppet Show*, so much so that floor manager Martin Baker and his colleagues got him a black chauffeur cap emblazoned with the words "MUPPET TOURS," which he wore proudly around the set. He behaved as if it was his personal responsibility to make everyone feel comfortable and entertained, especially groups of kids. "Any time there were visitors there, he was a welcoming buddy," Baker recalls. "I would always turn to Richard to do the tour, if he wasn't busy, or he would offer. He was an incredible ambassador that way."

Hunt wanted to make sure all the visitors had a memorable time. If he wasn't leading a tour, he was plucking a puppet off its wooden rack and bringing it to life. Other performers also acted out characters for visitors, but Hunt was the reliable master of these spontaneous performances. He could do thumbnail impressions of all the characters, from manic Animal to shy, tiny Robin. He would walk down the row of puppets and bring them to life one by one, operating them from the outside by grabbing the chin in his left hand and the top of the head in his right.

Hunt had a particular knack for thawing out shy youngsters, talking to them through the puppet, making them almost forget he was there. He easily learned and remembered an entire class's worth of names. Performing Janice one day, for example, he asked the audience if any of them were from California, knowing full well they were. When a young girl timidly raised her hand, Hunt elicited a giggle by saying, "Well, fer sure. It's Danielle, right? You look real laid back, Danielle. I'll bet you're a surfer. Far out!"

Yet even when there were no visitors, Hunt was always "on." He would perform for anyone who happened to be around, from his colleagues to the crew: he would make silly faces; do a soft-shoe à la Fred Astaire; imitate the Three Stooges; break into his own comic patter—whatever came to mind. These unceasing antics came out of his own personality, his restless need to amuse himself during the inevitable downtime on set, as well as his unquenchable need to entertain everyone all the time.

Most importantly, Hunt's buoyant energy served a very helpful purpose: keeping up everybody's spirits, maintaining a playful, productive atmosphere. This was especially needed on guest star days, as they had limited time with the guest and had to keep to a tight schedule to get all their material in the can. "It's very hard to shoot Muppets," says Brian Henson. "The whole crew could turn against you. But with Richard there, you knew that wasn't going to happen. He was the morale maintainer."

After a lunch break from 1:00 to 2:15, the performers and guest star filmed segments for the rest of the afternoon, increasingly conscious of the clock. Often the shoots took longer than planned, especially when the numbers were more elaborate than usual. Sometimes it could take almost eight hours to get just two minutes of footage in the can—which their tight schedules didn't allow for. "When you're spending about three days to do a show, you really don't have one day to spend on just a two-and-a-half minute piece," said Henson. While their pace wasn't necessarily sustainable, it was worth it for the high quality of the work—at least for the time being.

Exacerbating their time pressures, union rules mandated that the crew go off the clock at 7:30 P.M. After that, Henson had to negotiate overtime in five-minute increments until 8:00, when everything shut down entirely. On ten memorable occasions, they ran past 8 P.M.—and found themselves standing in the dark.

Wednesday and Thursday (and Sometimes Friday)

While Hunt rarely arrived on time, he was reliably tardy later in the week: the guest star was gone, there were fewer visitors, and he generally scorned rehearsing. (The guest occasionally returned on Wednesdays to finish filming, but this was rare.) Hunt's lateness exasperated Baker, who was responsible for getting the performers to the studio on time. "The other four were easy," Baker recalls, as Hunt's colleagues dependably arrived about a half hour early. "But Richard was a full-time job." Baker tried all sorts of tricks to get Hunt to the set on time: calling him at home an hour before he was needed, even giving him a "false call" of an earlier-than-needed start time. It became a running gag. Sometimes Hunt would hide in the studio, or up on the roof, just to stress out the young floor manager. "I suppose Richard's not here yet," Henson would remark to Baker as rehearsal was about to begin. "What do *you* think?" Baker would reply.

Hunt's lateness once cost him an exciting experience. He and Nelson planned to fly back to London together on the SST, but Hunt, who routinely rushed to the airport at the last second, missed the flight. It turned out that Nelson knew the stewardess; he and Hunt had met her on a previous flight, setting up a visit to the *Muppet Show* set for her and three fellow attendants. To return the favor, she offered to show Nelson the cockpit. He was just settling in with *The New York Times* crossword when she came running back to his seat. Not only could he tour the cockpit, he could sit there for takeoff! Even the perpetually cool Nelson found it thrilling to soar into the sky in this powerful jet. It "burned" Hunt to hear what he had missed, says Nelson. "But it still didn't help him be on time."

Hunt generally came rushing onto the floor, out of breath, just as work began. He seemed to have an uncanny sixth sense of when he was needed, usually tipped off by one of his friends among the crew. "It was hardly ever, 'Where's Richard?'" Nelson recalls. Hunt would arrive just in time to rehearse, or just after everyone else had finished rehearsing—and do the bit as flawlessly as if he'd run it through a dozen times.

Hunt's lateness was one of the few things about him that frustrated Henson, but Henson didn't hold it against him for long. "That sort of thing did piss off my dad, but he was ready to roll with it," says Brian Henson. "My dad was like Kermit, embracing everyone for their quirky weirdness and their flaws." Henson understood that Hunt's tardiness was part of the whole package—and he wouldn't have had it any other way.

What's more, it was impossible to stay mad at Hunt, who could be so beguiling. Hunt came rushing in late one day just as work began, much to Baker's chagrin. "I said, 'Richard, Richard!'" Baker recalls. "He said, 'What are you shouting at me for? This is the earliest I've ever been late!'"

While segments without the guest might seem quicker to film, in fact the opposite was often true. Scenes where the characters interacted backstage at the Muppet theater were particularly tricky. "You're working in a confined space, so it's usually a problem to get things organized just right," says Goelz. "They're never quite as routine as you expect them to be." When technical problems and other delays plagued the recording session, Hunt buried himself in *The International Herald Tribune*—his second choice, as he complained about not being able to find *The New York Times*.

Hunt read his newspaper not only during downtime, but often right up until the cameras rolled. He would wait between takes, arm up and puppet in position, reading. Directors Peter Harris and Philip Casson (who each directed half of the show's 120 episodes) would chide Hunt via loudspeaker from the control room: "Come on, Richard, we're going on in five." Hunt would stay motionless as if he hadn't heard a thing. Only when the countdown began would Hunt fold up the newspaper, return it to his back pocket, and turn on his performance like a light switch.

But once Hunt was on, he was *on*. Hunt wowed his colleagues—and audiences—with one unlikely hit that debuted in the second-season: an orange-haired, freaked-out lab assistant. "Beaker is one of my favorite characters, because he doesn't talk," said Hunt. As with Sully on *Sesame Street*, Hunt appreciated the challenge of a character with limited speech, conveying volumes through Beaker's bulging eyes, bobbing head, and anxious squeaks. Hunt produced Beaker's trademark intonations by breathing in as he vocalized, making the character sound panicked and practically gasping for air.

Beaker provided Hunt the opportunity to pair up with Goelz, and for both to show more of what they could do. While Goelz had had an immediate hit with weird daredevil Gonzo the Great, his dry scientist Dr. Bunsen Honeydew wasn't quite as funny at first. Goelz based Bunsen on his Silicon Valley co-workers, people who were so focused on the minute details of their work that they tuned out the bigger picture. "It was hard to make that entertaining," Goelz recalls. The character needed a comic foil. "Once we had a victim, who suffered every time, then we were onto something."

Enter the unfortunate Beaker. Less a lab assistant than a lab rat, the hapless helper suffers numerous indignities: among them, he is shrunk, enlarged, electrocuted, cloned, superglued to the guest, abducted by a giant germ, and, on more than one occasion, blown up. "It's a hard life for poor Beaker," said Hunt.

Yet in Hunt's interpretation, Beaker knows what he's getting into. Hunt and Goelz would debate the dynamic between their characters: while Goelz thought that Beaker endured this abuse merely for a paycheck, Hunt imagined that Beaker was genuinely fond of the bumbling scientist. "Beaker is a character very few people understood," Hunt said. "They all just said, 'Oh, he's so *stupid*.' No, Beaker wasn't stupid at all. Here's this very kindly old professor who's always doing these things that never quite work, he's not really quite in this world, and Beaker grew an affection for him, and a dedication. He would do anything for this guy. He was there not because he was stupid, but because he cared about him." In Hunt's view, Beaker isn't a victim, but a willing participant—which perhaps eases viewers' guilt for laughing at his predicaments, keeping the sketches more in line with the Muppets' underlying warmth. "I love this guy," Hunt said about Beaker during an on-set interview. "When this series is over, he's the one puppet I want to take home with me."

While Beaker was one of Hunt's favorite characters, the second season also saw him film one of his favorite *Muppet Show* segments: the Buffalo Springfield song "For What It's Worth," retooled with a pro-environmental theme. "He said it was because the message was able to get out to the world," says Muppet performer Mike Quinn. As with *Sesame Street*, Hunt loved to entertain—but especially valued when it made a social impact.

About halfway through the second season, the Muppets hired a new performer who fit right into the troupe's silly hijinks, and became especially good friends with Hunt: Louise Gold. Gold stayed through the end of *The Muppet Show*, making her the show's longest-running female performer as well as its only British cast member. While the 5'9" Gold liked to joke that she was hired for her height, she brought strong acting and singing skills, as well as a convivial understanding of the Muppet sensibility, a sharp wit, and an impish sense of humor.

Hunt adopted Gold as an unofficial little sister. "I went in and Richard took me on, as like, 'You don't know anything, come under my wing,'" says Gold. When they performed, Hunt watched not just his own work but everyone else's, advising Gold on her performance. When they went to premieres or other such events, he often suggested what she should wear. "That was our relationship, that I was the naughty little sister, who needed to be looked after and shown how to behave. Who needed to be told things, even things I maybe knew." Gold enjoyed her dynamic with Hunt, and the two became quite close.

Though cast and crew aimed to finish the week's filming on Thursdays, about half of the episodes required Hunt and his colleagues to come in on Fridays as well.

Off-Duty (Saturdays/Evenings)

The performers had so much fun that despite their long workdays, they spent many off hours together as well. They ate lunch together, occasionally Italian food across the street at Signor Baffi's, but usually at the more convenient ATV canteen, where Hunt was an attention-grabbing figure, parading around loudly and laughing. While the canteen offered waitress service, Hunt and the other performers preferred to get their food at the counter and take it to their seats. He warmly teased the two older women who ran the grill, dubbing one "Elsie, Queen of Grease."

After a long day of work, the performers found it hard to wind down—and the gang was generally ravenous. Hunt often organized dinners, packing the car and driving everyone into London. They made "emergency runs" some Wednesday nights for chicken tacos at a "questionable" Mexican restaurant in Sloane Square, Goelz recalls, where the meat still bore the marks where the feathers had been plucked out.

Hunt and Nelson especially spent a lot of time together, and liked to look after newbies to the group. Second-season writer Joe Bailey credits the pair with his survival in London. Bailey had a hard time finding good food when the minibus dropped him off around 9 P.M. after a long workday: he didn't like pub fare, and the finer restaurants required reservations. Hunt would call to announce his impending arrival, then pull up in the Cortina with Nelson riding shotgun. The trio often ended up at the Portobello, though Hunt and Nelson didn't live there anymore. The hotel lounge was open after hours only to guests, but the night manager gladly bent the rules for Hunt. So after many a late work night, Hunt and his friends would feast at the Portobello, drinking cold beer and eating chicken-fried steak, pretending to be guests.

Hunt and Nelson provided cultural sustenance as well. They took Bailey to legendary venues like the jazz club Ronnie Scott's, where one night they spent so long at the bar gabbing with the musicians, soaking up stories about "being on the road with 'The Count,' 'The Duke,' and 'Diz,'" that they never actually went in to see the show. Hunt and Nelson also hung around with the likes of rock-jazz fiddler Jean-Luc Ponty and the rock band Little Feat. "We did some fun moving around in London, met some neat people," says Nelson with characteristic understatement.

Another night Hunt and Nelson took Bailey to the 100 Club, a lively basement nightspot that showcased everyone from old-school jazz musicians to New Wave punk rockers. On the docket that night was legendary jazz violinist Stéphane Grappelli. Though by then a sixty-nine-year-old veteran of a storied career alongside Django Reinhardt, Grappelli played with the ease and freshness of a young man, swinging through classics like "Honeysuckle Rose" and "I Got Rhythm." Hunt, Nelson, and Bailey stayed through two sets, then sat happily in their seats, drinking it all in.

Suddenly Hunt exclaimed, "Let's go backstage and see him!"

"We can't do that," Bailey replied.

"Sure we can!" Hunt cried. "We're the Muppets! We can go anywhere!"

Hunt talked their way into Grappelli's dressing room, where the renowned musician turned out to be a huge Muppet fan. "He told us how much he loved the show and tried to watch it wherever he was," Bailey recalls. While Hunt and Nelson talked with Grappelli about jazz history, Bailey remembered that he was wearing a special staff-only *Muppet Show* T-shirt under his turtleneck. Bailey wriggled out of his shirt and handed it to the famed fiddler, who lit up and promised to wear it the following week while performing at Switzerland's Montreaux Jazz Festival. "So thanks to *The Muppet Show*," crows Bailey, "I got to give the great Stéphane Grappelli the shirt off my back."

Hunt and Nelson enjoyed hosting parties at their homes, now that they had the room to do so. While sitting around at a July 1977 party at Nelson's London apartment, Madeline Kahn—filming her *Muppet Show* episode that week—remarked that she envied the puppeteers their anonymity. "Whenever I leave my apartment, I'm on duty," she said. Goelz was so inspired by this idea that he had T-shirts made for everyone emblazoned with the phrase "OFF-DUTY."

And when a studio acquaintance discovered a bargain price on Hunt's favorite champagne, vintage Dom Perignon, that was all the excuse he needed to throw a party with a grand table of food, including a variety of rare local cheeses. Typically, he was late to his own party, making a grand entrance with more champagne and vast cartons of strawberries, trailing a bevy of friends.

Arguably the height of Hunt's time in England was when the Muppets received one of the biggest accolades of all: appearing before Queen Elizabeth as part of the Royal Variety Performance at London's Palladium Theatre on November 21, 1977. The event aired on NBC two days later as "America Salutes the Queen."

Hunt was amped up beyond even his usual exuberance for the event, snorting cocaine and smoking pot beforehand to make the evening even more exciting and surreal. Hunt wore a tuxedo to the black-tie affair, but paired the fancy suit with his trademark Adidas. For years afterward, he acted out an imaginary scene in which the Queen was scandalized by his sneakers: He would imitate her greeting him, then falling into a screaming faint—"Aaaaah!"—a story which was always a big hit.

Even when (or perhaps because) the stakes were so high, Hunt preferred to fly by the seat of his pants. He left his twenty-page script backstage while performing Statler and Waldorf with Henson, opting to rely on his prodigious memory. He stuck to the preplanned dialogue as the major Muppet alter egos—Kermit, Fozzie, Gonzo, Scooter, and Floyd—told pig jokes at Miss Piggy's expense, and lip-synched to the cheerful paean to friendship "We Got Us." But as a group of full-body walkaround monsters—including Hunt in his Sweetums costume—did a combative dance to a piece of classical music, bumping into each other and sparring with the stage manager (performed by Nelson), Hunt took things into his own hands—literally.

Hunt, as Sweetums, was supposed to pick up Goelz (playing first violinist in the orchestra) and mime throwing him off the stage, though in actuality Goelz would jump of his own power, as they had rehearsed. But during the show, Hunt picked up Goelz with such force and energy that he truly did hurl him up in the air and off the stage—a four-foot drop! "He was so ramped up for the show that he threw me with great force, and I just went flying," Goelz recalls. "I landed in the aisle; I didn't land on people, thank God."

Host Bob Hope brought the Original Five onstage after the show's finale, accompanied by four walkaround Muppet monsters. Louise Gold was vexed to meet the royal family inside the Mean Mama monster costume, especially as the only British cast member. Gold burst through the line and started pawing at Prince Charles, wrapping him in a hug, growling "Prince! Prince!" The other performers quickly grabbed her and pushed her back behind them. "Only somebody like Louise or Richard would have had the guts to do that," says Goelz. "The rest of us would have been afraid."

Though Hunt was generally unintimidated by celebrity, it did thrill him to hang out with artists he had long respected, and to have them respect his work in return. Guest star Peter Sellers, the famed British comic actor, turned out to be as big a fan of the Muppets as they were of him, with tapes of all the episodes at home. At a big dinner to celebrate wrapping Sellers's episode, the Original Five were in the midst of their usual fast-paced banter when Sellers meekly raised his hand and asked, "Can I play too?" Hunt loved to tell this story, as it reflected his own attitude, opines Muppet performer Brian Meehl. "For a mega-star to be so humble and little-kid-like meant a lot to him."

Hunt was delighted to spend time with jazz singer Cleo Laine, another second-season guest. He took visiting Closter buddy Ernie Capeci to see the fine art collection at Woburn Abbey, a grand, castle-like estate, then pulled the car up to another vast edifice a few miles away. "This is the rectory," he said with a wink. The door opened and Laine came running out, crying, "Oh, Richard, Richard!" Capeci was floored to realize it was Laine's house. Capeci held his breath, awe-struck, as Laine and her husband, fellow musician John Dankworth, pawed through the jazz records he had just bought.

While Hunt largely kept his work and social lives separate, they came together in one incident that could have torpedoed his career. Partying with a friend who was also a journalist, Hunt gossiped about a *Muppet Show* guest—and word got back to the Muppet powers-that-be. While the specific guest star is unknown, it was likely Rudolf Nureyev, consid-ered the greatest male ballet dancer of his generation, whose second-season appearance was a huge coup for the show, one of the first big names to appear. When Hunt met Nureyev backstage at *The Muppet Show*, the dancer boldly looked Hunt in the eye and said, "You like to suck cock, don't you?" Hunt repeated this remark to his sometime-lover Charles Kaiser, at the time a journalist for *The New York Times*, who found the anecdote so delicious that he repeated it widely for years, gleefully retelling it in his 1997 book *The Gay Metropolis*. Hunt knew Kaiser through their mutual friend Charles "Chuck" Gibson, a script typist on *Sesame Street*, so the story could have easily made its way back to the company.

Regardless of the exact guest at the center of the incident, word got back to *Muppet Show* producer David Lazer, infuriating him. Lazer han-dled the guest stars, and feared tarnishing the Muppets' good-hearted image and making performers wary of doing the gig. Lazer was also the person responsible for castigating, disciplining, or outright axing *Mup-pet Show* personnel. "Everyone said, 'You're going to get fired,'" Brian Henson recalls. Lazer called Hunt into his office, excoriating Hunt so harshly that he was reduced to tears. Lazer had planned to then bring Hunt to Jim Henson, in the next office, for the boss to deliver his own stern lecture. Upon seeing Hunt's distressed state, however, instead of chewing him out, Henson gave Hunt a big hug, saying, "We're not going to talk about this, but it's never going to happen again, right?"

Once the second season wrapped in mid-December, Hunt flew home for a six-week Christmas break, celebrating at the company Christmas party on December 19 at Tavern on the Green, as well as the Hunts' own Christmas celebration.

He had a lot to celebrate. Muppetmania had finally arrived in America: the Nielsen ratings for *The Muppet Show* were through the roof, and the Muppets seemed to be in every major media outlet, with both *Good Morning America* and *People* magazine visiting the Muppet workshop, and the Macy's Thanksgiving Day Parade featuring a Kermit balloon.

Hunt had a fairly set routine when he flew back to the States. He would land in Newark and drive straight home to Closter, wolf down the Entenmann's chocolate doughnuts and orange juice he picked up along the way, then go up to his small bedroom and sleep for about two days. But things were very different now at 52 Closter Dock Road: he owned it.

With his *Muppet Show* wages added to his *Sesame Street* earnings, Hunt was now looking at more money than he'd ever made in his life. His mother remembers him opening an envelope from work and laughing: "How can they give you so much money for something you love to do?"

One of Hunt's first major moves with his newfound wealth was to buy the family house from his mother, putting it in his name and assuming the financial responsibility, making sure the family never again needed to worry about losing their home. This move was for himself as much as the rest of the family, a childhood dream of security come true.

Hunt's purchasing of the house symbolized a changing of the guard. Jane, a forty-nine-year-old widow, wanted a fresh start, so Hunt rented her a Manhattan apartment at 142 West End Avenue, in the modern housing development of Lincoln Towers, just steps from the theatrical offerings of Lincoln Center. She soon met musician Arthur Miller, who moved in with her about a year later.

Meanwhile, Kate came back to Closter from Martha's Vineyard with three-year-old Amanda in tow. Lyn and Adam had moved out. Rachel, finishing up high school at Hunt's alma mater, Northern Valley, split her time between the house and her mother's new apartment. Despite being in Manhattan, Jane's place seemed positively serene compared to the Closter house, a lively way station for far-flung visitors. "That house was party city," Rachel recalls. Hunt often dropped in with a crowd of friends, as ever.

Yet Hunt didn't necessarily bring everyone home to Closter. Hunt had a new lover he had met at Henson Associates: Dennis Smith. A tall, athletic blond with striking green eyes, Smith worked as a stylist and designer in the photo studio, most notably designing the sets for the Kermitage collection, a photo series of Muppet takeoffs on famous paintings. The two men had very similar backgrounds: Smith was just six months older than Hunt, graduated high school at the same time, and grew up less than an hour from Closter in Kinnelon, New Jersey.

Smith was one of four longtime friends working at Henson Associates. Joe Tripician joined up first, doing everything from shopping for Miss Piggy's eyelashes, dispatched to the garment district with a swatch of fabric in hand, to developing Henson's in-house video system; since most of the *Muppet Show* puppets were still built in New York, they videotaped the puppets as they were being made, then overnighted the videos to London for Henson's feedback. Tripician's girlfriend, Merrill Aldergheri, made herself so useful when she visited him at work that she, too, soon wielded the video camera. Aldergheri's biggest task was cataloguing the publicity done about the Muppets, a job which grew out of hand as their popularity increased exponentially. Overtime wasn't enough; she took home piles of clippings, farming out the work to two of her closest friends: Kathy Karwat and Karwat's boyfriend, Dennis Smith. Karwat, committed to pursuing a painting career, had no interest in a formal position; Smith got hired in the graphics department.

Hunt and Smith quickly hit it off, drawn together by their shared off-beat sense of humor. Tripician recalled Smith improvising a mock *Saturday Night Live* commercial: "When I'm on the beach, there's nothing I like more than to cool off with a big steaming can of tuna." Yet Smith admired that Hunt's sense of humor was even more out there than his. "Dennis looked up to Richard," says Aldergheri. "He was impressed by his strong, funny personality, how he was willing to go a lot farther with a joke."

Hunt and Smith had a strong connection, but nowhere they could go to be alone. The problem was solved when Smith broke up with Karwat and rented a loft on the corner of Sullivan and Spring Streets in Soho, a neighborhood just being discovered by artists. The apartment had roaches galore, a bathtub under a counter, and a toilet in the hall, but

Smith was ecstatic at his freedom to play the field, regaling friends with tales of his exploits.

Smith and Karwat remained close friends, drawing even closer when Smith took up Karwat's medium of painting—and found his calling. The friends spent hours painting acrylics in Smith's loft, with Smith often sketching out drafts before stretching a canvas. Hunt was one of the first to appreciate Smith's work, paying thousands of dollars apiece for a number of his paintings. Hunt's patronage bolstered Smith's confidence as he launched his career. Smith showed his work at Soho's Phyllis Kind Gallery; the Metropolitan Museum of Art later acquired two paintings and a drawing.

Smith's paintings reflected his sense of humor: wryly whimsical, vividly tinted caricatures of imaginary people and situations, as if colorful cubist Paul Klee had paired up with quirky comic Edward Gorey. Friends would watch the paintings evolve when they hung out in the loft, listening to downtown bands like Television and the Talking Heads. "Every painting had a different story behind it," says Tripician. "The story would evolve with their lives." *Corn Eaters*, for example, in which three monstrous-looking people sprawl under a tree gnawing on oversized ears of corn, took inspiration from a film Aldergheri made of a man eating corn on the cob. Another painting was a map of heaven and hell, with an airplane going off course, threatening to disturb heaven; another featured a smug-looking entomologist surrounded by tiny bugs.

Hoping to meet patrons, Smith frequented the exclusive uptown disco Studio 54, sometimes accompanied by Hunt, hobnobbing with a wild clientele of artists, rock stars, and models. Smith also frequented Manhattan's gay bathhouses, sometimes with his lover Nelson Bird, who would later play a pivotal role in Hunt's life.

Hunt was feeling great in early 1978 as the troupe filmed the first half of the third season of *The Muppet Show*. He performed some memorable moments in this batch of episodes: Beaker got superglued to guest star Gilda Radner, and Scooter took over Kermit's hosting duties. Hunt debuted a smart-mouthed lunch lady named Gladys, an homage to the ATV cafeteria staff. And Hunt befriended the show's newest puppeteer:

Steve Whitmire. Like Hunt, Whitmire was just eighteen years old when he cold-called the Muppets, scored an audition, and joined up.

Hunt was now one of five main performers on the biggest television show in the world, making (and spending) more money than he had ever seen in his life, working and playing alongside some of entertainment's biggest names. But life was about to get even more exciting, as he got the chance to realize another of his ambitions. The lifelong movie buff was going to be in the movies!

Hunt performs Scooter on *The Muppet Movie* set, with Michael Earl as Janice and Dave Goelz as Zoot, 1978.

CHAPTER 8

Millions of People Happy

FITTINGLY ENOUGH, as Hunt worked on *The Muppet Movie*—a film he described as being "all about dreaming and looking for your dreams"—Hunt was living out a dream. The members of the Muppet troupe were elated to realize their vision of bringing their characters out of people's living rooms and onto the big screen.

These were golden days, basking in the warm sun of New Mexico and California, a welcome change from London's damp chill. The performers also luxuriated in the relatively slower pace of the work. While they were used to cranking out a thirty-minute episode of *The Muppet Show* in just three days, the ninety-minute movie began filming on July 5, 1978, and took eighty-seven days throughout the summer and fall to complete—meaning that the movie allowed them nearly ten times as long to produce a single minute of footage. Goelz likened doing television to "calisthenics" that got you in shape and honed your instincts, so you could bring your best abilities to the "craftsmanship" of making a movie. Here, each shot had just one camera and ideal lighting, and rather than rushing with one eye on the clock, the performers could do multiple takes to ensure they got the shot just right.

Making *The Muppet Movie* was a special time in terms of the dynamic of the Original Five, so practiced at working together that they could read each other in a glance, bouncing off each other playfully, their spirited rapport spurred on by director James Frawley. The performers genuinely believed in the earnest message of the movie: be yourself and follow your heart. Hunt's interpretation reveals as much about his own philosophy as about the movie: "The film's underlying current is about looking inside yourself and seeing what it is you want to do or be in life, and then pursuing it," Hunt said. And if you're lucky enough to find your tribe along the way, so much the better. "Through this film, Kermit starts pulling all these other bizarre characters together who were looking for *their* dream." But as Hunt knew all too well, nothing comes too easily or without a price—that's just life. "And then when everything starts to screw up, as it does every day of our existence, it ties back into existence."

The movie was dear to the Original Five because it was *their* story, a thinly disguised version of how Henson assembled his tribe. Kermit the Frog takes a cross-country road trip from the swamp (a play on Henson's Mississippi roots) to Hollywood, gathering collaborators along the way, largely following the real-life order in which Henson brought on the performers: Oz's comic alter ego Fozzie the Bear; Nelson's groovy stand-in Floyd Pepper; Hunt's eager young doppelgänger Scooter; and Goelz's wacky alter ego Gonzo, among the other major Muppet characters.

However, the viewer is not to interpret this story too literally. Even solely within the movie's fictional universe, you have a "true" and an "untrue" version of events, accentuated by the framing device of having the film's characters in a theater *watching* the dramatized version of how they came together. The movie tips off viewers to this explicitly. Just before the movie-within-a-movie begins, Kermit's young nephew Robin (arguably a stand-in for the viewer) asks, "Is this about how the Muppets really got started?" Kermit replies obliquely, "Well, it's sort of *approximately* how it happened." Henson and writers Jerry Juhl and Jack Burns are winking at the audience: take what you see with a grain of salt. The movie also rarely resists an opportunity to break the fourth wall, from having the characters read the script to voicing the need for "a clever plot device," further complicating matters.

Hunt's characters interact wonderfully with these multiple layers. He plays all of his major Muppet characters—Scooter, Janice, Beaker, Statler, and Sweetums—and as on *The Muppet Show*, his characters both open and close the film. This time, however, instead of delivering the final quip, Statler and Waldorf utter the very first lines, making it immediately clear that the movie is no less vulnerable than the show to the critics' barbs: "I'm Statler." "I'm Waldorf. We're here to heckle *The Muppet Movie.*"

Hunt's Sweetums is the sole character to move *between* the layers: Kermit and friends leave behind the shaggy ogre during the movie-within-a-movie, but he catches up with them at the *screening*, tearing through the screen—literally ripping the barrier between the two worlds. He thus delivers the movie's final major line, "I just *knew* I'd catch up with you guys!" (Technically Oz's Animal delivers the film's very last line, after the credits, directly to the audience: "Go home!")

Hunt and his colleagues were thrilled to work alongside a storied roster of guests, from Hunt's pal Madeline Kahn to ventriloquist Edgar Bergen in his last onscreen appearance, with delicious cameos from Mel Brooks as a Nazi-like scientist and Orson Welles as media mogul Lew Lord, a play on *Muppet Show* bankroller Lord Lew Grade. Character actor Charles Durning hits just the right notes as antagonist Doc Hopper, who helps Kermit articulate his dreams.

While making *The Muppet Movie* was overall an idyllic experience, Hunt undertook some of the most demanding puppeteering in his career thus far. For the move to the big screen, Henson raised the stakes in terms of impossible puppet stunts. Not only does Kermit ride a bicycle, but Fozzie drives a car (driven by a stuntman huddled in the trunk, watching the road on a monitor). "We're taking the characters out of the show and bringing them into the real world," Henson said. Yet without the custom sets of *The Muppet Show*, the Muppet performers were challenged to hide from the camera. As the puppets became more visible, their performers had to go to even greater lengths to remain invisible, stuffing and contorting themselves into smaller and smaller spaces. They rolled around on dollies, or sprawled flat out on the ground with their arms up in the air for extended periods. "If you don't dig sore arms, don't work with puppets," Hunt quipped. But he had a unique, tongue-in-cheek solution: "When my right arm gets sore, I go out to a court and shoot left-handed baskets. That gets my left arm sore."

Hunt didn't necessarily have a solution for the claustrophobia that arose from some shoots which made him feel like he was practically buried alive. He crouched in an underground pit, covered by slabs of ply-wood which were then covered with dirt or sand; the performers stuck their arms up through holes in the wood, watching their performances on monitors from inside these veritable crypts. But Henson wouldn't ask his puppeteers to do anything he wouldn't do himself, and more, even wedging himself into an undersized, underwater diving bell in order to puppeteer Kermit sitting in the middle of the swamp.

The Muppet Movie's grand finale scene groundbreakingly brought together more puppets—and puppeteers—than had ever been assem-bled onscreen. Just as Henson gathered his Muppet tribe, so Kermit has gathered his community of fellow dreamers; while he begins the movie singing "The Rainbow Connection" all by himself, he ends up singing the aspirational anthem with over 250 fellow visionaries. To achieve this feat, the film used nearly every Muppet character created in the last decade, hiring nearly 150 extras to puppeteer them on the one-day shoot.

The mad rush for puppeteers led to some interesting figures squeez-ing into the custom-made pit, six feet deep by seventeen feet wide, at CBS Studio's Soundstage 15, including Hunt's brother Adam and the macabre director Tim Burton (then working as a Disney animator)—but one performer especially stood out. "Do you see that guy with long hair?" people whispered. "He directed *Animal House*." A huge puppet enthusiast, John Landis had engineered a meeting with Henson and Oz through the *Muppet Movie* publicist, and Oz had invited him to per-form Grover in the finale. (Landis would return the favor, offering Oz cameos in over a half-dozen films.) The gregarious Hunt struck up a conversation with the budding director, and through this connection landed a role in a future Landis film.

Coincidentally, Hunt brought a visitor to the set that day who would lead him to his *other* on-camera movie role. Hunt met future teen idols Rob and Chad Lowe, then fourteen and ten, at a Dodgers game during the *Muppet Movie* shoot, coming to their aid when fans harassed Chad for wearing a Yankees hat. "Things were getting ugly when a guy stepped in and rescued my brother and me from the mob," Rob recalls. Hunt invited the pair to come watch the finale, their first time on a sound-stage. Hunt's kindness and his subsequent friendship with the Lowe brothers would pay off when Rob Lowe made it big. So not only was

Hunt's first movie appearance as a puppeteer thrilling in its own right, it would bring about another longtime dream, twice over: performing onscreen as an actor.

By late 1978, *The Muppet Show* was "perhaps the most widely seen television program in the world," reported *The New York Times*. *Time* magazine called it "the most popular television entertainment now being produced on earth." Over 200 million people in over one hundred countries watched the show each week—which, *Time* pointed out, outnumbered the population of the entire United States. The troupe had achieved the dream Kermit articulates in *The Muppet Movie*: making "millions of people happy." What's more, the show had finally won a long-coveted Emmy for Outstanding Comedy-Variety Series, as well as receiving another four nominations. Literally, the whole world was watching.

This success was reflected in Hunt's new digs when the team resumed filming the third season in November. Hunt rented the top floor of *Muppet Show* choreographer Gillian Lynne's house in Bedford Park, just west of Central London, throwing a big party right after moving in. Despite his possessions still being in boxes, Hunt departed from his usual uniform of jeans or white painter's pants with striped polo or rugby shirts, hosting the party in a rust-colored velvet jacket, dark green shirt, and tie, trading his ever-present sneakers for expensive Bally loafers. "Holy cow!" thought Goelz. "He looks terrific when he buys clothes." Hunt liked Goelz's silver Volkswagen Polo so much that he bought the exact same model; after a long day on set, they had to be careful not to get into each others' cars.

By now, stars were reaching out to the show, rather than vice versa, making for a fascinating mix. In just these few weeks before Christmas, Hunt worked alongside an exemplary range of performers. He, Nelson, and Gold delivered an iconic performance with singer-activist Harry Belafonte on the song "Turn the World Around," for which the workshop created African-inspired puppets. And Hunt was surprised to discover that entertainer Danny Kaye didn't live up to his jovial reputation, telling folksinger Livingston Taylor that Kaye was in fact "persnickety and disagreeable." By contrast, English comedian Spike Milligan had the troupe in stitches for his entire shoot—so much so that Nelson's stomach hurt from laughing after he left.

During Milligan's shoot, controversial British director Stanley Kubrick was filming a top-secret movie at Elstree's EMI Studios. Hunt charmed his way onto the set, coming back wide-eyed to report that the movie—which would become *The Shining*—would be "the scariest movie ever," says Goelz. Hunt brought *Shining* cast members Shelley Duvall and Danny Lloyd to the *Muppet Show* set, acting out characters for them.

As Hunt gained confidence in his career, he started instructing even those who had predated him. Despite having been at *Sesame Street* from the beginning, Caroll Spinney was intimidated to make an appearance on *The Muppet Show*, struggling with the complicated choreography that had been written for Big Bird. Hunt made a suggestion that Spinney appreciated for the rest of his career. "Forget about what those people are telling you to do," Hunt said. "Just have Big Bird think he's a good dancer—the best dancer in the world. *Pretend* he can dance."

Spinney tried out this advice on a PBS special, dancing alongside ballerina Cynthia Gregory; not only did it work, but Spinney actually enjoyed himself instead of cringing with his usual self-consciousness. The trick was an even bigger success a few years later, when Big Bird sang and danced with Broadway's Carol Channing in *Night of 100 Stars*. "It was the best dance number I've ever done, and it worked because Big Bird believed that he could do it, and I believed in him," Spinney says. Spinney's wife Debi recalls that her husband followed Hunt's suggestion for the rest of his career: "He held Richard in great esteem for that, because it changed his performance forevermore." *Fake it 'til you make it*—a motto that Hunt certainly found helpful in his own improvisational life.

The success of *The Muppet Show* spilled over into other projects. Not one but two *Sesame Street* Christmas specials aired in the same week in early December: CBS's *A Special Sesame Street Christmas* guest starred a young Michael Jackson and an aging Ethel Merman, while PBS's *Christmas Eve on Sesame Street* featured a touching Bert and Ernie version of O. Henry's "The Gift of the Magi." Both were nominated for Emmys; the latter won.

But Hunt was heartened by a *third* Muppet Christmas special that aired on American television that month—albeit on the then-obscure cable channel HBO—despite having been filmed nearly two years earlier. *Emmet Otter's Jug-Band Christmas* rode in on the anticipation for *The Muppet Movie*, helped along by the fact that Paul Williams wrote the music for both. Goelz calls the charming holiday special "one of my top three projects of all time."

The Original Five portrayed a vast array of new characters in *Emmet Otter*, from the mild-mannered Frogtown Hollow Jubilee Jug Band (led by Nelson as the title character) to their delightfully wicked rival River-bottom Nightmare Band. Hunt used a falsetto for youthful Charlie Muskrat and a bad-boy Brooklyn accent for Fred Lizard. The special anticipated the technology Hunt and his colleagues would later use more prominently, such as the animatronic remote-controlled puppets which enabled Emmet Otter and his mother to row down the fifty-five-foot-long "river" the set designers built in the studio, a remarkable effect. *Emmet Otter* would become a cult classic—as well as starting the relationship with HBO that would lead to the international hit series *Fraggle Rock*.

The troupe had plenty to revel about at that year's Christmas party, held at Manhattan's Players Club, a Gramercy Park mansion and museum-like actor's clubhouse featuring an impressive array of stage memorabilia. They flew back to London in January 1979 for a quick month wrapping up *The Muppet Show*'s third season, with guests ranging from *Rocky* hunk Sylvester Stallone to country singers Roy Rogers and Dale Evans. The show was branching out into themed episodes, capping off the season with a Muppet version of Robin Hood starring Broadway and West End veteran Lynn Redgrave, in which Hunt's Scooter was both narrator and stage manager.

On break between seasons, Hunt gleefully roamed Manhattan in his new car: an eight-passenger Checker cab, painted black. Hunt loved to fill the car with friends and ferry them around town. Named after their trademark checkerboard trim, the boxy, oversized cabs were a New York icon. At first Hunt didn't realize how much fuel the car ate up, running out of gas with Fischer one snowy February evening on the way home from front-row seats at Broadway previews for *Sweeney Todd*.

Sometimes people would try to hail his cab, and he would see how long he could prolong the gag.

The press blitz for *The Muppet Movie* delighted Hunt. He was thrilled to have his actual face appear on television when the Muppets appeared on popular newsmagazine *60 Minutes* in March. "We're doing what everybody else in the world wants to do—act crazy," Hunt told host Morley Safer. "Except we get paid to do it. That's the big difference." How much was "the Muppet empire" worth, Safer asked a squirming Henson—millions? "Probably," Henson replied. "But I wouldn't swear to that."

Hunt and his colleagues appeared on *The Tonight Show* in early April when Kermit took over Johnny Carson's hosting duties; Hunt ad-libbed as Scooter, teasing guest Leo Sayer about his accent. And fifty-odd celebrities fêted the gang in *The Muppets Go Hollywood*, a gala at the Cocoanut Grove featuring a live stage show, airing in May as an hourlong special on both sides of the ocean.

Even as preparations and promotion for the movie release ramped up, the *Muppet Show* team started production on season four. By now, the Original Five, Gold, Whitmire, and new hire Kathy Mullen had really hit their stride. The stellar roster of guests showcased superstars—and superheroes. *Superman*'s Christopher Reeve showed off his vaudeville side, singing, playing the piano, and reciting Shakespeare; *Wonder Woman*'s Lynda Carter inspired Scooter to lead the other characters in taking a correspondence course on how to be a superhero. Audiences also enjoyed unusual theme shows, such as a noir murder mystery featuring Liza Minnelli.

The new season provided Hunt with more opportunities to sing, from dueting with opera diva Beverly Sills to scatting jazz with Dizzy Gillespie; and from conducting a band of singing babies as sleazy spieler Bobby Benson to rasping as an old woman in the elderly band Geri and the Atrics. Hunt even resurrected the treacly singing duo of Wayne and Wanda, now paired with Mullen. Statler and Waldorf, too, got in on the musical action, delivering a touching cover of the nostalgic Frank Sinatra hit "It Was a Very Good Year." And indeed it was a very good year—even if success came with its own costs and complications.

Hunt hired a limousine for the black-tie royal premiere of *The Muppet Movie* at London's Leicester Square Theater on May 31, attended by

Princess Anne, Mark Hamill, and a bevy of other big names. "We're going, and we are going to be stars," Hunt announced to his friends. But the traffic outside the theater foiled Hunt's plans—since the limo couldn't go to the door, the driver parked a few blocks away, and he and his friends had to walk the rest of the way. "The whole point of hiring a limo is to come right out of the limo!" Gold recounts laughingly.

Hunt attracted attention in the lobby afterward, a strong presence in a sea of reserved Brits. "He was like four people in one," recalls Mike Quinn, an eager teen puppeteer who often visited the set. Quinn appreciated how Hunt took the time to engage with everyone. "He could have been like some others were, 'Oh, there's that kid again, let's run away,'" Quinn says. "But he'd come over and have a bit of fun."

The Muppet Movie was a huge hit, grossing over 65 million dollars in its opening release. Audiences loved it—and the critics did too, with everyone from Vincent Canby of *The New York Times* to Roger Ebert happily suspending their disbelief. "We get to know all the Muppets better than we could on their television show," gushed Ebert.

By this point, Hunt was one of the most famous people in the world—except that hardly anyone had heard of him. Yet everyone had heard of Henson, and nearly everyone had heard of Oz, who got special billing in *The Muppet Show* credits, producer David Lazer's idea. Sadly, while the Original Five still worked together as a singular entity, off-screen they were growing apart.

"Jim and Frank had separated themselves," Hunt said of this period years later. "And that in turn was at the expense of the others because it's not announced, and it's not really implied, but there's a sub-level that makes you think that well, these are the important ones and we're just here." Hunt was careful to point out that he never experienced this separation while they were on the job—"Not in the work, not while we're on the floor." On set he felt the same magical camaraderie as ever. But off-camera, the dynamic had shifted—and it hurt.

This separation was "very hard on the rest of us, especially Jerry," said Hunt. Some of the distancing was about money. While Hunt felt he was paid "a very good wage," he couldn't help but notice that he and Nelson took home far less than Henson and Oz. "Jim owned the company and Frank was an essential so they were making much, much more money than we were," he said. This made Hunt feel less valuable to the company—and, it seemed, to his boss.

John Lovelady, building puppets in the Muppets' new 69th Street headquarters, also noticed the increasing sense of distance between Henson and his colleagues. When Hunt and Lovelady first joined up, Henson was accessible enough that if you needed to talk to him, "he would make the time to listen to you. And then he got bigger and bigger and bigger, and it was harder to find the time to do that," says Lovelady. "The bigger the company got, the less close we were." While some of this distance was unavoidable as the company expanded exponentially, and as Henson increasingly juggled multiple projects and offices on two continents, it was a disappointment for many at the Muppets.

Hunt's sense of this separation, and his resentment of it, shows not only how the company was growing and changing but how he was as well. The eager kid who had bounced into the auditions less than a decade earlier was becoming more jaded. Interestingly, Hunt charted this growth through his Muppet alter ego. "Scooter grew," Hunt said. "He was this little kid, and that was me when I first walked in. But then my father died. That changed me and that changed Scooter. Jim and Frank were starting to separate themselves and so there was much more of the cynical thing for the little kid." Not only had Hunt lost his father, but he had lost the sense of Henson and Oz as father figures, seeing them more as equals— even if they didn't necessarily share this view in return. "I think they were satisfying their egos, as well as setting up on a professional level that they were better than the rest of us," Hunt said. "It was uncomfortable to me because I always wanted to have some sort of thing."

Hunt had originally seen this puppetry gig as a mere way station on the path to becoming an actor. Now his work was more famous than he could have ever imagined—but hardly anyone knew who he was.

While some of Hunt's invisibility was due to the separation among the core Muppet troupe, as well as the media's focus on Henson and Oz at the expense of the others, some of it was just the irony of puppetry: the more skilled the performance, the less likely the viewer is to consider that an actual human being is bringing this character to life.

Even Oz noticed this invisibility—and considered it a mixed bag. "It's a very good thing because you can buy a can of beans at the supermarket and no one's going to bother you," Oz said. "On the other hand, when you want someone to bother you while you're buying a can of beans, it gets very depressing."

Nelson, too, found that the anonymity went both ways. He found himself seated next to Al Pacino on the Concorde from New York to London. When they got to talking, and Nelson explained what he did for a living, Pacino said, "You're on the most famous TV show in the world, and nobody knows who you are." "That can be really nice, actually," Nelson replied. When the plane landed, and a crowd of people mobbed Pacino for autographs, Nelson just grinned at him. "See you in baggage, Al."

No matter how successful Hunt became, people just didn't take puppetry seriously. Hunt liked to tell a story about a dinner party conversation he had with an elderly Brit at the height of *The Muppet Show*. "What do you do?" she asked. "Oh, I'm a puppeteer with the Muppets," Hunt answered. Hunt would deliver the punchline in his best imitation of the woman's posh accent and wavery falsetto: "How lovely, dear. But what do you do for a *living*?"

It really burned him sometimes.

As Hunt filmed more *Muppet Show* episodes that summer, the negatives of the job nagged at him. A perennial sunbather, Hunt hated the weather in England. He would point out the rarity of sunlight to his friends "by asking a group of five or six Brits which way was North," recalls Bailey. "Inevitably, they all would point in different directions."

Hunt's Jersey pal Terry Minogue noticed a certain hesitancy each time Hunt was scheduled to go to London. "Right before he left, he'd always get a little depressed," says Minogue. "As much as he loved doing the show, I think he wished they had done it here. He wanted to stay with his friends in America." The outgoing Hunt sometimes felt like he was talking to a brick wall when he ran up against the more reserved British temperament. Hunt compensated for missing the States by bringing friends and family overseas, piling them into the Volkswagen Bug and showing them the sights, impressing them with how well he knew the city and how comfortably he drove on the left side of the road. But as much as Hunt threw himself into enjoying London, he suffered bouts of homesickness.

So Hunt took it in stride in early August when the ATV technical staff suddenly went on strike. The team had to close down production and fly back to the States, at great time and expense, and hold tight waiting to see when they would return to work.

During the unexpected break, Hunt checked another item off his wish list. He bought a grey-shingled cottage in Truro, Massachusetts, on the outer end of Cape Cod, fulfilling a dream he'd nurtured since high school.

Hunt's four-bedroom cottage on a private road on Truro's Corn Hill was the best of both worlds: just a quick ten-mile drive down Route 6 from the excitement of Provincetown, the cottage nevertheless felt peaceful and remote. From Route 6, the largely undeveloped Corn Hill Road wound up a dramatic hill, ending at a majestic sand dune seventy-five feet over Cape Cod Bay, with sweeping views across the water all the way from Plymouth to Provincetown. The eighteen cottages on the hill—thirteen of which, including Hunt's, comprised the Corn Hill Association condominium complex—were built around the turn of the twentieth century as a summer resort for a group of Victorians from Boston. The charming cottages, famously immortalized by Edward Hopper in his 1930 painting "Corn Hill," had creaky, uneven floorboards, exposed wood walls, and single-pane windows. Hunt's living room boasted a big fireplace topped by an ornate mantelpiece.

Hunt could usually be found perched on the cottage's back porch, looking out over the water. He couldn't get enough of the sun, especially after his time in London, basking like a lizard on a rock. He would thumb through *The New York Times*, or a book or a magazine, or just gaze across the bay. He especially liked to watch the sunsets, no two alike, colorful as works of art.

Though Hunt cherished the peace of the Truro house, characteristically, he couldn't wait to fill it with his loved ones. "That place was Grand Central," recalls *Sesame* performer Brian Meehl. "Richard took such pleasure from sharing it with people." The Hunt family held annual vacations at the house every August. Hunt loved taking people out to the local restaurants, especially popular Italian joint Front Street, where he was friends with chef-owner Howard Gruber. Hunt even lured Nelson out to the Cape. "They're selling these houses, you wanna buy one?" he asked Nelson, who replied, "Richard, I'm not going to buy a house in a place I've never been!" Nelson started renting nearby, however, and purchased his own Cape home in the early '90s.

Unfortunately, Hunt's place was only a summer cottage—the condo association turned off the electricity from October to March, which meant that he also had no water, since it came through an electric pump. And no heat! But that didn't stop Hunt, who liked to have Thanksgiving at the house, appreciating how deserted the area became with all the other cottages uninhabited. The family slept in sleeping bags on the living room floor, cuddled together for warmth in front of the fireplace. They washed dishes in the bay, joking that the sand was a useful pumice in scrubbing off the turkey residue. The cottage would be a cherished respite for Hunt for the rest of his life.

The ATV strike allowed Hunt and the other *Sesame Street* performers some much-needed time to work on the children's television blockbuster. The team cranked out 130 episodes per season, often squeezing in *Sesame Street* for a week or two between other projects. "We were definitely the poor sister," recalls executive producer Dulcy Singer. This made the main Muppet performers "top priority" in *Sesame Street* scheduling. One time, both Oz and Mel Gibson were available—and Singer chose Oz. "I got a lot of kidding for that. And to this day I'm not sorry."

Despite being on a tight schedule, the performers still found time to play—which, ironically, was often good for their work. One day Hunt and Nelson were fooling around when writer Sara Compton came by. "What are you doing?" she asked. They replied, "One monster with two heads!" And so it was.

"The Two-Headed Monster is a great character," said Hunt. "It reflects our personalities and our relationship with each other." Since the character had two heads—and two temperaments, two opinions, and so forth—each sketch offered a lesson in cooperation, as the monster dealt with emotions, learned how to listen, and even decided where to go on vacation. Hunt and Nelson invented a comical, boisterous gibberish in which the character communicated with itself.

The production team encouraged this kind of organic collaboration. By late 1979, the head roster was essentially as it would remain for over a decade: executive producer Singer; producer Lisa Simon; head writer Norman Stiles; and director Jon Stone, essentially a modern-day show-runner. Like the Muppet performers, this team respected the unique skills everyone brought to the table, valuing the creative process.

Not only did the character of the Two-Headed Monster emerge through play, but its sketches largely developed that way as well. "We had been pals for a while, so we really had a sense of where we were going," Nelson recalls. "Usually we would talk over a bit before we did it, outline it, and then we'd just play with it." Particularly when Stone was directing, if the script was too wordy or overwritten, Stone might say, "We're going to lose all this, and here's the idea, and just do it." Since Hunt had little patience with elaborate run-throughs, this was fine with him.

Still, despite their efficient productivity, *Sesame Street*'s main puppeteers could only do so much with their limited availability. Acknowledging how much of their time and focus was diverted by other projects, Henson brought some new hands on board. Two in particular, Michael Earl and Brian Meehl, took on the bulk of the work for the next few years—and both became close friends with Hunt.

Hunt had met Michael Earl on the *Muppet Movie* set, bounding up like Winnie-the-Pooh's Tigger to introduce himself to the nineteen-year-old performer. "Hi, I'm Richard Hunt!" he said, expecting Earl to recognize the name. Earl, however, was familiar only with Henson and Oz—which came off to Hunt like a dare. "From that point on, I was basically a challenge: to get me to be impressed, to get me to like him," Earl recalls. The gay performer enjoyed the "fun and playful, cat and mouse" dynamic he had with Hunt. Earl played a number of hand puppet characters, but most importantly, he took over the front half of the elephantine Snuffleupagus from a grateful Nelson, with Bryant Young taking over what had been Hunt's role in the back.

Hunt quickly befriended good-natured Brian Meehl, who reminded him of his Jersey buddies. Meehl had originally been a mime with Mummenschanz, and was hired for body puppeteering, such as romping about inside the full-body dog puppet Barkley. He soon transitioned to hand puppetry and vocalizing characters.

Meehl, Earl, and the other new hires were so needed that the writers created characters to play to their strengths. Noticing that Earl could do a Southern accent, the writers came up with absent-minded cowboy Forgetful Jones (later played by Hunt). But Hunt resented that Earl was advancing so quickly—far more quickly than he had, playing lead characters from the very start rather than doing an apprenticeship. "He was like, 'That's not fair,'" says Earl. "'I had to start doing right hands and you just waltz in here and start doing leads.'"

Another critical piece of *Sesame*'s future snapped into place that fall when Hunt met young puppeteer Kevin Clash. The shy performer had just done his first Muppet gig, performing Cookie Monster in the Macy's Thanksgiving Day Parade, and ducked into the bathroom during the after-party to hide from his heroes—only to run right into them. "Lo and behold . . . Richard Hunt was there," Clash recalled.

"So you're working with Kermit [Love]?" Hunt asked. The puppet designer and builder still mentored and encouraged new performers, as he had done for Hunt. When Clash said yes, Hunt launched into a pep talk, reflective both of his bluntness and his underdog politics. "He said, 'Jim doesn't have any Black puppeteers. So you need to go out there, you need to tell him what you do.'"

When Clash rejoined the party, he didn't quite have the nerve to take Hunt's advice—but fortunately Love beckoned him over to meet Henson, having talked up Clash in his absence. "Can you send me a tape?" Henson asked. Before Clash could open his mouth, Love spoke for him: "Yes, he will."

When *The Muppet Show*'s technical strike ended in late October, the Original Five dashed back to England to finish up two episodes in just four days, with Hunt and Nelson thrilled to work with renowned trumpeter Dizzy Gillespie. Barely a week later they flew to Los Angeles to film *John Denver and The Muppets: A Christmas Together*, where Hunt hung out with Denver in his dressing room between takes.

Hunt finally had a few weeks off in December, closing out the decade by attending Henson's Christmas party at Manhattan's St. Regis Hotel as well as throwing his own holiday celebration in Closter, the cozy house crowded with family and revelers. He would find himself grateful for the breather, for 1980 would be a jam-packed year of work, full of emotional endings—and promising new beginnings.

"The All Time Get Around Sometimes Play Together Every Other Friday Night Vaudeville Show," Chats Palace Theater, London, March 29, 1980. Left to right: Jerry Nelson, Betsy Baytos, Steve Whitmire, Hunt, Kathy Mullen, Rollie Krewson, and Louise Gold.

CHAPTER 9

Endings and Beginnings

S TAR WARS actor Mark Hamill flashed Hunt the middle finger during the introductions at the Sunday morning read-through for his January 1980 *Muppet Show* guest star stint. Hamill already spoke Hunt's language: if you like someone, you tease them and pretend you can't stand them. "I had the confidence to know he wouldn't take that the wrong way," Hamill recalls. "He loved it!"

Hunt and Hamill had met three years earlier when Hamill toured the *Muppet Show* set—and Hunt had made an immediate impression. "Richard was to me *instantly* the most charismatic of all the Muppeteers," says Hamill. "He was like a force of nature. He reminded me of [*Star Wars* co-star] Carrie Fisher—he had the same exuberance for life and for making every moment thrilling and exciting." For Hamill's wife Marilou, the connection wasn't quite so instant; she was put off by how "aggressive" Hunt was about getting together, wary of his persistent calls to their hotel room. Once they became good friends, Hunt made this into a running gag. "He always teased us about that," she recalls with a laugh. "'Oh yeah, you guys were distant at first.'"

Hamill's experience playing *Star Wars* hero Luke Skywalker made him a strong Muppet guest, as he had plenty of practice being the only human on the call sheet, sharing scenes with reptiles, robots, or puppets such as Yoda, played by Muppet performer Frank Oz. But Hamill was grateful for a chance to play against type. *The Muppet Show* offered guests a venue to show off surprising talents; witness opera diva Beverly Sills tap-dancing (or balancing a spoon on her nose!) or tough guy Sylvester Stallone singing. When Henson asked Hamill if he had any hidden skills, Hamill quipped in his best Kermit the Frog imitation: "Well, I've been known to do voices." Totally deadpan, Henson replied, "Who do you do?" The room roared with laughter, and the writers put the real-life dialogue right into the script. What's even funnier, however, is that Henson was completely serious.

The troupe also had a riotous time filming a bit where Hamill and a puppet played by Nelson gargled out the tune of Gershwin's "Summertime." "I wish there was footage of us trying to gargle and then sing," recalls Nelson. "We were all cracking up at each other." They wound up with Hunt recording the gargling; on camera, Hamill did his own gargles over Hunt's, trying very hard not to laugh. "Gargling Gershwin, does it get any more degrading than that?" Hamill jokes.

1980 was Hunt's busiest year of work yet. The Original Five crammed ten episodes into seven weeks in order to finish the fourth season of *The Muppet Show* in late February, closing out with Diana Ross drawing a larger-than-usual audience. Hunt had barely two weeks to catch his breath before jumping back into work, filming the fifth and last season all the way to late August with only the occasional weeklong break. Amazingly, even as the Muppet troupe churned out a fantastic final season of *The Muppet Show*, they were also sowing the seeds for what would come next.

Freedom characterizes the final season of *The Muppet Show*. The troupe was riding high on the success not just of the show but of the movie; they could essentially do whatever they wanted and the world would gladly come along for the ride. They had room to experiment with imaginative themes: a young Brooke Shields gamely starred in a surreal *Alice in Wonderland* episode; serious British actor Glenda Jackson played a delusional pirate captain who hijacked the theater, with Hunt as Sweetums by her side; comedy-variety queen Carol Burnett upstaged a dance marathon; and cutting-edge punk singer Debbie Harry inspired young frog Robin and a whole troop of Punk Scouts. Symbolically, rather than starting each show with the star already in the dressing room, Nelson's elderly character Pops took over Scooter's greeting duties, working the front door and vetting each guest before letting them in.

Hunt appreciated, however, that the last-season *Muppet Show* guests weren't just the current biggest and brightest. Henson used the show's success to bring on guests who weren't necessarily as well known as they once had been. The show saluted vaudeville star Wally Boag, just a couple of years short of retirement; and while ventriloquist Señor Wences had been a mainstay of *The Ed Sullivan Show*, his *Muppet Show* appearance introduced him to a whole new generation. "Jim loved performers like this," says Nelson. "He wanted other people to see these people." The performers were thrilled to see them as well. When Señor Wences came for the Sunday read-through, for example, Nelson recalls, "We were all like little kids sitting there watching him."

Despite their joy in their daily work, Hunt, Nelson, and Gold identified as *actors*, and sorely missed putting on that kind of entertainment. "Puppets was always a dual-edged thing," Gold recalls. "We wanted to be performing."

So, as if their ten-hour days weren't enough, the friends put together an after-hours variety show at the East End musical theater Chats Palace, calling the March 29 performance "The All Time Get Around Sometimes Play Together Every Other Friday Night Vaudeville Show." Nelson set up the show through his friend Graham Binmore, a *Muppet Show* puppet wrangler who co-directed a local production company. Hunt, Nelson, and Gold put on an evening of vaudeville sketches and musical numbers, joined onstage by Mullen, Whitmire, and *Muppet Show* dancer Betsy Baytos, among others. Even Henson got in on the act, renting a drum kit and hiding under a newsboy cap at the back of the stage. "What a blast," Gold recalls.

Hunt liked to blow off steam at the end of a long *Muppet Show* workday with a big meal. He'd take his colleagues out to a restaurant, one or two people or as many as a dozen: usually Nelson, and often Gold, Goelz, Whitmire, Quinn, Baker, and whoever else wanted to come along. Sometimes they would haunt nearby restaurants, such as Chikako's, a

Japanese place in neighboring Barnet, or Hunt would pack the tiny Volkswagen Polo and speed back to London.

But wherever they ate—no matter how many people were eating three-course meals and drinking expensive wine, regardless of how many hundreds of pounds the meal cost—if someone went out to dinner with Hunt, there was one rule: they could never pay the bill. They couldn't even pitch in their share. If it was a one-on-one meal, and they were foolish enough to visit the restroom, they would come back to find that Hunt had paid. Sometimes Hunt would pay the bill beforehand; sometimes the restaurant staff would know him and understand that he would pay; or, usually, he would simply slip away during the meal and take care of it. Even if his friends argued with him, even if they *insisted*, he would never let them pay. "When you start making more money than me, then you can buy dinner," Hunt told his friends.

Hunt's generosity also applied to waitstaff. Nelson recalls one raucous meal, a big group of people at an expensive restaurant shortly before the kitchen closed. Hunt had no shortage of complaints about the waiter: the service was slow, the drinks were wrong, half of the steaks had to be sent back. Finally, after one last episode, Hunt snapped, "That's it. Not a penny over 15 percent!" While some patrons might have stiffed the waiter in response to bad service, this didn't even cross Hunt's mind.

While most of his friends and colleagues appreciated Hunt's generosity, some were frustrated by not being able to reciprocate. "We would constantly fight with him: 'Let us pay. Let us share this,'" Baker recalls. Hunt's friends tried to circumvent him; if they invited him out to dinner, for example, they might call the restaurant the day before and give a credit card number in advance—but he often figured that out, and outsmarted his friends by coming early and giving the restaurant *his* credit card instead.

Hunt's ex-lover Duncan Kenworthy was not just frustrated by Hunt's relentless generosity; he saw it as "a slightly neurotic thing," an inability to owe or be grateful. Hunt had spent his youth worrying about money; now that he had some, he never wanted anyone to feel left out for lack of funds. He never forgot where he came from—to an almost unhealthy extent. Kenworthy interprets Hunt's generosity as part of a long-practiced false front, a fear that he would be rejected if he showed his true, vulnerable self. While everybody generally liked Hunt, few people got very close, at least not during the *Muppet Show* years. "He was always coming forward like a freight train," says Kenworthy, "but there was this hurt little boy in there that never quite got out."

Hunt saw a good bit of Kenworthy around this time as Kenworthy was in London running Henson's Creature Shop, a puppet and special effects workshop. Kenworthy had called Henson during the ATV strike to see about a job, having worked at the Children's Television Workshop and produced an Arabic version of *Sesame Street*. Henson was happy to have him aboard, but before making anything official, Henson ran the decision by Hunt. "He knew enough about my and Richard's relationship," Kenworthy recalls, "that Jim, very sensitively, said to Richard, 'I'm going to offer Duncan a job, is that okay with you?'" Hunt had no objections, and Kenworthy returned to England.

In another sign of having "made it," Hunt and Muppet designer Amy Van Gilder rented a stunning duplex at 11 Heath Villas, just up the road from the Creature Shop and Henson's sumptuous Hampstead rowhouse. Hunt's new place was ensconced in the peaceful Vale of Health enclave, surrounded on all sides by the greenery of Hampstead Heath. Hunt's living room overlooked the Vale of Health pond, with a view of the moor that looked like something out of *Wuthering Heights*.

Like the Closter and Truro houses, Hunt's Hampstead apartment was a gathering point. Most of the Muppet gang lived locally: Henson and Whitmire were in walking distance; Gold lived an easy couple of miles over in Kentish Town; and though Nelson was out in Letchmore Heath, near Elstree, he was generally game to come to London. Hunt often had friends over to watch British television; even the most banal local programming amused him greatly. He and Van Gilder kept a rubber dinghy in the living room, which they liked to take out on the pond. He always kept orange juice in the refrigerator, his idea of healthy eating. He ate breakfast food at all hours: bowls of Alpen muesli soaked in milk, or smoked salmon atop one of the few things he actually cooked—scrambled eggs.

Often keeping Hunt company in Hampstead was Ian Smith, whom Hunt dated during his last year on *The Muppet Show*. As he often did with lovers, Hunt took Smith all around—to the set, to friends' houses, out to big dinners—but only those in the know understood that they were together. Smith had a boyish smile and a wild mane of dark curls that belied his prim and proper nature.

As had been the case with Kenworthy, opposites attracted—and led to some passionate arguments. Stuart Fischer recalls the pair bickering "like a married couple of eighty years," arguing over mundane things such as what to wear or when to leave the house for an engagement. Fischer recalls one argument in which Hunt berated Smith about his accent, namely how he pronounced the word "pasta." In Italy the word is pronounced just as it is in the States, "PAH-sta." Yet Smith and many of his fellow Londoners pronounced it with a short "a," like "cat": "PASS-tah." "Everything in London is 'ah,'" Hunt screamed, his voice rising in volume. "But *this* one you pronounce wrong! Why do you pronounce this wrong?" Fischer, watching, laughed until he cried.

Hunt threw legendary parties in the Hampstead apartment, with guests ranging from members of the rock band Yes, whom he and Nelson had met backstage after a show, to West End actor Peter Land. Hunt flew around busily at these gatherings, alighting briefly to talk to each guest, making sure everyone's champagne flute was filled, then racing away again. The parties were kid-friendly, often with a movie like *The Wizard of Oz* playing in one of the bedrooms.

Hunt took lavish vacations in his limited free time. On one *Muppet Show* break, Hunt and Nelson borrowed a houseboat from an acquaintance at the studio and spent a week on the water in Beaulieu sur Mer, in the Côte D'Azur of France. In a three-star restaurant that looked like a castle, they ordered sumptuous entrées which were so good that they went ahead and ordered a second course: first stuffed sea bass, then filet mignon, washed down with a couple of bottles of expensive wine. "The whole meal was really expensive, like $200 [about $1,000 in 2023 dollars] for the two of us," Nelson recalls. "But we were living large in those days."

While Hunt enjoyed living large, he was a stalwart friend, around for both the highs *and* the lows. One night Hunt and Nelson performed Scooter and Pops at a party for *Muppet Show* designer Malcolm Stone, during which Nelson received word that his daughter Christine had had a bad episode of her cystic fibrosis and had started bleeding in her lungs. Hunt drove a distraught Nelson back to Letchmore Heath to pack a bag and reserve a seat on the next SST Concorde back to the States. Hunt then took Nelson to his own place, and the two went out to Hampstead Heath. Recalls Nelson, "We went out in the park and just talked, sat and talked, until it was time to go to the plane."

As *The Muppet Show* drew to a close, the seeds of the next projects were being planted.

On May 24, between the Paul Simon and Linda Ronstadt episodes, Henson flew to Scotland for the christening of his godson Freddie Stevenson, the son of his friend Jocelyn Stevenson, a writer who wore various hats at *Sesame Street*, including editing *Sesame Street Magazine*, writing a number of *Sesame*-related books, and freelancing for the show itself. Stevenson's brother-in-law Peter Orton—who ran the international division of the Children's Television Workshop, distributing *Sesame Street* around the world—prevailed upon Stevenson to seat him next to Henson at the dinner following the christening. Orton spent the meal bending Henson's ear about his big idea: a deliberately international television show. This would be a great contrast to *Sesame Street* and *The Muppet Show*, whose worldwide proliferation had largely developed on the fly. This new show could be consciously international right from the start—a concept with great potential both economically and creatively.

"Hmmm," said Henson.

This idea would become Hunt's next major television project with the Muppets: *Fraggle Rock*.

More seeds for the Muppet future were sown in mid-June when Henson, Oz, Spinney, and Hunt performed at the 1980 World Puppetry Festival in Washington, D.C. Puppeteers from all over the world—twenty nations from Japan to India to Czechoslovakia to Brazil—converged for the weeklong gathering, held in tandem with the thirteenth meeting of the international puppetry organization UNIMA (l'Union Internationale de la Marionette), and co-sponsored by UNIMA-USA and Puppeteers of America. Henson was instrumental in putting on the festival, as Henson Associates took responsibility for the legal aspects, the publicity, and the lion's share of the costs. Henson didn't put anything in writing with festival organizer Nancy Straub, preferring to rely on his word. The historic gathering would become renowned as the biggest and most daring American puppet festival of all time. "No [American puppetry] festival has so far equalled or surpassed the 1980 World Puppetry Festival for scale, scope or boldness of vision," UNIMA's magazine *Puppetry International* wrote over thirty years later.

The Muppets headlined the festival's opening gala event on June 8 at the Kennedy Center, with Henson and Oz as Kermit and Fozzie, Spinney as Big Bird roller-skating as he carried Oscar the Grouch, and Hunt right-handing for Fozzie as well as playing Sweetums. When Straub ran up the aisle to announce the next speaker, it was the Royal Variety Performance all over again—Hunt, in his Sweetums costume, jumped off the stage and nearly landed right on her. "That would have been a dramatic, tragic or comedic collision," she wrote.

While Hunt was still disgruntled by his career's ironic combination of fame and anonymity, the festival was a turning point for him in terms of realizing that he was, in fact, more well known and appreciated than he had thought, at least within the field. Puppetry's up-and-coming next generation was at the festival in full force. Pam Arciero, soon to be a *Sesame Street* performer as well as Hunt's good friend, was at the festival with the University of Connecticut theater department performing *The Ring of the Nibelung*. She was excited to meet Hunt, having followed his career for some time. They walked outside the Kennedy Center, stopping next door in front of the Watergate Hotel. Hunt pulled out a joint as they stood and looked at the building, marveling at the events there that had led to Nixon's resignation. "I was thrilled to hang out with Richard," Arciero recalls. "I think I was always thrilled to hang out with him."

And seventeen-year-old budding puppeteer David Rudman, who would also work on *Sesame Street* as well as befriend Hunt, was not only familiar with Hunt's work but *recognized* him, much to Hunt's great delight. Rudman, a Chicago native, was in the area visiting relatives and got tickets to the Kennedy Center gala. At a reception before the show, Rudman saw Henson and Oz surrounded by a mob of people. Hunt stood in the corner, wearing an orange University of New Jersey T-shirt, sipping a glass of wine and watching the room with his bright eyes. Rudman, who had recently seen the Muppets' appearance on *60 Minutes*, thought to himself, "I think that's the guy who does Scooter."

Rudman walked up to Hunt and asked, "Are you Richard Hunt, one of the Muppet guys?"

"Yeah, how do you know me?" Hunt replied.

"I dunno, I just recognized you," Rudman said with a shrug.

Hunt's eyes lit up. "You recognized me? C'mere!" Hunt grabbed Rudman by the arm and dragged him over to Henson and Oz. "I got recognized!" he crowed.

Unfortunately, Henson and Oz were nonplussed. "They were like, 'Yeah, all right, whatever,'" Rudman recalls.

Hunt's major characters have some fine moments in the waning weeks of *The Muppet Show*. Beaker gets cloned inside a copy machine, so a half-dozen Beakers roam the Muppet theater, giving the anxious lab assistant an opportunity for unusual interactions such as accompanying the Electric Mayhem, interrupting the Swedish Chef, and, with Hunt on double duty, appearing in the box seats with Statler and Waldorf. In another episode, Statler and Waldorf take a turn hosting the show, learning how challenging Kermit's job really is.

On August 17, 1980—Hunt's twenty-ninth birthday—the *Muppet Show* squad kicked off their final week of filming. Hunt was thrilled to welcome song-and-dance movie star Gene Kelly, fresh off the last feature film of his career, *Xanadu*. Hunt's character Scooter propels the episode's running in-joke; Scooter has taken up trying to predict the future with a deck of fortune-telling cards, and tells Beauregard that the world is going to end. For indeed, to those in the know, the world of *The Muppet Show* was in fact ending. In the closing scene, Kelly reads the instruction manual for the cards and discovers that Scooter was wrong; the cards he drew don't mean that the world is ending, but instead that their laundry will come back "gray and dingy." Beauregard, however, is not convinced: "I know it means the end is near." Kermit corrects him: "No, it means the end is *now*." And truly, for the purposes of the show, it *was* the end.

But happily, Hunt and Henson's Statler and Waldorf get the last word. "Are you ready for the end of the world?" Statler asks Waldorf, who replies, "Sure, it couldn't be any worse than this show!" Even in a moment that might be sad, the show reminds the viewer not to take anything too seriously.

Why end a show that was still so wildly successful? Henson measured success by a different rubric. He had largely mastered the medium of the half-hour comedy-variety show, and wanted to move on to the next challenge: seeing what more he could do on the silver screen.

What did Hunt and his colleagues do to celebrate making one of the most successful television programs in history? Why, work even harder, of course—but play hard as well.

The Muppet gang fêted the end of *The Muppet Show* with a big dinner party at White Elephant on the River, a celebrity haunt in Pimlico on the Thames. But just two days after wrapping the last episode, Hunt and eighty-four colleagues flew down to Bermuda for a three-day retreat. For the first time, the London and New York wings of Henson Associates came together—not without tension, as both halves of the company often competed for Henson's attention. But Hunt, as usual, had friends at the gathering from both sides of the Atlantic.

Henson kicked off the retreat by reviewing the history of the Muppets, which he conceived of in seven-year cycles: first the local *Sam and Friends* era; then the move to New York, and the ensuing appearances on other people's variety shows such as *Jimmy Dean* and *Ed Sullivan*; then the debut and first seven seasons of *Sesame Street*; and finally their own comedy-variety show, *The Muppet Show*, which was now coming to an end. Where did they want to go from here?

The company split off into seminars to brainstorm about what might come next, kicking around such topics as what creativity meant to them and what they thought the world needed from the Muppets today. But these work sessions were balanced out with plenty of time to explore the area, lounge on the beach, and even take a cruise. Hunt and his colleagues were given commemorative green-and-yellow *Muppet Show* jackets like the one Scooter had worn on the show—a gesture which Hunt, of course, especially appreciated.

The retreat culminated in a gala six-course dinner with dancing and a local steel drum band. During the dinner, Henson got up to give a farewell address to the crowd—but when he shyly faltered, Hunt stood up and delivered the speech as if he were Henson, to help give the company a needed sense of closure at the end of this intense production.

Hunt later explained how he often served in this role. "Jim and I both knew instinctively when you come into another country, and you take over these people's lives for four or five years, and then you leave all of a sudden, it's like, what happened?" he said. "It can be very damaging to them, because it's too overwhelming, too quick, too resentful. So you need somehow to bring a focus.

"Jim knew this. He'd stand up at a wrap party, and he'd say, I want to thank you all for helping me with the show, and uh, uh, thanks. And he'd look at me, and I'd stand up, and I'd say, 'What he is *trying* to say was . . .' because I could articulate anything." Hunt's speech on behalf of Henson was well received by the dinner crowd, with nods of recognition as well as Hunt's favorite applause: laughter.

This wasn't the first time Hunt stood in for Henson—nor would it be the last. "It was a pattern that he had," Meehl recalls. "Jim was shy, and talking to all those people wasn't really his thing, so Richard would get up, pretending to be Jim, to give the speech. This was something he did!"

While Hunt at times worried that Henson didn't fully appreciate what he brought to the company, moments like these helped assuage such doubts. Hunt would later learn that Henson valued these kinds of moments, and Hunt's ability to speak for him, more than Hunt had ever truly understood.

Not two weeks after wrapping *The Muppet Show,* Hunt and his colleagues began filming the Muppets' second feature film, *The Great Muppet Caper.* While their first movie had been an American road trip, their second was a thank-you to England, shot on location around London and at Elstree's EMI studios, just across the street and slightly east of where they had spent the last five years. The Original Five were joined by Whitmire, Gold, Mullen, and Meehl, as well as a half-dozen assistants, with the happy addition of teen puppeteer Mike Quinn working alongside his heroes.

With *Caper,* Henson continued to raise the bar of what could be done with puppets on film. Since *Muppet Movie* audiences had raved about Kermit riding a bicycle—a relatively simple marionette trick—Hunt and his colleagues kicked off *Caper* on September 4 in Battersea Park with a Muppet bicycle parade featuring over a dozen characters, a complicated endeavor involving marionettes as well as remote-controlled anima-tronic technology, helmed by sixteen-year-old Brian Henson. Similarly, while in the first movie Henson had submerged himself in an underwater tank to film Kermit in the swamp, here Oz learned to scuba dive so Piggy could perform an underwater ballet. Henson's biggest challenge with *Caper*, however—dwarfing any puppet stunts—was making his debut as a movie director, helming a feature film for the first time.

Hunt checked off another wish list item when he appeared in *Caper*'s opening number—*without* a puppet on his hand. Hunt shows up as an impatient taxi driver in his blink-and-you'll-miss-it cameo, a perfect role for the Checker cab owner. He honks the horn and says "Come on" in his best New York accent. (He sounds almost like Oscar the Grouch, whose voice Spinney based on a New York cabbie.) Sitting behind Hunt is another Muppet performer, Kathy Mullen.

Indeed, *Caper* is peppered with a half-dozen cameos by Muppet performers: Jim Henson and Hunt's Hampstead roommate Amy Van Gilder dine out at the Dubonnet Club; Frank Oz works at *The Daily Chronicle*. These cameos, besides being hidden gems for the viewers, gave some satisfaction to performers like Hunt who yearned to see not just their puppet characters but their own faces on the silver screen.

Hunt was especially pleased to see Jerry Nelson's daughter Christine have a cameo in the film, sweeping her up in a big bear hug when she and her father arrived on set in Hyde Park. "Hi, Gumbelina," he said, using his longtime nickname for her. "You've gotten so beautiful." She returned his grin and blushed gladly.

Henson had written the cameo expressly for the nineteen-year-old, making sure Christine had a line of dialogue so she could get her Screen Actors Guild union card. "This is the most amazing experience I've ever had," Christine wrote in her journal. "I'm so lucky to be me!" Christine's health was so fragile, as she continued to battle cystic fibrosis, that her father had flown to JFK to get her and flown back with her.

Stylish Christine was appalled by the "shapeless" blazer, shirt, and pants provided for her by the wardrobe department. She went to her father, who walked her over to Henson. "Jim, the clothes wardrobe gave Chris to wear aren't quite right," Nelson said. "I think she looks fine the way she is." Henson looked over Christine's white jeans and patterned yellow sweatshirt and nodded. "I agree. Tell Rose [in wardrobe] it's okay."

With a microphone taped to the small of her back, Christine and her father rehearsed and shot their scene. Their cameo perpetuates the movie's running gag that Kermit and Fozzie are identical twins, though clearly they look nothing alike. Humorously, no one in the movie can tell them apart, relying on one difference: their headwear. Christine and Nelson, walking around the lake in Hyde Park, pass Kermit on a park bench. "Look, Dad, there's a bear!" Christine exclaims. Her father corrects her: "No, Christine, that's a frog. Bears wear hats." Christine nods understandingly. The cameo is especially touching as the dialogue establishes not only Christine's name but their relationship. Her father flew her back to America the next day, tears in his eyes as they said goodbye at the airport.

Hunt was renowned on set for buoying up spirits, but he truly outdid himself one night on *Caper* in late October. Filming had gone past 2 A.M.; performers and crew alike were tired, cold, and damp as they waited to reset for a new scene, restlessly biding their time outside of Knebworth House, the eerie 500-year-old Gothic castle that stood in as the movie's Mallory Gallery.

Suddenly, everyone heard a voice booming out from above. "Who dares to haunt my house?" The crowd looked up; a gauzy white apparition much like a ghost had appeared in one of the battlements and was leaning over the rooftop. People were taken aback, truly spooked—until they realized it was Hunt, wearing a sheet over his head, projecting his voice out into the night. He had befriended the owners and talked them into letting him up on the roof. Everyone hollered and cheered, totally reinvigorated. "It was brilliant," says Quinn. "It woke us all up."

Hunt also kept up morale with his ad-libs, coming up with one of *Caper*'s most iconic lines. A roomful of Muppets are all talking at once when Kermit yells "Quiet!" Everyone stops talking except Hunt's Janice, who continues obliviously: "Look, Mother, it's my life, okay, so if I want to live on a beach and walk around naked..." Writer Jerry Juhl told an audience of fans years later, "'If I want to live on the beach and walk around naked'—now that's a Richard Hunt ad-lib." The line was a standout moment in a movie criticized for underutilizing the characters' established personalities.

But filming had a somber moment on December 8 when word came that John Lennon had been shot and killed outside his apartment building—and *Caper* shut down for the day. Hunt, a Beatles fan who admired Lennon and what he espoused, took the news hard. "There are so few good guys in the world," he reflected later. "And you take those people for granted. The people we give attention and enormous interest and jealousy to are the people that are slick and selling. Meanwhile, people like John Lennon—'All we are saying is give peace a chance.' 'All you need is love.' People were saying, 'Oh, shut up, John, get yourself a haircut. We know that, don't tell us that.' No, you need to tell yourself that every day. And you need to live it. And you need to share it."

By now, Hunt had largely broken through the typical staid reserve of the British. He made a lot of friends all around London, from all walks of life. He was friends with one big family who were so "proper and normal" that he and Gold joked with each other about wishing they came from families like that. And he looked in on a local, down-on-her-luck woman and her young son, bringing gifts and listening to her woes.

While finishing up *Caper* in January 1981, Hunt met Neil and Sally Pearce at Chikako's, his Japanese haunt in Barnet. Hunt wasn't a patron that night; he was filling in for the owner, a friend, who was at his father's funeral. Hunt was acting the role of host and waiter, leading the Pearces to their table and taking their order. He was a distracted, slapdash waiter, but so charming that no one seemed to care, least of all Sally and Neil, a young couple on their first date night away from their new baby, celebrating Sally's birthday.

Hunt had so much fun getting to know the couple, a fireman and a homemaker, that once the restaurant quieted down, Hunt came and sat with them—and characteristically insisted on picking up the check. "I don't work here," he explained. "I work on *The Muppet Show*." But even then, they didn't have the whole picture. "We thought, 'Oh, back-room boy!'" Sally quips.

In return for their meal, Hunt asked for just one thing: to come to their house for a proper English roast. Hunt came to Sunday dinner a few weeks later, bringing along Ian Smith, whom he introduced as a "friend"; it was the first of many such Sunday dinners at the Pearces.

At some point well after the Pearces realized just how successful Hunt was, they asked him, "Why do you want to be friends with us? We're just this nobody couple from Walthamstow." Hunt replied matter-of-factly, "I like to be friends with nice people who treat me nice."

The Pearces visited Hunt at Elstree in mid-March for the filming of *The Muppets Go to the Movies,* a one-hour ABC special. Hunt met them in the parking lot, where he knew the attendant, and gave them a tour of the set—which was actually *The Muppet Show* set, in use for the last time.

In many ways, *The Muppets Go to the Movies* was the unofficial *Muppet Show* series finale, with the same characters, performers, writers, and director. When Floyd and Janice perform the Beatles' "Act Naturally" backstage at the Muppet theater, it seems straight out of a regular episode, just with two guests (previous guest Dudley Moore, joined by the marvelously versatile Lily Tomlin) instead of one. At the end, when the characters leave, and Kermit locks the stage door behind him—the only time viewers ever see this—it clicks shut with a certain finality.

Yet fittingly, as Henson had ended the show largely to pursue the movies, *The Muppets Go to the Movies* satirizes film genres from westerns to silents, space flicks to horror films, buddy comedies to romance. (Hunt's Janice introduces *The Wizard of Oz* as "My favorite flick of all time," a sweet moment as it was one of Hunt's favorite movies.) The special is an apt transition to as well as a blatant promotion for *Caper,* containing three scenes from the film and airing a month before the film's release.

However, despite all the advance publicity, when *The Great Muppet Caper* came out in America on June 26, it did less well than expected. Not only did it bring in less than half the box office sales of *The Muppet Movie* ($31,000 versus $65,000), but the critics were disappointed. Henson's heart just wasn't in the movie in the same way—and it showed.

What's more, too many cooks had spoiled the broth, writing-wise. Juhl co-wrote a first draft with Jack Rose, who had written for Bob Hope films; then sitcom veterans Tom Patchett and Jay Tarses rewrote the script, with all four writers credited for the final composite version. Since Juhl was the only writer to really *know* these characters, many felt that the film didn't contain the same character-driven humor fans had come to love. While *Times* critic Vincent Canby lauded Kermit and

Piggy's romance, the majority of critics echoed Roger Ebert's assessment that the Muppets "lose their special quality" in the film. Critics similarly disparaged the celebrity roles and cameos, opining that they felt random. These middling reviews and box office sales heightened the pressure on Henson's next project—but not on Hunt.

Now that *The Muppet Show* was truly over, and *Caper* was in the can, Hunt's separation from his colleagues widened. He was the only Original Five member not to work on Henson's next big project: *The Dark Crystal* (Whitmire, Mullen, Meehl, and Quinn worked on it as well). Having directed his first full-length feature film, now Henson turned his attention to co-directing, with Oz, the company's most ambitious project yet: a full-length puppet film that did *not* feature the Muppets. *The Dark Crystal* was a risky endeavor. Would audiences appreciate the dark fantasy flick, without their beloved characters? Would they know what to make of it? Henson had long pushed the boundaries of puppetry—could he push them too far?

Why wasn't Hunt more involved with *The Dark Crystal*? First, it wasn't necessarily the best use of his talents. Henson planned to dub the puppet characters many times over, requiring flawlessly meticulous technical puppeteers who stuck to the script word for word. Hunt's talents shone brighter when he performed and voiced a character at the same time, with room to play with the part.

Another interpretation (not mutually exclusive) is that this lack of involvement was actually a compliment: Henson trusted Hunt to hold down the fort at *Sesame Street*, the beginning of a trend of Henson delegating and handing off projects to Hunt and others. "Jim wanted anyone that could sub to go back to *Sesame Street*, so they could do stuff without Jim and Frank being around, because that was the hard part," says Duncan Kenworthy, an associate producer on the film.

Though Hunt didn't have a major involvement in *The Dark Crystal*, which began filming at Elstree in mid-April, he stayed intermittently in the Hampstead apartment and was still around when needed—and when he made himself needed. Hunt wasn't afraid to hold Henson accountable, to play the role of the naughty eldest son. "Through all these years I was the bad boy," he recalled. "I was the one who was always questioning everything. If there was an injustice towards some-

one else within a job, or someone was being ignored, I'd bring it up."
Mike Quinn had started working with the Muppets as a sixteen-year-
old apprentice, but when he was upgraded to puppeteering the Skekis
Slave Master in *The Dark Crystal*, his wages stayed the same. When
Hunt found out, he was livid, going straight to the production office for
a few choice words with Henson and the production manager. "'This is
ridiculous! You pay him properly!'" Quinn recalls him saying. "They
looked all sheepish, and sure enough, next paycheck, I was looking at
three times the amount."

Hunt was remarkably patient with Quinn when the young puppeteer
substituted as Waldorf alongside Hunt's Statler on a half-dozen Polaroid
commercials shot at Wembley Studios in late May. As Quinn needed
take after take to make their characters nod in unison, Hunt remained
calm and encouraging. "He didn't stress about the takes," said Quinn.
"He'd find a way to recover." And with Hunt on the set, any shoot lived
up to the slogan, "Polaroid means fun."

Hunt did puppeteer a Pod character in *Dark Crystal*'s crowded Pod-
ling Village sequence, filmed in late June. Much like the *Muppet Movie*
finale, they grabbed "anyone who was in town," recalls Kenworthy, who
also puppeteered in the scene despite being a producer rather than a
performer. That weeklong shoot, however, was Hunt's only participa-
tion in the film, and he soon went back to the States to enjoy the sunny
summer.

Hunt was likely in his favorite spot on the July 4th weekend, reading
The New York Times on the back porch of the Truro house, when he
came across a tiny article about a rare cluster of illness among some gay
men, the first such coverage in the mainstream press. The piece presumably raised his concerns even as it partially explained them: Hunt's
lover Dennis Smith, despite being a self-described "health nut" who ate
well and exercised regularly, had complained for months of a flu-like
malaise. Smith ran fevers, waking up bathed in sweat; doctors ran two
bone marrow biopsies to try to figure out what was wrong.

Yet if Hunt felt a momentary pinch of fear, presumably it seemed distant, even surreal, from his perch overlooking the shimmering water.
Behind him the house was noisily stuffed with dear ones, at the height
of the summer season. Everything was fine! He was on top of the world.

PART IV

Hunt and Rob Mills on the *Fraggle Rock* set, around 1983. Top photo: Hunt performs Junior Gorg's voice and face remotely. Bottom photo: Beside Hunt, Mills wears Junior Gorg's full-body costume minus its heavy head.

CHAPTER 10

Top of the World

W HILE BACK IN NEW YORK the temperature hovered above freezing, Hunt ushered in the new year of 1982 basking in the southern California sun and in the attention of millions of people, standing and waving on the Muppets' float at the head of the New Year's Tournament of Roses parade, in full-body costume as Sweetums. As if to illustrate that year's parade theme of "Friends and Neighbors," Hunt jumped off the float at every opportunity, dancing down the street, engaging with the tens of thousands of spectators along the route, conscious of the cameras beaming out to countless more at home. "You sparked spontaneous joy with everyone with whom you came in contact," the parade's advertising director wrote Hunt in a thank-you note. "And out of costume, you were totally charming."

Life was good.

Hunt's twenties had been a decade of elated improvisation, learning on his feet. He had scrambled along as his career leapt upward, working and playing hard; it had been fun, but fleeting, almost too fast to enjoy. Now he could settle in and savor what he had accomplished—and strategize how best to build upon it. He was thirty years old, eager to see what might come next, how he could make the most of this unimaginable success.

Hunt felt on top of the world—almost literally, stretched out in a lawn chair twelve stories high, sunning himself on the roof deck of his brand-new Upper West Side apartment. He had long kept his eyes open for just the right place, even as he assumed ownership of the Closter house, rented his mother a place in the city, and bought his beloved Truro cottage. Finally in fall 1981 he found an urban perch that met his exacting standards, the perfect rental, a place he would call home for the rest of his life.

Apartment 12B at 645 West End Avenue, between 91st and 92nd Streets, checked all the boxes. The Italianate prewar building appealed to Hunt's aesthetic sense, with marble ceilings in the lobby and stained-glass roses on the bathroom windows. He was perfectly situated: just a half hour over the George Washington Bridge from Closter, and an even quicker drive downtown to Dennis Smith's place in Soho or, later, Nelson Bird's West Village apartment. He could roll out of bed and zoom down to the *Sesame Street* studios, and still be approximately on time, or at least acceptably tardy. He could catch a show at Lincoln Center, where he and his high school friends had dreamed of being performers in the city; now he was living the dream. The urban location even satisfied his need for nature, just steps from scenic Riverside Park overlooking the Hudson, and a few blocks from Central Park in the other direction.

Hunt often had the sprawling Classic Six all to himself. His roommate Andrew Schwartz had signed the lease five years earlier as a Juilliard student, sharing the space with a revolving door of roommates; he initially sublet to Hunt to take a yearlong gig as principal bassoonist with the Jerusalem Symphony, and frequently played or taught out of town for months at a time. The two men rarely overlapped in the space. "Richard was, in a way, a perfect roommate because he wasn't here all the time either," says Schwartz. They were respectful, warm but slightly distant roommates, their respective quarters occupying opposite ends of the apartment. Hunt had no desire to live alone; indeed, the more people he had gathered around him, the happier he was.

Hunt especially relished his new home as a place to entertain, in both senses of the word, as ever. He loved to bring his family and friends together, throwing parties at the slightest provocation: to celebrate birthdays and holidays, to blow off steam after wrapping a show, to watch Muppet work debut on TV, or just to share a new routine or song.

He'd invite some friends early to help pull off the event, barking instructions over the roar of the vacuum cleaner as he ran it across the rug: *Okay. You go down to the bodega. Buy the skinny, tall bottles of soda, the quarts, not the half gallons; the half gallons go to waste.* Other friends would be dispatched to the liquor store, the grocer, even the record shop; soon, almost seamlessly, guests mingled throughout the roomy apartment, the walls echoing with talk and laughter. At some point Hunt would hustle everyone into the living room, people sitting and standing wherever they could, drinks in hand, as Hunt emceed a show, introducing his guests' performances as well as putting on his own act.

Hunt treated Manhattan like Closter, driving around and stopping at friends' places. "He'd honk the horn and we'd look out and go, 'Uncle Richard's here!'" says Mark Hamill. Mark, his wife Marilou, and their kids would pile into Hunt's Checker cab for, say, a scenic drive through Central Park. "He used to call and say, 'I'm ten minutes away, I can only stay for fifteen minutes, and I leave tomorrow, this is your only time to see me,'" says Marilou in a typical story. But Hunt's friends were happy to accommodate him. When he called as Marilou was about to pick up her aunt from the airport, she dispatched someone else to run the errand: "It was my only time to see him!" While Hunt was unfazed by celebrity, treating Luke Skywalker like just another sibling, he did appreciate having carte blanche to drop in on such in-demand people. "Hey, guess who I saw this weekend?" he would say after spending time with famous friends like the Hamills or James Taylor. Mostly he was bragging—but sometimes it seemed as if he didn't quite believe it himself.

Hunt also made new friends at parties in the vivid downtown art scene. "Richard felt that we were lucky to be here at that moment, because that was a unique time in New York," says Jesper Haynes, a Swedish photographer whom Hunt met playing chess at a "very decadent" party in a Tribeca loft thrown by a British bank robber. Around sunrise, Hunt drove everyone home, but called Haynes an hour later in a panic: a coke-addled fight had broken out, and someone had pulled out a gun. Did Haynes know these guys? Would they come after him? Thankfully, nothing came of the incident except a new friendship. Hunt would call up Haynes and invite him to join the gang, the overstuffed

Checker making its way around town, hitting a string of parties in a single night.

Yet as Hunt settled into his new home, he left the nest in a sense at the Muppets. The troupe's rocket trip to stardom had boosted them well beyond the core family of the Original Five. Now they were expanding even more rapidly, taking on a whole new generation of performers. Henson dreamed big for his company, hoping to follow his muse and experiment creatively while pleasing audiences and striking deals that kept the cycle going. Simply too much was going on for the boss to be everywhere at once; Henson started to step back and entrust his experienced colleagues to step up to the job. While just a decade ago Hunt had been an eager young apprentice in a small ensemble, now he found himself one of the most senior members of a large company, taking on a host of new responsibilities—whether he wanted to or not.

The most striking example of the changed Muppet family dynamic was a promising new show: *Fraggle Rock*. Henson largely entrusted this show to a carefully assembled team. With the sharp eye that had hired them, he now saw ways in which the members of his company could stretch and grow and take on new tasks. Henson singled out *Fraggle Rock* as "the first show that I personally didn't have to be involved with every day." Essentially, the show was a satellite project, though Henson did occasionally perform, write, and direct.

The team members were honored to assume the new responsibilities, despite the inevitable challenges, and to gather together to make the show happen. Years later, Hunt pointed out *Fraggle Rock* as "the first time there was a conscious effort on a lot of different people's parts to come to the same place." While other shows may have "evolved that way," he said, here it was deliberate. But could the team rise to the occasion? Could they make this show succeed, and largely without their "fearless leader"? Challenge accepted.

Hunt stepped up in a major way before *Fraggle Rock* even began: he led the first round of auditions, a big deal as heretofore this had always been Henson's job. Now, it largely became Hunt's job.

From *Fraggle Rock* onward, Hunt led the first round of auditions on most major Muppet shows and movies, screening and whittling down the candidates, deciding who would go on to meet the boss. Leading auditions suited Hunt perfectly, as he had long been the Muppets' social ambassador, showing visitors around the set, welcoming the guest stars, and guiding the newbies. What's more, Hunt had developed in himself what he had long admired in Henson: a keen eye for a person's talents, temperament, and potential. Hunt delighted in goading or startling people into showing their true selves. He could quickly suss out whether someone had the requisite technical puppetry skills for the job, as well as a compatible attitude, a willingness to play along when things got weird. Most performers who joined in this period recall Hunt as their first impression of the Muppets—and if that didn't scare them off, then nothing would.

"Shut the fuck up," Hunt barked at a babbling Rob Mills at the *Fraggle Rock* auditions in Toronto in fall 1981. Though Hunt had once been a bouncy puppy, at auditions he could come off more like a gruff guard dog. "He pushes me up against the wall, takes a Polaroid of me," says Mills. "He's being really belligerent. 'I don't care who you're working for. Who do you think you are?' I'm going, 'This is an audition?'" From this brusque beginning, Hunt and Mills developed a beautiful working partnership.

Terry Angus and his mother were waiting his turn when a woman burst out of the audition room exclaiming, "Crazy, the man's crazy!" ("If they want crazy, give 'em crazy," his mother quipped.) Hunt's boisterous demeanor rattled Angus as he hustled through the audition: "Hi, how ya doing, I'm Richard Hunt, nice to meet you, come over here, we're going to take your picture, now sit down here—all right, show me what you can do." Angus brought out a homemade Kermit, speaking humbly through the character: "Excuse me, Mr. Hunt, I really don't think you should be treating everybody like this. Couldn't you be nicer, more approachable?" "Yeah, what are you gonna do about it, frog?" Kermit gulped nervously. "Erm, nothing. Good job. Way to go." Hunt roared with laughter. "That's great. I definitely want you to see Jim."

Fraggle Rock hoped to do a number of things the Muppets had never done before: not only to make a show without Henson at the helm, but to make a show that would be consciously international from the start. The opening and closing segments would be original to each country, with the puppet dialogue dubbed into the local language, so the whole show would seem made at home. By contrast, *Sesame Street* had spread across the globe through haphazard, unstandardized co-productions, while *The Muppet Show* had been dubbed into its different versions after the fact. The Canadian Broadcasting Corporation (CBC) paired up with the then relatively unknown American cable channel Home Box Office (HBO) to bring *Fraggle Rock* to the small screen.

While this global concept was a great monetary opportunity, Henson raised the stakes and made it a moral one, as well: He wanted to use the show to promote world peace. *Fraggle Rock* first-season producer Duncan Kenworthy initially laughed at the hubristic optimism of this "impossible, enormous, grandiose" idea. Ideally, the show would teach kids around the world to deal with conflict, develop empathy, and recognize interdependence. Hunt appreciated bringing his talents to this worthy cause; he followed global affairs through his ever-present newspaper, and had despaired at the assassination of Nobel Peace Prize–winning Egyptian leader Anwar Sadat, a huge setback for peace in the Middle East.

Fraggle Rock tackled this noble aim with joyful irreverence, both onscreen and off. Alumni describe the show as one of the most collaborative and *fun* projects they ever worked on, a fitting environment for a show aiming to promote global harmony. Both the high-minded aspirations and the fun hijinks were apparent as the *Fraggle Rock* team shot the first twelve episodes in Toronto throughout the first half of 1982.

If you wanted to create an international show to end war, with puppets, humor, and music, what might that look like? The show's creators—Henson, Kenworthy, head writer Jerry Juhl, writer Jocelyn Stevenson, and puppet designer Michael Frith—came up with three different groups of characters that were interdependent but didn't know it. "The audience is the only one who can see it [the interdependence]," says Stevenson, at whose son's christening the show had been conceived. "Which, we were hoping, would make people go, 'Oh, wait a minute.'"

Reflecting real-world power differentials, the three groups are different sizes: the two-foot-tall Fraggles; the twenty-two-foot Gorgs; and the antlike colony of tiny, hardworking Doozers. Juhl, who had brought loose plotlines to *The Muppet Show*, here laid the groundwork for a story arc that would emerge over the course of the show's ninety-six episodes: the groups gradually and poignantly come to recognize each other's shared humanity. (While Juhl and Stevenson penned the majority of the episodes, a half-dozen other writers also contributed.)

A mere handful of performers brought this vast roster to life, using puppeteering techniques ranging from traditional to high-tech. Just five performers—Jerry Nelson, Dave Goelz, Steve Whitmire, Kathy Mullen, and Karen Prell—used hand puppets to play the five main Fraggle characters, arguably the show's stars: confident Gobo (Nelson); introverted Boober (Goelz); indecisive Wembley (Whitmire); dreamy Mokey (Mullen); and enthusiastic Red (Prell). Meanwhile, these same five performers used radio-controlled remote technology to play the show's five most prominent Doozer characters. (Both the Fraggles and the Doozers also had a broad community of background and supporting characters.) Whitmire, Mullen, and Prell's presence signified a step up for them within the troupe, as well as, for the latter two, a step up for women within the Muppets.

Practically ever-present onscreen, Nelson played a major character in each of *Fraggle Rock*'s three character groupings, a half-dozen minor parts, and sometimes even multiple characters at once. Nelson's gregarious Gobo Fraggle is the closest thing *Fraggle Rock* has to a main character, who crucially unites the different tribes. "He's kind of the cement that holds it all together," Henson told Nelson. "That's where I need you." Nelson's ubiquity signaled that Henson trusted him to anchor the show, as well as making up for his lack of a major character on *The Muppet Show*, a needed salve for his earlier sense of separation.

Hunt's biggest role on *Fraggle Rock*, both literally and figuratively, was Junior Gorg. The oversized characters of Pa, Ma, and Junior Gorg exemplify the show's use of collaboration, as each Gorg required two puppeteers to bring it to life. Hunt voiced Junior while remotely manipulating his facial expressions, controlling his eyelids with a joystick and his mouth with a waldo mitt, opening and closing his hand as if it were inside the puppet; meanwhile, a few feet away, Mills performed the body inside a full-body costume and heavy Gorg head. (Nelson voiced Pa Gorg, with Gord Robertson inside the full-body costume; Cheryl Wagner, and Myra Fried in season one, voiced Ma Gorg, while Trish

Leeper performed the body. Mills, Robertson, and Leeper had previously worked together as a trio of mimes, and initially auditioned as a single unit.)

Hunt may have tested Mills roughly at his audition, but the young performer quickly passed muster as they worked together to embody Junior Gorg. Their partnership struck their colleagues as magic; they seemed so perfectly in sync. The duo could read each other instantly. "I would talk, and he could hear the pitch in my voice," said Hunt. "Out of nowhere I would go [growl] and he would immediately, almost instantaneously posture himself. Then if it went a different way, if it was sweet rather than gruff, he was right there. And that's an amazing thing." Hunt's history as full-bodied characters such as Snuffleupagus and Sweetums likely helped him understand Mills's experience inside the costume.

The pair's synergy was even more remarkable given that Hunt abhorred rehearsal, so the two would work out scenes on set, drawing from their shared vocabulary of old movies and TV shows. "The director would say, 'I want you guys here, you're doing that,'" Mills recalls. "Richard would come over and say, 'Okay, ignore everything he said. I need you to do a big Gleason,'" referencing Jackie Gleason from *The Honeymooners*. "I would know exactly what he meant." Their performance was so smooth it would fool directors, especially new ones, who would try to give notes on line delivery to Mills inside the costume. Hunt, over at the remote control table, would laugh and say, "Yes, but you have to come over and tell *me* the note."

Hunt could be protective of Mills, making a rare show of anger one day as they filmed a scene in which Mills was supposed to step over a prop that he couldn't see, and thus kept tripping and falling over in take after take. "Finally Richard got up and said, 'He's fuckin' blind! He can't see it, and you can't get him to do it!'" recalls Robertson, who cites this as evidence of Hunt's faith in Mills's abilities. "If Rob couldn't do it, it couldn't be done, and this was not safe." Mills, however, had no such qualms: "Me being the dumb mime, I kept trying!"

Hunt identified closely with the gargantuan character. "Junior Gorg came a lot from me," he said. Like Hunt as a child in Closter, Junior is doggedly friendly, wanting a pal—but the Fraggles perceive the huge, eager creature as a threat, and his behavior doesn't help. "He's all by himself, and so he's quite lonely, and wants some friends, so he pretends he's chasing the Fraggles; in reality he just wants 'em to stick around and play," said Hunt.

Though Junior's character came from Hunt, Junior's voice came from the Muppet costumer Calista Hendrickson's young son Robin. "When he was a little boy, he started tawkin' like dis to me," Hunt said. "And I went, 'Say, dat's a gweat voice! Dis is the way Junior tawks too!'"

On *Fraggle Rock*, a good idea could come from anywhere, especially when head writer Jerry Juhl was around. As on *The Muppet Show*, Juhl liked to watch the performers develop their characters and then build on that. When Juhl saw headless Gorgs running around the studio—Mills and Robertson in costume, with the heads taken off and their own heads tucked down inside the body—he wrote a first-season episode in which the Gorgs' heads disappear ("The Great Radish Famine"). This striking visual was achieved not by special effects, but by pinning the neck hole closed with a swatch of matching fabric—locking in the performers until their dressers let them out. "We cursed ourselves for our inventiveness," says Mills. Hunt was pleased not to be the one inside the costume, for a change. "Richard made a point of putting his feet up on the remote control table and said loudly, 'I don't have anything to do except read the lines. Have fun in there,'" Mills recalls.

Hunt served as a mentor to Mills, Angus, and the other new hires. He held regular meetings and even his despised rehearsals, giving unflinching feedback. "He was like this big sheepdog rounding up the flock," recalls performer Karen Prell. "He'd have them all rehearsing something, and then say, 'You suck!' He liked to get people out of their comfort zones, because that's where the best performing and fun and creativity would happen."

Hunt could be an intimidating teacher, but he could also be wonderfully mischievous. When the newbies seemed anxious on one of their first days of filming, Hunt cut the tension—with a water pistol. "Everyone's really nervous, and suddenly I get this squirt of water in the ear," says Mills. "He was picking people off, and then pretending, 'Oh, not me.' I said, 'I'm getting you at recess.' It was *on*."

At the break, the performers ran out to stock up on squirt bottles. The battle took on epic proportions, ending up in the parking lot, the performers noisily carrying on like a pack of kids. Hunt wore a raincoat, shielded himself with an umbrella, and ran carrying a bucket as water slopped over its sides. Even the fire department next door got roped in, as Mills, Angus, and others borrowed a hose and soaked Hunt full force until he raised his hands in surrender with a good-natured, gap-toothed grin.

Hunt's ability to connect with people, and to connect them to each other, made him almost a diplomat figure on *Fraggle Rock*, approached by everyone from new performers to crew to writers to directors for his blunt and helpful advice. In a sense, Hunt's unofficial role as *Muppet Show* tour guide became codified on *Fraggle Rock*.

Hunt's welcoming role often entailed guiding visitors around the set. You really did need someone to help you find your way through VTR Productions/Eastern Sound, a labyrinthine warren not unlike *Fraggle Rock*'s onscreen maze of caves and tunnels. Just steps from the center of Toronto, where its two subway lines intersected, 38/48 Yorkville Avenue looked from the front like a traditional Victorian three-story brick house, with a peaked roof and bay windows. But various piecemeal additions had been built on over the decades, each seemingly heedless of the others, intersecting at unexpected junctures, making for a Byzantine layout.

Hunt was a perfect guide because he felt at home all over the studio. He could be found sunning on the roof; giving tips and cracking jokes in the Canadian puppeteers' lounge; talking shop with producer Kenworthy, who recalls that he and Hunt had come to a "very easygoing" rapport in the years since their involvement; getting the scoop on the CBC in set decorator Stephen Finnie's office; or hanging out up a rickety flight of stairs in his own tiny dressing room, which Finnie had decked out with velvet drapes and an ornate chandelier.

Overall, Hunt enjoyed Toronto, even if he did scoff that it hardly measured up to New York. However, he rarely stayed in town outside of work. Nor did he stray much from the studio's Yorkville neighborhood, gentrifying from its days as a Greenwich Village–like folk haven where Joni Mitchell and Buffy Sainte-Marie had played smoky coffeehouses. Hunt stayed just two blocks from the studio at the posh Four Seasons Hotel, lunching at nearby restaurants such as French bistro Le Trou

Normand and a homey sushi joint named Mori's, where Hunt convinced Angus to eat octopus. "You gotta try new things, Scosch," he admonished the Nova Scotian. (Angus's wife Cheryl was "Scoschette.") Regulars at Mori's had their own sake boxes, with their names inked in calligraphy on the side; Hunt's box said "Beaker."

Hunt was such a cheering presence at the Muppets that by this point, when Henson needed a comedian, he didn't hire someone from outside—he had Hunt do it. The *Fraggle* team stayed in Toronto in August, joined by Henson and Oz, to film the ABC special *The Fantastic Miss Piggy Show*. (Jerry Nelson was notably absent, spending every last minute in New York with his ailing daughter Christine.) Rather than having a laugh track, Henson wanted a live audience for the show, and he wanted them in good humor. Who better to warm them up than someone who was always making jokes on set? Hunt delivered an hour-long comedic monologue seemingly off the top of his head, impressing—and, more importantly, greatly amusing—the audience of largely *Fraggle* personnel.

Hunt might have been in a particularly good mood that summer because he was falling in love, embarking on what would be his most significant romantic relationship ever. "Nelson was his name," said Hunt in a late-in-life interview. "And the most important person in my life."

Hunt never forgot the moment he met Kenneth Nelson Bird (whom everyone called "Nelson"), recounting the tale years later. Late one Friday in spring 1982, Hunt flew home from *Fraggle Rock* and jumped straight into the car to join Dennis Smith at the Cape, driving through the night with "a bunch of lunatic people" crammed into his Checker cab. He jerked the car to a stop in front of the Truro house just after dawn, ran upstairs, and burst into the master bedroom, exclaiming to Smith, "These people are gonna drive me crazy!" The forecast called for a rainy weekend; they'd all be cooped up in the house the whole trip!

Then he noticed the slim, self-possessed man watching him with mild eyes. "I look over in the other bed and there's this guy, just leaning on his hand, looking at me, very quiet. Dennis said, 'Oh, Richard, this is my friend, Nelson. Nelson, this is Richard.' I looked over at him. He said, 'Hello, Richard.'"

At first this new person made him uncomfortable. "There was just this calm. It bothered me. It was too familiar. I didn't know what it was. I do now. I do think I'm one of those people like Jim [Henson] who believes strongly in souls having come through. We had known each other. And so that was the beginning of this relationship."

Like Smith, Bird was a trim, blond artist. But where Smith was wry and wisecracking, Bird was inscrutably calm—which would become a huge influence on Hunt.

Meeting Bird catalyzed what Hunt would call a "major spiritual shift" in his life, a grounding, learning how to quiet down and pay attention. "This is the key to it all," said Hunt. "I was this loud crazy guy, bouncing off the walls. I'd be talking and he would grab a piece of my sleeve and I'd go [exhales]—and it was an amazing thing. So he brought me to life—this is the importance of this, because it is major importance—by bringing calm to me.

"Now, I still was nuts. But he started this road."

Hunt had his hands full at *Sesame Street* in fall 1982 as the children's television blockbuster, like *Fraggle Rock*, reflected the new Muppet dynamic. The show's spacious new digs at Unitel (later Teletape) Studios, on 57th Street between 10th and 11th Avenues, heralded that it was here to stay. Yet ironically, *Sesame's* success worked against it in terms of getting Henson's attention, as the show seemed like less of a creative challenge. Henson and Oz were more focused on seeing what they could achieve on the big screen, coming to *Sesame Street* for just a jam-packed couple of weeks each season. Jerry Nelson was overwhelmed by the loss of his daughter Christine to cystic fibrosis at age twenty-one on September 5. Michael Earl had left the show, though he would freelance occasionally on Muppet projects. New hire Martin P. Robinson took on the oversized Mr. Snuffleupagus. Hunt, Meehl, and Spinney did what they could, but there was simply too much to be done. Something had to change.

Not only did Hunt have a lot of work to do, but the work itself could feel unfulfilling. He struggled with playing Aristotle, *Sesame Street's* short-lived attempt at a vision-impaired Muppet character. "Oh man, that fucking blind puppet again," he would complain. He appreciated the concept, but had trouble making the character seem present without being able to direct its gaze. Hunt worked hard on Aristotle, even studying Ray Charles as a model, but the character soon became a "dead Muppet," retired to the file cabinet. Was this really showing the world the best he could do?

Hunt kept his eye out for opportunities beyond the Muppets—especially when *The Dark Crystal* met a tepid reception in December. Was Henson's Midas touch wearing off? Audiences didn't know what to make of the movie, alienated by its unfamiliar fantasy world, uncharismatic characters, and overall dark mood. Reviewers compared it unfavorably to the recent animated *Lord of the Rings* movie as well as the *Star Wars* franchise. *New York Times* reviewer Vincent Canby, who had adored the Muppets' previous two movies, said the screenplay was "without any narrative drive whatever" and the movie as a whole was "without charm as well as interest." And this from a Muppet enthusiast!

Hunt later surmised that Henson had simply aimed higher than he could reach with *The Dark Crystal* and his subsequent fantasy film *Labyrinth*. "I don't think he personally got to where he wanted, really," Hunt said. "I think he was reaching very hard out there trying—obviously there was something he wanted to tell. Something he wanted to connect to, something he wanted to make work and, to a large degree, he did make it work—but not quite." The stakes were simply too high, the cost too great, without room for the freewheeling improvisation of the early days. "They were just so expensive," Hunt observed. "It's difficult to just be able to play around in there." Hunt noticed the toll this disappointment took on Henson. "I think he was extremely frustrated. Because he was always able to do anything he wanted. And they weren't quite there."

Given Hunt's drive to find performing work outside of puppeteering, he was excited to land a role in the latest John Landis film *Trading Places*, having met the director while shooting the *Muppet Movie* finale. Hunt shot his scenes in New York in January 1983.

Hunt was optimistic that *Trading Places* would do well, given the popularity of its director and cast. The screwball comedy starred *Saturday Night Live* denizens Dan Aykroyd and Eddie Murphy as a prosperous stockbroker and destitute wisecracker who literally trade places.

Hunt played a frazzled commodities trader named Wilson. As comic lackey to the movie's old-school henchmen, Hunt acted alongside classic actors Ralph Bellamy and Don Ameche, who came out of retirement for the part, while Hollywood royalty Jamie Lee Curtis provided the film's romance. (Oz also briefly appeared, as he often did in Landis's films.) Hunt anticipated the big names would draw eyes to the movie—and hoped this would help him come out from below the frame.

Still, Hunt was unqualifiedly pleased to see *Fraggle Rock* resonate with viewers across North America upon its January 1983 debut. So audiences could see it too: *Fraggle Rock* was something special. The team returned to Toronto in February with a new confidence, spending three months filming the next dozen episodes, finishing out the first season.

Their assurance was boosted by a new producer: Lawrence Mirkin. (Kenworthy had returned to London to oversee the *Fraggle* co-productions.) A dual U.S. and Canadian citizen, as well as a self-described "extremely collaborative" producer, Mirkin was well suited to bring everyone together. This Henson-like hand at the helm fostered an atmosphere on set in which everyone worked "in service of the best idea," as Mirkin puts it, whether that idea came from the head writer or the puppet wrangler. Mirkin honored the scary, exhilarating creative process of making something out of nothing—or, as he prefers to see it, "nothing but possibility."

Fraggle Rock lived up to its episode title "All Work and All Play," with cast and crew filming one episode per week. Hunt strolled over from the Four Seasons each Monday morning to see what was in store. As on *The Muppet Show*, the week kicked off with the read-through, unveiling the scripts for that week and the next. Hunt wouldn't mince words if he thought something sounded out-of-place or inauthentic. "Oh, like I'm going to say *that*," Hunt would scoff on behalf of his character. The writers often incorporated his feedback, and the next draft would contain a revised line. Tuesdays the cast recorded songs in the morning, which were mixed in the afternoon—leaving just three days to film.

In order to cut through overtime red tape, Mirkin decided that Wednesdays and Thursdays would stick to strict hours of 8 A.M. to 7 P.M.—but on Fridays they would work as long as it took. "Just tell your families you don't know when you'll be home," he advised the cast and crew. Of *Fraggle Rock*'s ninety-six episodes, a quarter finished on time; half took an extra two to four hours; and the rest ran over until two or three in the morning. "I didn't want to have a 9-to-5 job so I took an 8 to 8:30 job," Nelson jokes. "8 in the morning until 8:30 at night! Sometimes 12 at night!"

Doozer-centered episodes ran over most often, ensnared by technology. "If you knew it was a Doozer show, don't make dinner plans on Friday night," recalls *Fraggle* writer Sugith Varughese. Much to Hunt's frustration, Gorg episodes also often ran over. While Henson rightly praised the "technical wizardry" of the Gorg puppets, they could run into time-consuming snags, such as draining their batteries when a shoot went long. Hunt would complain if it looked like he might miss his 9 P.M. flight back to New York. "I'm doing this under duress!" he would cry out dramatically. Still, he always stayed until they wrapped the episode, even if it meant another night in town.

Once the work was done, no matter how late, most everyone trooped one block over to the WWII-era gastropub The Pilot for the *Fraggle* tradition of Frosty Fridays, blowing off steam over beer and food, with Nelson picking up the tab.

Hunt and Nelson especially liked to make newer *Fraggle* personnel feel at home. They spent a memorably raucous evening in the Four Seasons bar with production assistant Pete Coogan, teasing the young Brit mercilessly, refusing to let him buy a round, entertaining him with their rapid-fire banter. The very next day, Hunt was delighted to find Coogan on his flight to New York. Hunt gave his first-class ticket to Coogan's seatmate and settled into coach beside him for an uproarious ride—and, by the time they landed, a new friendship.

When cast and crew finished the first season in late April, Hunt and Nelson took it upon themselves to put together the traditional end-of-season gift, getting T-shirts made for everyone—a task usually done by Henson, another sign of how they had stepped up.

Hunt was often impatient to race home from Toronto because his personal life demanded his attention. While Hunt's involvement with Nelson Bird was promising, he kept it private for the time being. Hunt spent most of his time at Bird's apartment, on far West 11th Street by the Hudson River. Hunt didn't bring Bird around to meet his family and friends, his usual ritual with lovers (even if he didn't introduce them as such).

Meanwhile, Dennis Smith, Hunt and Bird's mutual ex-lover, was struggling with the mysterious illness that was going around. Smith had taken a leave from Henson Associates, ostensibly to focus on his art, but seemed too sick to ever return to work. The hospital required visitors to wear surgical masks, not knowing how the illness might be transmitted. And what diagnoses the doctors could provide seemed even more baffling. Hunt's friend Stuart Fischer was nearing the end of his medical residency when Hunt called him to ask about a friend's obscure diagnosis: bird pneumonia. "In those days, it was nothing," says Fischer. "You'd have to work in an aviary to get it!"

By the time Hunt came home from *Fraggle Rock*'s first season, he and Bird held vigil at Smith's bedside in Glen Ridge, New Jersey. Smith lay atop a sheet of reticulated foam from the Muppet workshop; he had sent in his mother to get it, hoping to stave off bedsores. Always attentive to his health, Hunt presumably couldn't help but feel a twinge of worry. How was he any different from his friend?

Hunt as Wilson in the movie *Trading Places*, 1983.

CHAPTER 11

Making Connections

B Y THE TIME the Muppets started working on their third major motion picture, *The Muppets Take Manhattan*, their auditions drew a wide—and weird—variety of performers. Hunt jumped straight from wrapping *Fraggle Rock*'s first season to working on the film; he flew home from Toronto Friday night and led auditions on Saturday morning, April 30, 1983, at the Minskoff Rehearsal Studio in Times Square. Puppeteer Wayne Martin was surprised to find himself trying out alongside actors, mimes, even makeup artists—everyone *but* puppeteers. Hunt looked over Martin's resume, asked him to put on a puppet, then, to Martin's surprise, conducted the interview directly with the puppet. After just a few minutes he said, "You've got it. Thank God you're a real live puppeteer, not an actor!" (Martin would play a dog in the movie's large wedding scene.) Two days later, Henson and Oz held an all-day workshop to look over those who remained.

The Muppets Take Manhattan filmed from May 27 to September 16 in Hunt's beloved city. Though some of the film's New York landmarks, such as the Port Authority Bus Terminal, were actually indoor sets at Empire Studios in Long Island City, Queens, the performers drew large, excited crowds as they filmed on location at iconic spots like the New York Public Library, Central Park, and the Empire State Building, with children shouting greetings to their favorite characters. While crowd control could sometimes interfere with the work, it was hard to complain about such a warm and enthusiastic audience.

The Muppets Take Manhattan heralded a number of changes for the troupe. Reflecting a shift in the dynamic of the Original Five, Oz directed the film as his solo debut—and Hunt seemed to have mixed feelings about his colleague's ascent. "When I became a director, Richie said, 'What are you doing? You're so great at puppeteering,'" Oz recalls. Yet Oz considered the experience not wholly different from being on the other side of the camera, given the group's collaborative working style, especially among the original core. "When Jim and I had worked in the past, I'll mention some ideas to him," says Oz. "We both did that to each other. Also not only us, but Dave Goelz, or Jerry Nelson, or Richard Hunt . . . In a way, it's more of a shared sense of creativity with each person guiding. It just happened to be that I was the one guiding it."

The Muppets Take Manhattan also marks a transition in that many new generation members were on board alongside the originals. Nelson spent much of the sweltering shoot hiding out with his girlfriend Jan Berguson in Truro; Hunt prodded his friend into the city for their main scene together, with Nelson dubbing in his other lines later. But the enthusiasm of the next generation more than compensated, as Whitmire, Mullen, Prell, Meehl, Earl, Martin Robinson, and even David Rudman and Pam Arciero, whom Hunt had met at the 1980 World Puppetry Festival, all worked on the film. During breaks, Hunt entertained in his tiny dressing room, trouncing his colleagues in epic matches of Trivial Pursuit.

What's more, *The Muppets Take Manhattan* signaled a change in the Muppets' sensibility and audience. On the one hand, the film repeats Hunt's racy ad-libbed gag from *The Great Muppet Caper*, with Janice again the last loud talker after the rest of the group has gone quiet: "Look, buddy, I don't take my clothes off for anyone, even if it is arrr-tistic." But the segment in which Miss Piggy imagines her friends as toddlers portends the Muppets' shift toward a younger crowd; the scene would inspire the wildly popular Saturday morning cartoon *Muppet Babies*, which exacerbated the public perception of the Muppets as being just for kids.

One of *The Muppets Take Manhattan*'s most delightful elements is its cameos, with brief appearances by dancer Gregory Hines, comedian Joan Rivers, a number of *Muppet Show* guest stars, even then-mayor Ed Koch. In response to feedback that the *Great Muppet Caper* cameos had

seemed gratuitous, Oz made sure that the actors were chosen specifically for their parts. This perspective sweetens the cameos played by
the Muppet performers and their friends and family: for example, *Muppet Show* producer David Lazer, frequent liaison for the guest stars,
escorts Liza Minnelli into Sardi's; Oz looks bemused in a boardroom;
and Kermit and Piggy ride in a Central Park horse-drawn carriage
driven by Henson himself.

Hunt's mother, Jane Hunt, asked Oz for an audition and landed a
part just perfect for her: the stage actor plays a patron at Sardi's restaurant, the legendary theater hangout. Wearing a blue dress and a big
smile, she throws herself into the role, joining the whispering campaign
about Kermit ("A big producer, dear") and shrieking wonderfully at the
sight of rats running through the restaurant, even swatting at one with
her menu.

In a playful gesture, Oz cast director John Landis as a Broadway producer with just a single line, one of the film's most memorable: "A
frog—with an afro?" But Landis would provide even more exposure for
Oz and Hunt when his new film *Trading Places* turned out to be one of
the biggest movies of the year.

Hunt loved to tell the story of being recognized by a man on the street
for his role in Landis's film. "You. *Trading Places*. You're in that last scene."
Hunt ate up the attention, thrilled to be seen not just as a puppeteer but as
an actor. "Yes, I was in *Trading Places*. What was it about my performance
that made you remember me?" "Oh nothing," said the man. "I'm a projec-
tionist. I've seen that movie at least two hundred times!"

It was a running joke with Hunt that his work was cultishly famous
in some ways and absurdly obscure in others. It made a certain kind of
cosmic sense.

Hunt took all his friends to see *Trading Places* when it came out in
June, radiant with pride. "When he talked about *Trading Places*, it was
satisfying to him in a way that nothing else was," says Mark Hamill.
"Because it was a big hit movie and he was great in it." *Trading Places*
turned out to be 1983's fourth-highest-grossing film, no small feat in a
year led by blockbuster *Return of the Jedi*. Finally, *finally*, people were
seeing Hunt act.

Hunt's star moment comes in the frantic climactic scene, shot on the commodities trading floor of the World Trade Center, packed with real-life brokers. The Duke brothers (Ralph Bellamy and Don Ameche) order Hunt's character Wilson to buy up stock in orange juice, but as the price suddenly plummets they about-face and exhort him to sell. The room is jammed with traders trying to dump the increasingly worthless product. "Selling! Sell! Sell . . . ing . . . !" he cries as he wilts in a dramatic faint.

Yet for all the hilarity of his performance, Hunt wasn't happy with it. "Should I do something like this?" he had asked Landis, before doing what he thought was a practice run. "All right, I'm ready to do it now," he told Landis, who said, "Oh, that's okay, we got it." Hunt was "absolutely horrified," says Hunt's friend Terry Minogue. "He was embarrassed by that scene, because he knew he could have done better, made people laugh more. He talked about that a lot." Hunt could be his own most demanding critic, wanting to be seen at his best—especially when his face, for once, was finally so widely seen.

Hunt could hear the clock ticking as Dennis Smith, just thirty-two years old, died in Glen Ridge, New Jersey, in July 1983, the first person in Hunt's circles to pass away from the mysterious illness that people were now calling Acquired Immune Deficiency Syndrome, or AIDS.

Smith's death seemed to catalyze Hunt into being more open about his personal life. That same month, he came out as gay to the Hamills over lunch at Sardi's. "He was afraid to tell us," says Marilou. "He thought we'd think differently of him." He had been dropping hints to feel them out on the topic, telling them a tall tale about *Superman* star (and *Muppet Show* guest) Christopher Reeve being supported by a "sugar daddy" early in his career. "My reaction was, 'I should be so lucky to have a sugar daddy,'" says Mark Hamill. "He later told me that I passed the test by not saying anything disparaging."

Also driving Hunt to be more open was his relationship with Nelson Bird, an unprecedented romance after years of more casual connections. The relationship became more serious, or at least more public, after Smith's death. "This was the first time he was in love with somebody where there was the possibility of a long-term relationship," says Hunt's friend Ernie Capeci. "And he was all about falling in love."

Two years younger than Hunt, Bird had spent his childhood outside Montgomery, Alabama, and his adolescence in the affluent Birmingham suburb of Vestavia Hills, where his father Alvin, who went by Buddy, was a physicist while his mother Betty looked after him and his two sisters. At all-white W. A. Berry High School, Bird showed his creative promise by participating in the art club and co-editing the literary magazine ("Treasure Chest"); from there, he went on to art school in the north.

By the time Bird met Hunt, he paid the bills as a graphic designer for an ad agency, but considered his creativity to be his true priority. "What he needed was a patron," said Hunt. "He was a writer and an artist and he never wasted time but he didn't like to have a specific job." Hunt became one of Bird's most avid supporters, hanging one of his abstract paintings over the bed on the Upper West Side.

Bird was aptly named, with delicate, avian features, a feathery cap of sandy-blond hair, and a cool, inscrutable gaze through narrow eyes. The two men were similar in some ways—and exact opposites in others. "We've always been alter egos," Hunt said of himself and Bird. "We were very much alike and totally different."

Hunt's dynamic with Bird is visible in a home movie shot by *Sesame* production designer Victor DiNapoli, on an idyllic August afternoon at DiNapoli's house in Long Island's tony Hamptons area. The two men are sunbathing in matching red shorts, Bird smiling wryly as Hunt goes off on a manic comedic monologue.

Hunt relentlessly cajoles the reticent Bird to join in. "Say hello," he urges. "*Say hello.*" He orders Bird to introduce himself. "What's in a name?" Bird parries back, mimicking Gertrude Stein. "A name is a name is a name is a name." Bird's mild amusement pales beside Hunt's endless energy. Anything becomes a prop when it enters Hunt's realm: he walks along the high railing of the deck, nearly losing his balance, turning the near fall into slapstick. As Blondie plays in the background, Hunt recites from Tennessee Williams's *The Glass Menagerie* in a cooing southern drawl ("I used to have twenty-seven gentlemen callers . . ."), pumps vigorously on a swing, and persists in trying to get Bird into the routine. At one point he announces, "And now our rendition of Tweedledum and Tweedledee." He leans into Bird and drapes an arm around him: "I'm Tweedledum." After a pause, wearing an indulgent, exasperated smile, Bird obliges: "I'm Tweedledee." Hunt's teeth flash briefly in an unguarded grin, just before his patter starts up again.

When Hunt started bringing Bird around to meet his friends, they were surprised at how serious the two men were—and how dissimilar. "To say Nelson was a cold fish was giving him the benefit of the doubt," says Hunt's friend Stuart Fischer, who recalls Hunt being "hysterically funny" and Bird barely cracking a smile. It didn't help that the reticent Bird rarely interacted directly with Hunt's friends, even at small dinners; Hunt tended to serve as intermediary.

Hunt felt upset that his friends didn't connect with Bird. "Nelson's very quiet, very private," Hunt said, tellingly referring to Bird in the present tense years after his passing. "He never really could open himself up and that always bothered me because he was such an incredible human being and I wish people could see—I was the only one that could. It was devastating to me, devastating." Hunt liked to have all his loved ones together in the same room, bringing his boyfriends around for years without naming them as such. Now he had someone so valuable to him, yet it was a tricky balance between this individual and his vast network of family and friends—not to mention a balance between Bird and what had always been Hunt's primary relationship: work.

Hunt stepped up on *Sesame Street* in fall 1983 as the show largely became another Muppet satellite project—and Hunt was increasingly tasked with keeping it afloat.

Hunt's responsibilities increased sharply with the departure of his friend Brian Meehl, who felt burnt out after working two years straight with barely a two-week break. Meehl had witnessed the toll of the unrelenting pace on the core crew: Hunt partied hard, a grieving Nelson drank hard, and Henson and Oz showed an obsessional devotion that he simply could not sustain. "I was looking at these guys, going, 'They're not happy,'" says Meehl. When Henson asked Meehl to audition for *Fraggle Rock*, he replied, "Jim, I'm done." Henson gladly fostered creative freedom, sending Meehl off with a celebratory toast in his office.

Sesame people joke that Meehl was so vital that they needed a half-dozen people to replace him. But what really happened was that others realized, as Meehl had, that the pace was simply not sustainable. To keep up the Muppets' presence on the show, they needed more hands on deck. The next generation of puppeteers was coming to *Sesame Street*.

Hunt was grateful for the help. Filming 130 episodes per season was a round-the-clock job, and he made no secret of his aspirations beyond puppetry. "You're kind of replacing me, because I'd rather be an unemployed actor," he told Martin P. Robinson, the earliest of the new hires. Like many of the newbies, Robinson came in through puppet designer and builder Kermit Love, still a mentor to budding performers as he had been to Hunt.

Pam Arciero also came in through Love. She had initially auditioned for *Sesame Street* in 1981 and been told, "Sorry, we're not looking for any female puppeteers." (Granted, they were mostly looking for a new Snuffleupagus.) But she persistently accompanied Love to the set, pitching in and getting to know people. Arciero's second audition reflected a change in attitude at *Sesame*, as the powers that be decided to bring on a woman to replace Meehl as Oscar the Grouch's crabby gal pal Grundgetta.

As with *Fraggle Rock*, the auditions for *Sesame Street* were now largely Hunt's purview. Much like his own audition, he and Jane Henson met with the candidates and played around with puppets, giving the potential hires a chance to show who they were and what they could do. Though Hunt could be intimidating, he laid off the gruff guard dog act once performers proved they were serious. By the time Arciero auditioned for the role of Grundgetta, Hunt was so warm and inviting toward her that she felt at ease.

Once Hunt and Jane Henson winnowed down the first round of candidates, they led a workshop for roughly 300 puppeteers. That, too, hadn't changed much since Hunt came aboard: at once both a training session and an extended audition, the leaders put the candidates through their paces as they went over their lip-synch, singing, and improv skills. After sixteen weeks, just two performers remained: Arciero and Camille Bonora. Arciero won the role, but there was plenty of work for both— and both were taken under Hunt's wing.

In his own charismatic, original way, Hunt thrived in the role of teacher. He became an invaluable mentor to the next generation of performers—and they became an invaluable community to him. As in his own family, Hunt became the cool big brother, reveling in the empowerment of seniority. Robinson was just three years younger than Hunt, but to Hunt, veteran of a decade, he was a babe in arms: "He was the old hand, I was the new kid," Robinson recalls. Hunt didn't let anyone forget that he had earned his stripes, and he expected them to do the same. He harangued Robinson about going straight to major roles, such as the *front* of Snuffleupagus, claiming exaggeratedly that he'd had to wait eight years before getting his own characters. Hunt could be visibly annoyed by the eager young puppeteers, even downright suspicious. He put new hires through a hazing period, gauging their limits and weak points, assessing their characters. You had to prove to him that you had a sense of honor, that you were truly committed to learning the work.

But if you passed his test, most times you couldn't tell the difference. "If he was nice to you, he hated you," says Arciero. "If he liked you, he would tease you and torment you and punish you and make fun of you. That's how he showed his love." When the busty puppeteer right-handed with him on Forgetful Jones, he would joke, "Get those things out of my way!" Similarly, puppet wrangler Noel MacNeal recalls retrieving a puppet from Hunt after a sketch. "I went over to get the puppet and Richard just tossed it to me. I said something like, 'Oh, I'm glad I had both hands out,' and he said, 'Hey, if I didn't like you, I'd be nice to you.' I said, 'Well, Richard, then you must effing love me.'" Hunt burst into a genuine hearty laugh. "I knew then, *Okay, we're cool.*"

Hunt taught his pupils how to right-hand with him, as Henson and Oz had taught him a decade earlier. Since Hunt generally abhorred rehearsal, you had to be present and alert. If the right hand had a task, for example, such as moving a cup, "He just goes, 'Do it,' and you better do it right," Arciero recalls. But Hunt dispensed plenty of advice, unofficially helping to direct the scene: setting people up in the shot, suggesting where to stand, how to enter with a character, where to place the monitor; these tricky technical details seemed second nature to him. Hunt took special care to show his mentees how to do things, to guide them so they could eventually do it themselves. As usual, Hunt was collaborative rather than competitive, interested in fostering independent skill in others, knowing that if everyone was at their best, it made for the best work overall.

Happily, working with the next generation gave Hunt a new appreciation for the value of his experience. He didn't always respect his field, especially as compared to on-camera acting. "At that time, he discounted what puppetry was, and discounted his own skill, which is why he felt like rehearsing was not that important," says Arciero. When the young, trained puppeteers came in, saying, "Oh my God, you're Richard Hunt," Hunt realized that people did indeed know him and his work, even if he had been hidden below the frame. He felt *legitimized*—and it felt good.

The *Sesame* performers couldn't help but grow close as they worked such long hours together. They started shooting at 9 A.M., took a lunch break from 1 to 2, and then kept working for as long as it took, sometimes as late as 9 or 10 P.M. They produced an enormous amount of work, often trying to film two shows a day, sometimes filming as much as twenty-two minutes of footage in a single day, a high-pressure pace.

The tight schedule didn't allow the performers to stray far from the set, so they holed up in the Muppet lounge just beside it, a narrow triangle of a room with boxes of puppets heaped in its narrow end. They would squeeze onto the couch, rehearse in front of the mirrored dressing table, and play Nintendo with the sound low so as not to disturb the filming. Nelson, especially, could play Thunder and Lighting for hours; Henson, when he popped in, showed a surprising affinity for Duck Hunt, never missing a shot. Hunt used the lounge to read his newspaper, coach his colleagues as they practiced, or smoke a joint, often all at once.

Hunt was capable of showing tremendous dedication, even if he didn't always do so. He pushed himself past his physical limits when filling in as Nelson's vampiric number-lover Count von Count on a song with country star Loretta Lynn, "Count on Me." Lynn had trouble keeping to the prerecorded track, straying off the measure in take after take. After about five dozen tries, the studio had cleared of everyone but Hunt and Arciero as his right hand. Hunt had recently been diagnosed with an abdominal hernia, which hurt him so badly that he barely had the strength to hold up the heavy puppet; nevertheless, he insisted on sticking it out until they were finished, despite Arciero's repeated offers to switch jobs. The shoot ended up requiring over eighty takes. "When he got done, he was exhausted and drained and in terrible pain," Arciero recalls. "It was literally the most agonizing. But he wouldn't give it up, because he was Richard."

Though the performers spent long hours together at work, they often took their meals together as well, lunching at nearby French restaurants such as Bretagne or Brittany du Soir—Hunt picking up the check, as usual—and going to dinner together, often with their significant others, including Bird, after the workday was done. Arciero calls these the "sweet days," where they worked so hard and treasured their downtime with each other, celebrating birthdays and special occasions; her *Sesame* colleagues even surprised her with a baby shower. "It was family."

Despite appreciating his new colleagues, Hunt's heart didn't always seem to be in his work at *Sesame Street*. The half-dozen eager newbies arrived promptly at 8:30 for a half-hour call in advance of the 9 A.M. start time—at which point Hunt would streak into the studio, *The New York Times* rolled up in his back pocket. When shooting, he'd often set himself up in the shot, check the monitor, say "Okay," then go right back to reading, arm aloft and puppet held high, as his colleagues got ready around him. As at *The Muppet Show*, he'd read through the countdown, throwing down the paper mere seconds before the cameras rolled, totally present to the scene. "He's so amazing, and he read the paper to the last minute," Arciero remarked admiringly one day to associate producer Arleen Sherman, who quipped, "Yeah, think how good he'd be if he actually paid attention!"

Part of Hunt's inattention stemmed from his annoyance at still finding himself below the frame, puppeteering rather than on-camera acting. And this particular puppetry didn't necessarily demonstrate his best work. Hunt had little patience for characters like the absent-minded cowboy Forgetful Jones, for example, whom he had inherited from Earl and found too dim-witted to do much with.

But Hunt *really* loathed the little red monster he took over from Meehl. Elmo had debuted a few years earlier as a nameless Anything Muppet, repetitive and largely incoherent. "They wanted Elmo to speak in only one word," says Meehl. "He'd obsess about a word the same way

Cookie Monster would obsess about a cookie." Meehl would repeat the word in a faint whisper: "Casa, casa, casa." In comparison to his later cuteness, early incarnations of Elmo seemed off-putting and even creepy, Meehl recalls: "He sounded like some dirty old man on a phone!"

Hunt ditched Elmo's weird simpering whisper for a deep, gravelly voice, similar to his half of the Two-Headed Monster. Now the puppet came off like a macho caveman, barking out choppy grammar: "Elmo squeak balloon too hard." "Rhyme for boys is noise!" The character didn't work, and no one was more aware of it than Hunt. "I hate this damn puppet!" he would complain. "I'm suffering with it!" If Hunt couldn't find the key to this character, Elmo was in danger of joining Aristotle in the graveyard for dead Muppets.

Not only did Hunt have his hands full with *Sesame Street*, he flew to Toronto in nearly every spare moment as *Fraggle Rock* filmed its second season from fall 1983 into the following spring. He had a brief winter break, during which he flew to Las Vegas and shot the film *Oxford Blues* alongside Rob Lowe, but mostly he did some deft juggling to balance his two major work obligations. The shows also juggled to accommodate his crowded schedule, such as when *Fraggle Rock* switched around scenes during the week for him. Hunt continued to stay at the Four Seasons when in Toronto, while Nelson, Goelz, and others had rented local apartments, indicative of his frequent back-and-forth.

Hunt's hectic schedule could stress out his colleagues. He sometimes flew in late the night before filming, or even the same morning, and his last-minute dashes to the airport meant that he didn't always make his flight, let alone study his lines ahead of time. Hunt's behavior irked newer writers like Sugith Varughese, who thought Hunt "played fast and loose" with the dialogue. Why did the writers take scripts through multiple drafts, perfecting every syllable, "when at the last minute, Richard flies in at 7 in the morning, and makes it up as he goes along?" While "making it up" is an exaggeration, it is true that Hunt treated scripts more like guidelines than precious documents set in stone.

Yet even when Hunt's schedule let up, he liked to improvise because he simply thrived on the fly. "Richard seemed to rely on inspiration and instinct," says Goelz, who watched Hunt bring many characters to life. Hunt walked into the music studio totally cold one Tuesday morning to play a one-time, second-season character, the tiny yet rebellious Turbo Doozer. He didn't know the song, hadn't come up with the voice, didn't know the character at all. Yet over the course of the forty-five-minute recording session, Hunt used elements of his own attitude and body language to create the tough-talking, Marlon Brando–sounding character. "By the time he sang the song, Richard could ad-lib in that little Doozer," Goelz recalls.

Indeed, Goelz and Hunt played a pair of *Fraggle Rock* characters that had grown out of improvisation: smart-mouth rats Gunge (Hunt) and Philo (Goelz), who live alongside resident guru Marjory the Trash Heap (Nelson). Appearing in about a quarter of the *Fraggle Rock* episodes, Gunge and Philo are one of Hunt and Goelz's funniest pairings, right up there with *The Muppet Show*'s Bunsen and Beaker.

Though Gunge and Philo are an inseparable duo, originally the show had planned for only one such character. During development, the performers played around with the puppets to determine the casting. Hunt snatched up a rat puppet and voiced him like a Jersey wiseguy, coining the character's tagline: "Nyaah!" Goelz grabbed an identical puppet and did exactly the same. "Richard immediately had a character that was so good I just *copied* him," says Goelz. Since only one such role was available, the two began arguing—in character—over who would play him: "I'm gonna do it!" "No, I'm gonna do it!" Their dynamic was so enjoyable that the writers made it a duo and cast them both.

Hunt could more easily squeeze Gunge into his tight schedule, as Marjory and her minions usually appear in just one or two scenes per episode. But in spring 1984, the show centered an entire episode around the smart-mouth rats. Writer Varughese intended "Home Is Where the Trash Is" as a send-up of Samuel Beckett—and Hunt was the only one to figure it out. "I didn't tell anybody, and Richard right away was like, 'You're doing *Waiting for Godot* here.' I was like, 'Yup.'" Varughese was starting to earn Hunt's trust.

Despite Hunt's erratic schedule, he was an integral part of backstage antics. When Martin Baker stepped down as associate producer on *Fraggle Rock* at the end of the second season, cast and crew sent him off with a homemade video. Mocking a documentary format, Henson, Whitmire, Goelz, executive producer Diana Birkenfeld, and others wear completely straight faces as they say outrageous and untrue things about Baker. They paint the staid married man as a deranged figure, running around with both men and women, shoplifting, ruining the show's budget, shocking even his psychiatrist.

But Hunt, as usual, outdoes his colleagues. Hunt had been pranking Baker since driving him crazy with his chronic lateness on the *Muppet Show* set, and had to get in on the fun. "Martin, he's everything in my life," Hunt tells the cameraman confidently, standing in front of a parking garage. "I think it was about nine years ago that I first met him, and God, he's made all the difference." But when Hunt finds out that Baker is leaving, he immediately becomes very upset. "He's leaving? No, no. Martin's the most important part of the show for me. He can't leave. He *can't leave*. Oh, Jesus Christ!" Hunt runs into the parking garage, yanks open the door to the staircase and starts running up the stairs. The camera pans up, revealing Hunt atop the six-story garage on its open-air top level. "MARTIN! WHY??!!" Hunt shouts. He grasps at his hair, distraught. Is he going to jump? Hundreds of feet up, he crouches down and dangerously dangles an arm and a leg over the side of the garage.

The camera shakily follows Hunt's presumed trajectory down the side of the garage. Cut to Hunt lying on the ground below. "I'll always love you, Martin Scorsese!" he exclaims. "It's Martin *Baker*," whispers the cameraman. Hunt screws up his face. "Who?" His eyes close and his head flops back: The End.

Summer 1984 brought Hunt a chance to catch his breath. In June, Hunt took Bird to Italy, first Rome and then Positano, in a romantic trip he would treasure for the rest of his life.

Hunt also spent a lot of time in Truro, where the very weather seemed almost like another colorful Cape character. During one weekend visit, Hunt, Bird, Meehl, and Meehl's wife Cindy were startled awake when a bolt of lightning struck the roof. The Meehls leaped out of bed and met Hunt in the hallway; Cindy was so alarmed, thinking the house might explode, that she hadn't even dressed. Hunt and Meehl laughed afterward about taking the time to put on their pants. But curiously, whether out of confidence, apathy, or just sound sleep, Bird stayed in bed.

And the weather made itself known when Hunt—or as he called himself for the day, the Reverend Richard Hunt of the Church of the Holy Mackerel—officiated Jerry Nelson's wedding to Jan Berguson, on July 16, 1984, in front of about 200 people on Truro's Corn Hill Beach. Technically, the couple had wed a week earlier, on Jerry's birthday, in a tiny ceremony with a justice of the peace in a friend's Provincetown living room. By contrast, they were calling this event "the show-biz wedding."

Hunt had raced into town late the night before, planning out the event with Nelson: Hunt would do a spiel, read a Cherokee wedding poem Nelson had picked out, and declare Jerry and Jan married; the newlyweds would kiss, and then everyone would eat.

The weather, however, had other plans. As Hunt sermonized in his best gospel preacher persona, dark clouds gathered and thunder rumbled ominously in the distance. Friends held umbrellas over the bride and groom as Hunt declaimed the first line of the wedding poem, his arms flung out wide: "Now you shall feel no rain!" At that very instant, "the heavens opened up, and it *poured*," says Jan. "Now *that* was show business."

Hunt was gratified to see himself on the big screen again that summer in *Oxford Blues*. He took friends to see the movie with great fanfare: "We're going to the movies, we're going to the movies!" Hunt had gotten the role of Larry through Rob Lowe, now a budding Brat Pack star and the film's biggest name. He had an easy onscreen rapport with his real-life friend, snarkily teasing him as the two characters work together as red-jacketed valets. However, Hunt appeared only in the opening scenes of the film. He would take his friends to see the movie, sit raptly through the first fifteen minutes—and then stand up and say, "All right, we're done!" and usher everybody out.

The Muppets, too, were on the big screen that summer, as *The Muppets Take Manhattan* opened to lackluster reviews and even smaller box office returns than *Caper*. While *The New York Times* critic Vincent Canby appreciated the cameos, he judged the film to be less "extraordinaire" (as Miss Piggy would say) than its predecessors. Goelz muses that the film seemed less authentic than what had come before, as if the franchise might have been starting to go through the motions: "*Manhattan* was like a restatement of *The Muppet Movie*, but not as heartfelt." Viewers did enjoy the Oscar-nominated soundtrack by *Sesame Street* writer and composer Jeff Moss, as well as the Kermit and Piggy wedding finale, with almost as many characters crammed into the chapel as in the finale of the first Muppet film.

Hunt's *Sesame Street* and *Fraggle Rock* communities came together in Toronto that summer with the filming of *Follow That Bird*, the first feature-length *Sesame Street* film, for which Hunt also led the auditions. But when the two shows picked up again in late September, they seemed to be headed in markedly different directions.

The Reverend Richard Hunt of the Church of the Holy Mackerel officiates Jerry and Jan Nelson's wedding, Truro, MA, July 16, 1984. Behind Jerry and Jan are their respective brothers Martin Nelson and Stephen Berguson.

CHAPTER 12

Changes

WHEN HUNT DECIDED to throw a party to celebrate twenty-five years at 52 Closter Dock Road, the family realized that so many people had passed through the house, it couldn't possibly fit them all! They rented out the Masonic Lodge in nearby Tenafly for the September 1984 event. The whole family came—which took some doing. Hunt had recently coaxed youngest sister Rachel back up to the area from Florida, finding her a doctor for some persistent health issues. "Richard kept the Hunt family together," Miller says.

Hunt inspired another anniversary party around this time too. He noticed that *Sesame* stalwart Caroll Spinney, who played Big Bird and Oscar the Grouch, was approaching his fifteenth year with the Muppets, and proposed to Henson that they celebrate the occasion. "This was pretty unusual," Spinney wrote. "I can't remember another party at Muppets being given for something like that." Henson held a festive get-together at the company's Manhattan townhouse, with a pianist, finger foods, caviar, and champagne. "It was very special," Spinney's wife Debi recalls. "And it all happened because of Richard."

Hunt enjoyed his work on *Sesame Street*, and his newer colleagues had deepened his appreciation for his craft, but he still often felt like he was putting on puppet shows at children's birthday parties. Fortunately, by this point he had the power to do something about it.

* * *

When Hunt stood in the doorway of *Sesame Street*'s Muppet performer lounge at midday on November 26, 1984, after another unfulfilling session of shooting Elmo, the red puppet dangling lifelessly from his hand, he already had his eye on Kevin Clash.

The young puppeteer, whom Hunt had met after the 1979 Thanksgiving Day Parade, had recently joined the show full-time. But Clash had worked intermittently with the Muppets in the intervening years as other commitments permitted, so by the time he joined up, he had already proven himself to Hunt. Clash also showed his skill through how quickly he picked up two of the roles he inherited from Meehl: the pretentious oration of the inept inventor Nobel Price, and the strident twang of Clementine, the cowgirl companion to Hunt's own Forgetful Jones.

It may have been a symbolic moment; but at the time, Hunt just wanted to dump the puppet. As established, Hunt had little affection for the babyish, cherry-red monster. "Richard saved his energy for the hipper, more established characters, and he just hated doing Elmo," says Clash. Though Hunt enjoyed his role as senior hand, he had little time for characters that didn't connect. And he had reached a status where he didn't have to waste that time; he could exert artistic control and pass along the role, a move which awed the newer puppeteers.

Hunt opened the door to the lounge and held up Elmo. "I'm done," he said. "Who wants this?" It certainly wasn't the first time Hunt had passed on his roles. "He was always throwing characters to us, to get us out there, to learn," Clash says. "He'd come in and say, 'You know, I don't wanna do this pig. You do the pig. I don't wanna do this monster. This is what you have to do, go on out there and do it.'" Yet this impromptu audition seemed different. Clash recalls his nervousness: "If he doesn't know what to do with it, how am I going to do it?" But with his keen eye for sizing up puppeteers, Hunt knew Clash could adeptly take on the new role. Hunt threw the puppet across the room; Clash caught the flying red bundle of fur, gave it a giggly falsetto, and a star was born. Hunt later took Clash into the control room to speak to producers Dulcy Singer and Lisa Simon about the switch.

It is hard not to see the gesture as a grand metaphor, Elmo in midair, the imminent changing of the guard captured in a snapshot. Children's television was becoming increasingly watered down, pitched to a younger audience, less satiric and more simplistic. Public funding was dwindling; *Sesame Street* had to worry about things like market share, which hadn't been a concern when they were the only game in town. In a sense they had spawned their own genre, created their own competition. To stay on top, they would have to adapt, to change along with the times.

Hunt couldn't help making fun when the discarded puppet became *Sesame's* runaway star. "When the character got really popular, Richard would tease me," says Clash. "We'd have kids come in to visit *Sesame*, asking for Elmo, and he'd come in: 'They want Elmo. Go and get Elmo.'"

But if Hunt thought *Sesame Street* was getting too saccharine, he was positively nauseated by Henson's latest offering, which debuted in fall 1984: the Saturday morning cartoon *Muppet Babies*. "Richard hated *Muppet Babies*," says Arciero. "That was like the destruction of the Muppets, as far as he was concerned. Anything getting too cutesy made him crazy."

Sesame Street at least had Muppet characters who were clearly meant to be children, such as six-and-a-half-year-old Big Bird and three-year-old Elmo. But *Muppet Babies* took the original, edgy main gang of *Muppet Show* characters—some of Hunt's finest work—and diluted them into toddler versions of themselves. Now Kermit, Piggy, Gonzo, Fozzie, and the like were animated, doe-eyed infants, voiced by outside actors in cloying, high-pitched tones. Scooter had a tomboyish twin sister named Skeeter. Even Beaker, Janice, Statler, and Waldorf made appearances in toddler form.

Clearly aimed at a very young audience, each half-hour episode was composed of multiple segments loosely related to a theme, requiring very little attention span. To save money on animation, the show incorporated clips from other Muppet productions, films in the public domain, and popular movies such as *Star Wars* and *Indiana Jones*, with Henson easily obtaining the rights from friends like George Lucas and Steven Spielberg.

The co-production with Marvel and CBS was incredibly successful, scoring at or near the top of the Nielsen ratings for its entire eight-season run. *Muppet Babies* spawned a host of knockoffs, inspiring animated baby versions of characters from Saturday morning staples like *Looney Tunes*, *The Flintstones*, and *Scooby Doo*, and even generating its own short-lived spinoff. The show's popularity also likely influenced the aging down of *Sesame Street*.

Like Hunt, Oz wasn't fond of the concept either, though he had directed *The Muppets Take Manhattan*, which contained the toddler scene that had inspired the cartoon. "He felt it was inappropriate to take characters from one medium with adult characteristics and move them into another," says Muppet designer Michael Frith. "*The Muppet Show* was intended for families, not just kids." While families had watched *The Muppet Show* together during evening prime time, kids were often parked alone in front of the television for the animated Saturday morning fare.

Muppet Babies especially burned Hunt because so much of what he brought to the Muppets was their rebellious edge. Without that, where was his place in the troupe? Was this what had become of some of his best-known characters? Was this his legacy? God, he hoped not.

By contrast, Hunt appreciated that *Fraggle Rock* was geared toward all ages, rather than just for kids. The Canadian Broadcasting Company (CBC) had put the show not in its children's but its variety department, which hired adult-oriented personnel like producer Lawrence Mirkin, who, in turn, didn't hire children's writers for the show. "We respected that there were kids watching it, but we never wrote for kids," says Varughese. When a director asked Henson if he thought kids would understand some vocabulary in the script, Henson replied, "Well, I think it'll make sense in the context, but if not, they'll ask a parent."

Indeed, many adults watched *Fraggle Rock*; in Canada, it often beat out popular newsmagazine *60 Minutes* for its Sunday evening slot. And in the States, the adult cable channel Home Box Office (HBO) signaled an industry shift toward private programming when it co-funded *Fraggle Rock* as its first original content, a trend which would lead to much racier material such as *The Sopranos*. This grown-up audience allowed *Fraggle Rock* to deal with heavy issues such as war, death, and sex—or at least innuendo. Quips Varughese, "It allowed us to write Ma and Pa Gorg horny."

When Hunt returned to Toronto in November 1984 to work on *Fraggle Rock*'s third season, he kicked things off as a provocative antagonist in "Wembley and the Mean Genie." Hunt often played such roles on *Fraggle*

Rock, the closest the show got to having villains. Indeed, this was often Hunt's role in the Muppets as a whole: pushing back against the cuteness, bringing an edgier, maturer sensibility to the puppet productions.

The Mean Genie wonderfully exemplifies Hunt's *Fraggle* antagonists, written with notable complexity by Robert Sandler. As with many of these dark characters, the genie serves as a foil for the indecisive Wembley Fraggle (Whitmire), a people pleaser who worries so much about making everyone happy that he rarely satisfies anyone. The genie easily takes advantage of Wembley once freed from the bottle, testing the limits of his escape, stealing, lying and committing other egregious breaches of community conduct.

The genie's power reaches its apex when he hypnotizes all the Fraggles but Wembley—a spellbinding scene for the viewers as well as the Fraggles—and leads them in singing "Do You Want It," an anti-authoritarian anthem right up there with Alice Cooper's "School's Out." This is the Mean Genie's rock star moment, high up on stage, his gold hoop earrings and chains glinting in the dramatic lights. Hunt gives a standout performance, in a variation of his tough-guy New York accent.

Hunt stayed in character when they weren't filming, much to the amusement of his co-workers. "That was fun because in between takes, he had the genie always coming on to Wembley," says Mills. "'Yeah, I like them green eyes.' Steve is not knowing what to do, trying to improv along with him. Richard's like, 'I wanna get me some of that Fraggle.'"

Hunt's behavior fit right in with the show's backstage antics. Cast and crew were inveterate pranksters, trying to get a rise out of each other. Whitmire and Goelz in particular loved to prank each other as well as play tricks on Stevenson, who wrote the third season's "Scared Silly" to reflect these backstage hijinks. "Scared Silly was art imitating life," Stevenson says. When Boober Fraggle (Goelz) scares Wembley (Whitmire), Hunt's little rat Gunge encourages Wembley to get revenge—again, Hunt's edgy character influences the naive Wembley—just as Hunt often egged on his co-workers' pranks.

Hunt had a good laugh when Special Effects artist Tim McElcheran managed to get one over on Goelz and Whitmire. McElcheran filled an overhead light with confetti, rigged it to be activated remotely, and hung it right above Goelz's mark for a Boober scene. When Goelz and Whitmire were immersed in filming, McElcheran made the light flash and then drop the confetti on Goelz and Whitmire—who jumped out of their skins. Hunt and Nelson came around from behind the set, as if they had been in on it. "Two little scaredy-cats," Hunt announced loudly, pointing in turn at Goelz and Whitmire. "Scaredy-cat one, scaredy-cat two. Now we really know who is afraid of everything."

Hunt also appreciated *Fraggle Rock*'s musical opportunities. He paid homage to musical director Don Gillis with a five-episode character named Gillis Fraggle, the musical director of the Fraggle community. Hunt seemingly channeled his high school choir director Gail Poch as the character effusively conducted the Fraggle chorus. And Hunt praised the "amazing" prolific output of *Fraggle*'s respective composer and lyricist Phil Balsam and Dennis Lee. "Do you know how many people can write 200 songs, let alone 200 different songs?" he said at the wrap party. "There are some people, like the guy who wrote *Cats*, who wrote one song 200 times and made a fortune!"

By now, Hunt truly felt at home at *Fraggle Rock*. Cast and crew had grown into another work family, functioning as a strong, cooperative unit. "We had a sense that we were doing something good that would last," recalls Mirkin. "We all emotionally grew because of the quality of the work and how we worked together." Everyone involved with the project was proud to prove themselves to Henson, to put their energies toward such a lofty cause—and Hunt was an essential part of bringing people together.

Hunt connected with nearly everyone on set, dispensing advice and making sure things ran smoothly. He continued to hold meetings for the newer puppeteers, and kept an eye out for anyone who might need help. Floor manager Wayne Moss, for example, had never before been in charge of such a big studio. Hunt observed him for a while, then pulled him aside and said, "You might want to do this, this, and this," Moss recalls. When Henson singled out Moss as an exemplary floor manager to a group of HBO executives, Moss knew who to thank for the praise. "I attribute some of that to Richard taking me aside and giving me information," Moss says. "I learned from him as much as I learned from my own mistakes, all the way through."

Hunt's collaborative role on *Fraggle Rock* extended even to writers, as he worked with Robert Sandler on the third season's "Battle of Leaking Roof." Sandler used Junior and Pa Gorg to pay tribute to Laurel and Hardy, capitalizing on Hunt and Nelson's practiced comic patter. Pa and Junior go up on the roof to fix it; Robertson and Mills, inside the over-sized costumes, gamely climbed nearly to the studio ceiling. Pa—who is afraid of heights—gets stuck. How to get him back on solid ground?

"Richard Hunt gave me two of my favorite ways of getting Pa down," Sandler recalls. "One was, he [Junior] says to him, 'Okay, Pa! Take this rope, tie it around your waist, great, and when I count to three, I'm going to pull you down.'" When that doesn't work, Junior suggests he jump down: "Just as your feet hit the ground, you just jump up again, and go, 'Ta daaa!'" Sandler appreciated Hunt's knowledge of the character, as well as his unpredictable comedic imagination. "These suggestions were so silly that they were perfect Junior." The collaboration exemplified how the show functioned, which Sandler took to heart. "I learned an important lesson as a writer in that script: ask everybody around you, let them contribute to your success," Sandler concludes. "Let them make your job easier."

Directors, too, benefited from Hunt's input, especially when they didn't have much experience with puppets. "If new directors were feeling overwhelmed, Richard was one of the people they could go to, to get some clarification and suggestions," Prell says. While Hunt's assistance was generous, he also learned more about what went into directing an episode—knowledge which would prove valuable down the line.

The *Fraggle* personnel enjoyed each other's company so much they took side trips together. Hunt, Prell, and some of the Canadian puppeteers and workshop folks drove to Niagara Falls and gave themselves the full tourist experience. They took the famed Maid of the Mist boat tour of the falls, wearing matching plastic rain slickers, shrieking delightedly as they all got drenched.

Around this time, Hunt took a fascinating trip, the farthest he had ever gone, to a whole new continent: Africa. Henson was developing a TV special, *The Muppet Institute of Technology*, bringing in an intriguing array of consultants from science fiction writer Douglas Adams to modern jazz keyboardist Herbie Hancock. Hancock proposed filming some footage in The Gambia—so Henson recruited Hunt, producer Martin Baker, and cameraman Dave Barber to fly out to the tiny West African country. "That's how I ended up on a boat in the Gambia with Miss Piggy and Kermit, playing a portable keyboard as we floated on a river," writes Hancock. The Muppet folks also shot footage with a Beaker puppet and *Fraggle Rock*'s intrepid explorer Traveling Matt. Hunt, Baker, and Barber brought a suitcase full of Muppet paraphernalia, T-shirts, pens, and the like for the locals; Hunt spent most of the shoot mobbed by a group of kids, handing out gift after gift. The excursion was risky, health-wise: Everyone got a slew of vaccinations before flying over, but Barber fell into the water and had to be hospitalized for a couple of days, and Baker developed a nasty case of malaria. Still, Hunt wouldn't have missed the trip for anything—even though the special ultimately never got made.

Hunt spent the first three months of 1985 finishing *Fraggle Rock*'s third season and starting on the fourth—but racing back to New York whenever he could. On January 31, Hunt escorted Mark Hamill's wife Marilou to watch Hamill make his Broadway debut at the Longacre Theater in the musical *Harrigan 'N Hart* (sadly, the show closed after only four performances). And in one star-studded weekend, on February 16 Hunt hobnobbed with the likes of Andy Warhol at Henson's third masked ball at the Waldorf-Astoria Hotel; the very next night, Hunt and two dozen Muppet colleagues filmed "Night of 100 Stars," a TV special to raise money for the nonprofit Actors' Fund of America. The three-hour show took nearly seven hours to film; its luminary roster featured a Who's Who of the 1980s, including many *Muppet Show* guests.

Hunt felt especially drawn to New York as tensions ramped up between him and his lover Nelson Bird. Interestingly, art reflected life in that regard at *Fraggle Rock*. Just before Hunt took his summer break from the show, he filmed an episode featuring a character—or, rather, an alter ego—that surprisingly resonated with Bird.

Goelz's gloomy introvert Boober Fraggle was a character who preferred to stay inside the confines of his comfort zone, thank you very much, gladly skipping a lively party for an evening of soothing laundry. Stevenson came up with Boober's alter ego Sidebottom when she saw the name on the side of a truck. "There must be another side to Boober,"

Stevenson mused. "Yes, the side that he keeps on the bottom. And that's how Sidebottom was born."

Boober's risk-taking, fun-loving alter ego Sidebottom debuted in the second season "Boober's Dream"; a few months later, Juhl spun the concept into the wild farce of "Boober's Quiet Day," which Goelz singles out as one of his most demanding Muppet performances. Goelz played *three* different versions of Boober in the episode: the original Boober; Sidebottom; and the original Boober impersonating yet another character, The Old Gypsy Lady, replete with Eastern European accent. What's more, two Boobers often appeared onscreen at the same time, a technological feat using Ultimatte, an early precursor of green screen. Goelz also found the performance challenging due to its complicated plot and Boober's struggle to bring together the two sides of his personality.

After the episode aired, Bird approached Goelz and told him how much he appreciated it. "I just loved that show," Bird said. "I love Boober and I love Sidebottom." Goelz felt the correlation was apt. "Nelson was a very quiet, shy, retiring person. He didn't get out there like Richard did. He held back. I think Sidebottom was a projection for Nelson— uninhibited behavior was a disavowed aspect of his personality, and Sidebottom legitimized it. I was touched that Boober's dilemma seemed to express a truth."

When Boober wrestled with Sidebottom for the last time in the fourth season's "Sidebottom Blues," filmed in March 1985, Hunt featured prominently in the episode as Junior, singing a great duet with Sidebottom ("Fun Is Here to Stay") and getting hypnotized by Sidebottom into thinking he's a Fraggle. Ultimately, the lesson of Sidebottom is that you don't need to keep your fun side bottled up; and that repressing it only makes it more likely to get out of control if and when you do finally let it out. Unfortunately, Bird was wrestling with some of the same struggles—and it was affecting his relationship with Hunt.

"You know, we had a fight last night. It was kinda bad," Hunt would confess to his friends. The "alter egos" didn't always find it easy to get along. While Hunt could connect instantly with nearly anybody, sustaining that connection on an intimate level required a different set of skills. His usual practice was to keep people at a distance, entertaining them in perpetual performance mode, but that held little credence with

Bird. Hunt also found the fights exciting, their own adrenaline rush; he considered it a personal challenge to get a rise out of his maddeningly mild-mannered counterpart.

Both men were still dealing with Smith's death, with AIDS an unspoken threat hovering over their relationship. Hunt told friend Joe Tripician about seeing Smith in a dream. "Dennis visited me," Hunt said. "It was like one of his paintings. He was parachuting down on this umbrella with a big smile, and saying to me, *I'm thinking of you, and I'm okay.*" Tripician was struck that Hunt seemed not gloomy but uplifted by the dream, as if he had been gifted some extra time with his friend.

One evening, Hunt, Capeci, and Fischer were sitting around after dinner at La Ripaille, a French restaurant just a few blocks from Bird's West Village apartment, when Hunt mentioned he was driving out to stay the night in Closter. "Why aren't you staying at Nelson's?" Fischer asked. "He's going out tonight," Hunt replied. "You mean there's a mystery man?" Fischer asked. "I think I know who it is!" Jokingly, Fischer pointed to himself, smiling and nodding.

To his friends' shock, Hunt burst into tears. Fischer and Capeci had never seen him cry before, not even when his father died. They raced to comfort him, alarmed to see the king of comedy lose his composure; clearly there was more going on than they knew. They entreated Hunt, "Come on, we're your friends, you can tell us anything!"

Hunt finally admitted that he and Bird were on the outs: Bird had confessed to going to bathhouses at least twice a month throughout their relationship, if not more. And there was no pretending Bird didn't understand the risk; indeed, New York State would close down the city's bathhouses just a few months later. Bird's behavior endangered not just his own life, but Hunt's. Wiping his eyes, Hunt asked his friends, "How could somebody you love do that to you?"

For once, the garrulous Fischer had no words.

Hari and Nelson bird 1984

Hunt and Nelson Bird, 1984.

CHAPTER 13

Three Terrible Things

"THREE TERRIBLE THINGS HAPPENED," Hunt said to Marilou Hamill when they caught up in early 1986. "I'll tell you the worst last."

By summer 1985, Hunt and Bird fought constantly, with Hunt riled up and railing against Bird's maddening, implacable calm. Hunt felt betrayed by Bird's trips to the baths, afraid that they were both in danger. The couple seemed about to split, with Bird on his way out.

In an attempt to rekindle their romance, in late June Hunt took Bird back to Italy, where they had had such an idyllic time. First, they went to the gorgeous cliffside village of Positano, then busy, beautiful Rome; but in Rome they cut the trip short. The pollution in the city made it hard for Bird to breathe, Hunt told Stuart Fischer upon their hasty return, a story that immediately raised his friend's suspicions—especially since Fischer worked as an attending physician in the emergency room of Cabrini Medical Center and had seen many similar cases. "I said, 'Was the pollution bad for you?' and he said no. I said, 'How can one person have bad pollution and the other one doesn't?'" Fischer recalls. "That's when I knew that something was wrong."

Hunt dragged Bird along to his own checkup with Dr. Robert "Bobby" Friedman; the doctor took one look at the ashen-faced Bird and ordered him straight to the hospital. Rather than suggesting St. Vincent's Hospital, just a few blocks from Bird's apartment, whose seventh-floor

AIDS ward would become ground zero of the epidemic, Friedman called ahead across town to Cabrini, where Fischer was on duty. Fischer received the pair when they came in, ran an X-ray, and determined that Bird had pneumocystis pneumonia, an opportunistic lung infection that signaled a weakened immune system. Bird was admitted immediately.

Later that night, Hunt and Fischer walked out to Stuyvesant Square Park, where Hunt collapsed on a bench and cried. He cried not just for losing Nelson but for the distance that had grown up like a wall between them, their inability to connect as they once had. And he cried for himself—knowing what this might portend.

Hunt told his sister Kate the news while the two were driving across the George Washington Bridge in a hard rain. "He said to me, Nelson had HIV, and therefore he was assuming that he did." They were quickly reminded, however, that life may be short regardless of one's health. Just minutes later, the car hydroplaned and crashed into the guard rail. The siblings were shaken but unhurt. Hunt looked at Kate and said, "Well, I guess God doesn't want me to die *today*."

Not everyone took the news as well as Hunt's sister. Hunt had rarely spoken about his sex life to Jerry Nelson, despite their close friendship. "I had never thought about that aspect of Richard," says Nelson. He had met Hunt's lovers when Hunt had brought them around—he had been amused by the "Nelson" connection between him and Bird—but hadn't given the matter much thought. Nelson wasn't just surprised to learn that Hunt might be HIV-positive—he was furious. Hunt had been unafraid to call out what he perceived as self-destructive behavior in Nelson, particularly his drinking, and Nelson felt irked by what seemed like hypocrisy, an unwillingness on Hunt's part to hold himself to the same high standard. Despite this tough passage, Nelson and Hunt valued each other too much to let this hurt their friendship. They continued to enjoy each other's company, particularly at work and on Cape Cod, where Nelson often rented a house a short walk from Hunt's Truro cabin.

But even as Hunt feared for Bird's life and for his own, he ran the roost at *Little Muppet Monsters*, a new Saturday morning program which began filming in July.

Little Muppet Monsters had *Muppet Babies* to thank for its existence. Given the cutesy cartoon's wild popularity, it seemed a sure thing to expand the Muppets' Saturday morning presence to a full hour with a companion program. But while CBS wanted more animated Muppets, Henson wanted to bring live-action puppetry to the Saturday crowd, so they settled on the awkward compromise of half and half. The new show would feature both puppet and cartoon versions of the Muppet characters, often back to back, with jarringly unfamiliar voices for all the animated characters but Hunt's, the only Muppet performer to voice any of the cartoons. The rest of the troupe was in England working on Henson's second major fantasy film, *Labyrinth*, while Hunt kept the home fires burning.

As performance director, Hunt basically ran the puppet half of *Little Muppet Monsters*. He oversaw the puppeteers, assigning roles, setting up shots, and doling out suggestions and advice, while also playing one of the three leads. The segments seem like a smart *Muppet Show* spinoff for the younger set, a cuter, gentler version of its affectionate anarchy. The show reflects its own behind-the-scenes dynamic: Hunt plays Tug Monster, called Big Brother Monster in Frith's original designs, good-naturedly bossing around younger siblings Molly (Camille Bonora) and Boo (David Rudman). Though the show features cameos from classic *Muppet Show* characters, Hunt's Scooter is the only one to interact directly with the new kids, as Hunt was the only "original" around the set.

Once an eager apprentice himself, now Hunt coached the next generation of Muppet performers. "*Little Muppet Monsters* was Richard in his mentor role, and loving it," says Rudman, freshly graduated from college and working intently on his first major Muppet character. "He loved being the guy to help all the younger puppeteers with everything, from acting to performing to singing the music in the show." Hunt had a keen eye for casting, surprising the performers with his familiarity with their work. Assigning Cheryl Blaylock a small rat, he said, "Cheryl, do your little Judy Holliday voice," she recalls. "I'm like, 'How'd you know I did Judy Holliday?'" The next generation appreciated how encouraging Hunt was, giving everyone a chance to try a role, never pigeonholing or typecasting. Hunt taught his apprentices how to wring more humor from the script, whether through line delivery or sheer physicality, cracking each other up. "I learned a lot, and it was all because of Richard," says Rudman, who drove Hunt and Bonora to and from the East Harlem studios, the three leads talking shop as they made their way through Central Park.

After a day's work and a late dinner, Hunt usually drove downtown to visit Bird at Cabrini. In typical Hunt fashion, he used his charm and his acting chops to simply rise above the rules. Arriving around nine at night, well after visiting hours, "I would bring a good shirt and tie, and I'd walk through the emergency room, and they'd think I was a doctor. . . . They'd say, 'Evening, Doctor.'"

The epidemic seemed to be everywhere. Even Hollywood hunk Rock Hudson, President Reagan's pal, announced in July that he was HIV-positive, a turning point in the public eye—though over 12,000 Americans had already died of AIDS-related causes. Three of Hunt's friends were sick at Fischer's thirty-fifth birthday party later that month; Hunt brought a pale, thin Bird, briefly paroled from Cabrini, to watch their friends and family perform. Jane Hunt sang "Rose's Turn" from *Gypsy*, a fiery portrayal of a stage mother gone rogue. Hunt's old Closter friend Glenn Mure sang a challenging Donizetti aria that called for nine impossibly high C's; he nailed them all and soared upward again at the end for a tenth, hauntingly holding onto the high clear note. Hunt was especially touched by Fischer's recitation of James Agee's "Knoxville: Summer 1915," a nostalgic small-town vision that called up Hunt's childhood in Closter.

Meanwhile, as Hunt had his hands full in New York, the guests staying at his Truro house went out to dinner and came back to find the place in flames! The hot water heater had exploded. Despite the Truro fire department's best efforts, the house couldn't be saved; Hunt would have to raze it down to the foundation and completely rebuild. His peaceful respite had disappeared—just when he needed it most.

On August 16, the night before his thirty-fourth birthday, Hunt came to visit Bird at Cabrini as usual—but immediately sensed that something was different. "I walked in on the night he died and I knew he would," Hunt said. "So I stayed through the night. And sat with him. He was half-conscious and then he came back to consciousness in the middle of the night. I told him how much he meant to me and he'd brought me to life and he didn't take his eyes off me, reached out. It was the moment of my life. I said, 'You know what tomorrow is, don't you?' This poor guy. He said, 'It's your birthday.' I said, 'I'm gonna be here and I don't want you to give me no trouble.' It was very important. It's a very strong part of me. And it's when he died."

Bird's death was like a line drawn across Hunt's life. Afterward, he was never quite the same. To some, Bird's death permanently dimmed Hunt's usual ebullience, particularly after he cleared out Bird's apartment and found all his vials of medication unopened, as if Bird had made no effort to fight the disease. "After that, the childlike Richard disappeared," says Fischer. "There was always a cloud over his head." And yet to others, Bird's death only magnified Hunt's carpe diem attitude. "From the first time I met him, he lived very much like 'I'm on borrowed time,'" says Hunt's friend Jesper Haynes. "When Nelson died he realized that this could possibly happen to him too, so he was like, *I'm going to really live while I can.*" This attitude influenced the people around him. "It rubbed off—this energy that was so up and positive and life-affirming, in the middle of all this death around."

Hunt brought this uplifting energy especially to the set. At the wrap party for *Little Muppet Monsters*, the outtake reel from the summer of filming was "all Richard," says Rudman. "It was Richard being hilarious after every take, or the take would screw up and Richard would say something funny." Though other aspects of Hunt's life were in turmoil, one would hardly know it from his daily antics at work.

Hunt tried to maintain a veneer of normalcy by renting a house in the Hamptons for the annual Hunt family gathering. If they couldn't go to Truro at the end of the summer, they could at least gather and go to the beach. Unsurprisingly, despite the beautiful scenery, the vacation felt tinged with gloom.

Compounding Hunt's sense of loss, around this time he and his colleagues found out that HBO had axed *Fraggle Rock* in a wave of cutbacks: their fourth and current season would be their last. Exacerbating the frustration, the decision hadn't been mutual between the show's two major funders. "CBC would have been perfectly happy keeping it, and in fact tried to find some other way to carry on with it," says Nelson.

"Another season would have been ideal." Cast and crew had expected to have more time to extend the show's narrative arc and tie up story-lines, but it was not to be.

Hunt threw himself into his work, flying to Toronto in mid-September to conduct auditions for *The Muppets: A Celebration of 30 Years*, a land-mark retrospective commemorating the accumulated work of the whole company. In a sense, Henson had invited the viewer to the ulti-mate Muppet wrap party: nearly every character from the last three decades gathers at a black-tie gala, eating and drinking, affectionately roasting each other and watching clips of their past performances.

These large banquet scenes required so many performers that Hunt conducted even wider and weirder auditions than usual, including one man doing martial arts. "We're looking for puppeteers, but thank you!" Hunt told him. One act prompted Hunt to ring up Stephen Finnie in his office: "Get your ass over here quick." The *Fraggle Rock* set decorator dashed over. Hunt introduced him as a producer to a pair of identical twins in matching black-and-white polka dot dresses, saying, "We think you should do your act again so Mr. Finnie can see it." The twins burst into "Me and My Shadow," dancing in perfect sync, earnestly straight-faced but inadvertently hilarious. "Finnie's just sitting there, getting redder and redder, trying not to burst out laughing," says Mills. "Rich-ard keeps nudging him and he's like, 'Stop it.' Finally they say, 'Thank you very much, we'll be in touch.'"

The company began shooting almost as soon as the cast was set, a lively production reminiscent of the salad days, bringing together Hunt's far-strewn colleagues, directed by *The Muppet Show*'s Peter Harris. At the end of the week of filming, the seasoned team brought the show to life with a wrap party at the Four Seasons, which doubled as a celebration of Henson's fiftieth birthday (though it was actually his forty-ninth). The party was a nice moment of resolution, taking time to appreciate what they had all created together. Flying home, Hunt and Arciero gripped the armrests as their plane bounced through pockets of turbulence. "You know," he remarked, "if this plane goes down with both of us on it, we'll definitely get a mention in *The New York Times*."

Hunt kept his eye on the ratings that fall as *Little Muppet Monsters* took its place—right behind *Muppet Babies*—in the CBS Saturday morning lineup. The show suffered from an identity crisis, a weird hybrid that never quite cohered. Cartoon viewers tuned out during the live-action segments, while the animation alienated Muppet fans, especially the ersatz voices. Ultimately, the physical puppets seemed so *alive* that they outshone their cartoon counterparts. As story director Scott Shaw points out, "The juxtapositioning of live-action and animated Muppets invited an unfavorable comparison, to which the cartoon versions inevitably suffered; the puppetry was just too good."

CBS wasn't overly attached to *Little Muppet Monsters*; when Marvel was late delivering the animation for the fourth episode, CBS aired another *Muppet Babies* instead—and the ratings soared. "So they said, 'Forget *Little Muppet Monsters*,' and they just started playing *Muppet Babies* back to back," co-creator Kathy Mullen says wryly. Though Hunt and his colleagues had filmed material for a full season of thirteen episodes, only the first three ever aired. Disappointed, Hunt later described *Little Muppet Monsters* as "this failed show that didn't work."

Hunt was frankly grateful that fall to let his busy schedule distract him from his grief, flying back and forth between *Fraggle Rock* and *Sesame Street*. He took a renewed interest in his pupils. *Fraggle Rock*'s Terry Angus recalls "quite a chewing out" after one rehearsal in which they were off their game. "He said, 'I lost a good show, we had two damn good puppeteers, and you guys better shape up.'" Now both those "damn good puppeteers"—David Rudman and Camille Bonora—were on board at *Sesame Street*. Perhaps as recompense for the flop of *Little Muppet Monsters*, Hunt took his generous mentorship to the next level on Rudman's very first day.

Hunt saw some of himself in the young, eager Rudman, soaking up learning like a sponge. Hunt had looked after Rudman since the young puppeteer had recognized him at the 1980 World Puppetry Festival; he had helped Rudman create the audition tape that got him hired, and given him pointers when he came in for occasional projects. Hunt later named Rudman as one of the "Original Eight"—the updated expansion of the "Original Five"—alongside Steve Whitmire and Kevin Clash. (He also singled out some noteworthy "girls" such as Bonora, Kathy Mullen, Karen Prell, and Louise Gold.)

Like most new puppeteers, Rudman was supposed to begin doing right hands. But when Rudman visited the set the day before his debut, Hunt said, "You know what, I'm not going to go to work tomorrow, I have a doctor's appointment, and I'm going to give you all my characters." "Can you do that?" Rudman asked, incredulous. "Yeah," Hunt replied. "I'm going to do this for you." Though a few years earlier Hunt had given Michael Earl and Martin Robinson a hard time for advancing too quickly, now he not only handed off two Anything Muppet characters to Rudman, but shepherded the switch past the producers. So on his very first day, Rudman played a dentist singing "Who Are the People in Your Neighborhood?" as well as a background Muppet in another song. "This was unheard of," says Rudman. "I'm a little quieter, so he probably felt like I needed a push, to get me out there. He was looking out for me."

And yet, in their own way, Hunt's colleagues were looking out for him too. They made a tremendous showing at the memorial service Hunt put on for Bird that fall, with even a sizable Toronto contingent packing the side chapel at St. John the Divine and the reception on the Columbia campus. The turnout impressed Bird's parents, who had flown in from Utah. "I know that you're not all here because of Nelson," his mother Betty Bird told a group of *Sesame* puppeteers at the reception. "It speaks of your love of Richard, and Nelson was lucky to be in on that, and to get a side effect of that." The memorial was part of Hunt's increased openness about his love for Bird. "Nelson talked to me all the time, but he didn't talk to anyone else," said Hunt. "So when he died, I started talking."

At the service, Hunt stepped into his usual role as emcee. "It was Richard running a show," says Mills. "He was bearing himself up with the fact that he was running around trying to get everybody organized." As a quartet played an off-key version of Samuel Barber's *Adagio for Strings*, Hunt stepped away from the stage and hid his face in a corner, his shoulders shaking. But when one of his sisters went to comfort him, she discovered that, true to form, Hunt had found humor even at this somber event. "He wasn't crying at all," says Mills. "He was trying very hard not to laugh at the quartet's efforts to get back in key." Hunt's mirth ebbed during a friend's mournful rendition of "My Old Kentucky

Home." He was particularly moved by Fischer's recitation of James Agee's "Knoxville: Summer 1915," which Hunt and Bird had watched him recite just a few weeks earlier.

Ironically, speakers onstage gestured toward an empty urn; the funeral home—one of the few that would deal with the epidemic—was so backed up that they hadn't yet done the cremation. "It was like something out of a British farce," says Fischer. "It was the essence of comedy under the worst possible circumstances." But even these faint glimmers of wry humor weren't present at Bird's funeral in Alabama, which Hunt attended with his sister Kate, where the cause of death was never mentioned.

By this point, Hunt was almost inured to the epidemic; death had become the new normal. "After Nelson, which was the most important person in my life, it all became—not matter of fact, but very much what I'd expect World War II was all about," Hunt said. "Every week someone would say, 'Oh, Joey down the block just got it.' 'Oh, that's terrible.' But it had become, like, part of the life." Hunt stressed that he didn't want to seem unsympathetic: "I don't think many people have gone through as much as I have so they responded on a devastated level. People were in shock. I understood that, and I didn't want to appear cold or callous because I wasn't; I was very saddened by the whole experience." Yet, as on the plane with Arciero, he could seem oddly calm in the face of danger. He and Closter friend Geni Sackson were walking down a Toronto street when a car came speeding out of a parking lot, tires squealing, heading right for them. "He pulled me back," says Sackson. "We just missed getting slammed. We both said 'Oh well!' and kept walking. Our lives could have ended, and we just said, 'Oh, well!'"

Though Hunt assumed he was HIV-positive, he did not actually know that for a fact—nor did he want to know. An AIDS test had become available earlier that year, but Hunt, like many, steadfastly refused to be tested. Since there was no reliable treatment, a diagnosis was little more than a death sentence. But he looked after his health carefully, trusted Dr. Friedman, and kept current about what might help, adopting a regimen of supplements. "He used to say, 'Oh, I've got this problem, and I'm taking all this stuff,'" says *Fraggle Rock* floor manager Wayne Moss. "It sounded very homeopathic." Hunt was matter-of-fact about cramming a handful of pills into his mouth and knocking them back all at once with a shot of orange juice, making even that mundane ritual entertaining.

Soon after Bird's funeral, Hunt visited Gold in London and went to see his psychic Betty Balcombe, asking her if Bird had liked his memorial service. "She said, 'Oh, he didn't come. He wasn't there,'" Gold recalls. "It made me laugh, because it was very Nelson not to come." Gold appreciated that Balcombe said this, rather than falsely telling Hunt what he wanted to hear.

Balcombe helped Hunt find a way to hold onto his connection to Bird—literally. She told him that Bird wanted him to find a certain "calming" green stone. "He wants you to have this stone because it will be a connection between you," Hunt recalled. Hunt searched all over for just the right stone. He had just about given up when a Toronto acquaintance said she might have seen something fitting that description in a crystal shop in the Boston suburb of Brookline. Eerily, Hunt was scheduled to go to Boston the very next day. His friends picked him up at the airport and told him they were going straight to a new restaurant—which, in another cosmic coincidence, was just three doors down from the crystal shop, though his friends lived clear across the city.

Hunt believed in this sort of synchronicity, and sure enough, he had completed his quest. "I walked in and looked around and saw this stone—I wish I hadn't now—and I knew in a moment." The small, translucent, sea-green trapezoid looked like "the same kind of shapes and colors that Nelson painted." The stone affected Hunt much as Bird himself had: "It calmed me down. It had this enormous effect on me." Hunt kept the quartz chloride in his pocket for the next four years. "I always carried it with me. Every time there was a problem, I would hold the stone."

Though no one could replace Bird, Hunt kept trying. "He was in and out of relationships," says Oz. "That was hurtful to him. He needed a lover who really cared for him." Unfortunately, many of the men Hunt spent time with appreciated his largesse more than his large heart. One chiseled blond from New Jersey even borrowed Hunt's precious Checker cab—and wrecked it. "He got really depressed," says Nelson. "These guys were taking advantage of him, because he was free with his money. I said, 'Why are you hanging out with people that'll do this to you?' And he said, 'I just want somebody to love.'"

Hunt and some friends were getting ready for a party at his apartment on January 21, 1986, when *The Muppets: A Celebration of 30 Years* aired on CBS. He went into the kitchen to answer a call from his mother, watching the special at her place. "It brought back all those years of working with the Muppets, and he cried, and we cried," says Clash. "But of course he came back in and started acting crazy, and we all acted stupid getting the rest of the stuff we needed for the party."

The Muppets: A Celebration of 30 Years finally enabled Hunt to see how truly integral he was to the group, laying his old doubts to rest. "That's when I saw all of us," he said. "We're *equally* as important to the whole thing. And it allowed me my place." Hunt credited this realization especially to the "outside perspective" producer Andrew Solt brought to the project.

The retrospective highlights the various elements Hunt brings to the Muppets—his rapport with the guest stars, his musicality, even his full-body puppetry—spanning his career from *Ed Sullivan* right down to *Little Muppet Monsters*. The special also honors the deeper, soberer moments of the Muppets—"The times when we don't try to be just funny," says Kermit—many featuring Hunt in a central role.

Hunt's career is encapsulated in an unwittingly symbolic series of shots during the "Rainbow Connection" finale. As the gang in the banquet hall sings together one last time, Hunt appears as old man Statler from early in his career, alongside fellow old men Waldorf (Henson) and Pops (Nelson); then he appears as kiddie Tug Monster from his most recent production, alongside young'uns Boo (Rudman) and Molly (Bonora)—reflecting his work both with those who taught him and those he taught.

The special posits the anniversary not as an ending but a beginning. "We start our second thirty years tomorrow, so rehearsal begins at 9 A.M. sharp!" Kermit exhorts his colleagues as the special closes. But Hunt knew that, barring a miracle, he wouldn't have another thirty years with the company, even if the anniversary special helped him appreciate the fifteen years he had already put in.

Still, it felt like old times in February back at Elstree's Studio D, now owned by the BBC, filming the Easter special *The Tale of the Bunny Picnic*, directed by Henson. Jocelyn Stevenson, who wrote the special based on the company's picnics on Hampstead Heath, remembers the filming as "a big fat laugh," especially with both Hunt and Gold on set. Hunt and Clash headed up the puppet staging. Hunt brought a needed edge to the special with another of his tough-talking, wisecracking older brother characters, Lugsy Bunny, who pushed back against Whitmire's adorably indecisive protagonist Bean Bunny, a familiar dynamic for the pair. Actors from the popular soap *EastEnders* came from their set next door to watch the Muppets at work, the stars looking as enthralled as little kids, their mouths hanging open.

When *Bunny Picnic* aired in late March, Hunt watched it at the Hamills', sitting on the couch between their sons Nathan and Griffin. By now he had come up with a dramatic way to retell the events of the past year. "He said, 'Three terrible things happened. I'll tell you the worst last,'" Marilou recalls. He recounted the wrecked car, the burned-down house—and finally, of course, losing Bird.

Hunt, with Jim Henson as Cantus Fraggle, directs an episode of *Fraggle Rock*, April 1986.

CHAPTER 14

Magic Be with You

O N MARCH 24, 1986, Hunt and Henson, as Kermit and Scooter, presented the Oscar for Best Animated Short Film at the ceremony in Los Angeles. Hunt remained hidden behind the podium while Henson made an on-camera appearance to open the envelope, a Kermit-green handkerchief in his lapel. Even after all his years performing, Henson still felt nervous about public appearances, Hunt recalled. "When we were doing the Academy Awards, Jim said, 'God, I don't mind the puppet, it's just getting up there by myself, I can't stand it.'" Though Hunt sometimes teased Henson about this sort of discomfort, he was happy to speak in his stead at major Muppet events.

While *Fraggle Rock* was reliably a playful, productive respite, Hunt was experiencing some loss on that front, too, as cast and crew reconvened in Toronto in spring 1986 to shoot the last dozen episodes. And on top of losing the show, Hunt lost his synchronistic partnership with Mills, who had to step down from performing Junior Gorg.

Playing Junior had always been a physical challenge for Mills, whose asthma made it hard to breathe inside the "horribly unforgiving" costume. Though Mills had usually been able to recover on hiatus, he came into *Fraggle Rock*'s last season straight from filming *Labyrinth*, where he had developed aspergillus, a persistent lung infection. Now doing Junior was "awful"; despite multiple inhalers and ephedra tea, Mills coughed uncontrollably in the suit before each take, gasping and heaving for breath. Finally Mills went to Larry Mirkin: "My doctor says if I do this, I'll drop dead," he told the producer, who at his suggestion hired local performer Frank Meschkuleit in his place.

Hunt took the news badly. He was angry that Mills hadn't told him directly, and frustrated that he didn't have the same easy rapport with Meschkuleit that he did with Mills. "No matter what Frank did, it wasn't good enough," Mills recalls. Hunt also insisted on working with Meschkuleit *through* Mills. "There I was, wheezing my way back and forth from the puppeteers' table to the set to give notes and direction to Frank while Richard scowled at us both. Not pleasant."

The situation came to a head one day outside Stephen Finnie's office. "Oh, you're happy you don't have to do Junior," Hunt said snarkily, having heard from mutual friends in the workshop that Mills had said it felt "great" to stop doing the role. "I just lost it and started yelling at him," says Mills. "Of course I wanted to finish Junior! But I was also so glad not to be coughing blood, not to have my ribs hurt with every breath, not to die in a furry outfit." Hunt, startled by Mills's outburst, took it to heart; the two tearfully hugged and made up. "Richard was a little better to deal with after that," says Mills. "A little."

Mills appreciated where Hunt was coming from, reflecting on it years later. "He wanted completion with that, which I totally understand," says Mills. "I wanted that too—but I just couldn't do it."

Though Mills was unable to breathe inside the Junior suit, the two were able to work together again as Junior in the episode "The Gorg Who Would Be King," in which the character is shrunk down to Fraggle size and therefore performed, like the Fraggles, as a hand puppet. "We got to switch roles for a bit," Mills says. Hunt performed Junior's voice and movements, while Mills operated Junior's radio-controlled eyes.

This conceit not only freed Mills from the taxing costume, but enabled the show to use the character in the other groups' worlds, a technologically impossible feat with the full-body puppet. Junior travels through the Fraggle caves, meets a Doozer, and even gets teased by Philo and Gunge. Junior's new size helps him empathize with his fellow creatures and understand why he feels so apprehensive about having to become "King of the Universe." When he returns to full size and becomes king, his first royal act is to abdicate the crown. Writer Laura

Phillips thinks Hunt pulled this off just right: "He knew exactly how to elevate Junior so he would be able to end the monarchy, though it was quite a leap for the character." Hunt also sings one of his loveliest *Fraggle* songs here, "How Wide, How Far, How Long." With this episode, Hunt helped the series take a major step forward in terms of equalizing and connecting the different groups, and modeling world peace.

But by far Hunt's strongest and most moving performance in the last season of *Fraggle Rock* was the role of Mudwell the Mudbunny, another collaboration with Mills. Hunt, who loathed excessive backstory, prepped Mills with just one pithy sentence: "You're doing this guy, it's me after I'm dead."

Hunt cited "Gone But Not Forgotten" as one of his favorite *Fraggle Rock* episodes, allowing him to explore and express his grief. "There was a show that was just on a personal level," he said. "The mud bunny. It was quite soon after Nelson died. I gave him a soft voice. So I played out my thing there." The episode is right up there with *Sesame Street*'s tribute to Mr. Hooper as a shining example of how to talk helpfully and realistically about death.

Again, Hunt saw just what writer Phillips was trying to communicate with the script. "Richard understood exactly what Mudwell was about and how I wanted the character interpreted," she says. Hunt's Mudwell the Mudbunny is an easygoing rabbit with a goofy laugh. Despite his relaxed demeanor, Mudwell seems perpetually busy, singing a seemingly innocuous tune ("Just a Dream Away") while sculpting in the mud. The episode is another pairing with Whitmire's Wembley, who befriends Mudwell—but Wembley is taken aback when the rabbit abruptly breaks off their friendship, for fear of causing him pain at their inevitable parting. "A Mudbunny never knows when the time will come," he says. "Bound to hurt anyone I made friends with when I have to say goodbye." Whether intentional or not, the parallels with the AIDS epidemic are hard to ignore. As Mudwell continues to shape the mud, it becomes clear that he's preparing his own casket—and then he lies down in it, and dies.

The usually sunny Wembley is plunged into grief. His friends share their coping strategies: Boober (Goelz) primal screams under the blankets, Mokey (Mullen) solemnly recites poetry. None of it helps. Tellingly,

Wembley turns to Nelson's character Gobo. (Remember, Henson had assigned this role to Nelson, telling him, "He's the cement that holds it all together. That's where I need you." By this point, Nelson himself was no stranger to grief.) Gobo tells Wembley of his heartbreak when his pet Thimblebug died, and the comfort he finds in holding onto its nest: "It's like a part of him is still alive." And the memento doesn't even have to be a physical object, Gobo advises. "It could just be a happy moment that you keep alive in your memory."

In search of resolution, Wembley visits Mudwell's grave, where Mills's character (a nameless lizard) emerges from a crack in the mud. Together they sing "Just a Dream Away," the words taking on new meaning: "It's just a dream away/You've got to leave to stay/We'll meet again someday/Just a dream away . . ." Wembley holds onto the song from his friendship with Mudwell, and connects with a new friend through singing it together. It's as if Hunt's character has passed down his legacy through Mills's character, who continues to pass it on. The scene fades out with Hunt's voice singing, "It's just a dream away . . ."

The episode deals with death gently—but unflinchingly. "It was a very delicate piece of writing," says Mirkin. "You didn't want to be maudlin, and you didn't want to say reincarnation, but you wanted to have all these things hovering." It was a fine line to draw on the all-ages show, and a challenging topic to tackle. "I thought that was such a brave thing to do, and potentially piss a lot of people off," says Muppet performer Mike Quinn. "But it was so nicely played by Richard. He knew what he was doing, for sure."

Hunt, like many of his colleagues, had grown quite a bit during the *Fraggle Rock* years. Henson trusted the members of his company to make this show largely in his absence, to stretch themselves as the work required, and they had indeed risen to the occasion. Hunt was no longer solely a performer, but a mentor, consultant, and important backstage liaison. Yet Henson saw even more potential in him. Mirkin and Henson were discussing possible *Fraggle* directors when Henson, in his casual way, brought up Hunt. "Jim was the one who said Richard could do this," Mirkin recalls. In Hunt's most striking embodiment of growth on the show, he took on his biggest role: that of director.

If *Fraggle Rock* had to go out early, they would use their last few episodes to complete the story arc of the show, to model world peace by
showing the different groups coming together, to truly connect their
characters before going off the air. They planned out the last few episodes carefully—and tapped Hunt to direct the penultimate episode of
the entire series, making sure to stick the landing as they brought the
show to its conclusion. Hunt directed "The Honk of Honks" in the last
week of April 1986.

Hunt had made a natural progression to the director's seat. He had
long watched directors and thought about what went into the job
and how he could do it. He had advised new directors, many of
whom were so unfamiliar with filming puppetry—especially the various technologies—that they would give notes on Gorg line delivery to
the performer in the costume rather than the one actually saying the
lines. Hunt could put on his puppet captain hat and quickly set up a shot,
telling everyone where to stand, while a new director was still sizing up
the set. Hunt shadowed Wayne Moss when the *Fraggle* floor manager
directed two early last-season episodes, the two of them putting their
heads together; when Hunt directed a few months later, Moss returned
the favor, with the show's practiced collaboration. (The two called back
their partnership in "Fraggles Look for Jobs," a satirical reel of inside
jokes shown at the wrap party, with Hunt and Moss humorously arguing
over which one of them was *really* the director.)

Indeed, Hunt was ready to direct because he knew everyone in the
room. Hunt had great communication and rapport with the cast and
crew, who respected him and wanted to see him succeed. He worked
easily with his friend Jocelyn Stevenson, who wrote the episode. What's
more, Hunt felt confident. He had seen his place in the Muppets recognized with the *30 Years* special, and felt proud to be trusted with helming an episode. And what he didn't know, well, he would take the advice
he had given to Caroll Spinney dancing as Big Bird: just *pretend* you can
do it.

Still, directing was a big leap. "Directing [is] a lot different than just
working the characters, because when you work your own character,
that's the only thing you have to worry about," Hunt said. "When you
direct, you have to worry about your own character and everyone else's

characters as well. Along with a bunch of other things like scenery and music and the script and cameramen and editing and trying to get a show that's seven minutes too long down to the allotted time." The episode is particularly challenging in that it contains scenes in every single one of the Fraggle worlds, each requiring different technology and techniques. "He was definitely stepping out of his comfort zone," says *Fraggle* performer Karen Prell. "But he embraced it, and went for it, as usual, like Richard."

Adding to the pressure, the episode contained Henson's character Cantus Fraggle—meaning that Hunt was directing *Henson*. Cantus Fraggle represents Henson in some ways. "Cantus *is* Jim," says Stevenson, who often wrote for the character. When the traveling minstrel makes his infrequent visits to the world of *Fraggle Rock*, everyone eagerly gathers around him and values his wise, thought-provoking perspective—a sweet parallel to the way Henson came in and out of the show. While Hunt may have been intimidated to direct his mentor, Henson enjoyed handing over the reins. "Then Jim could just relax, and have fun with his performing, and not worry about the directing," says Prell.

"The Honk of Honks" is a crucial episode in the overall arc of the show: the human character Doc sees the Fraggles for the first time, bringing together the disparate groups of creatures as never before, modeling interdependence for the viewers at home. This makes it a fitting episode for Hunt to direct, who so deeply valued people connecting and seeing their shared humanity, however snarkily he may have gone about it.

On this visit, Cantus announces that the Fraggles are going to sing one of their most important songs, as evidenced by its name: "The Song of Songs." But first, in this show's solemnly goofy way, Gobo Fraggle must assemble the titular Honk of Honks: one big horn containing horns from each of the show's different worlds (the Fraggles, the Doozers, the Gorgs, and the Trash Heap). Gobo's centrality is a nice nod to the importance of the character and of Nelson. The episode builds on the relationships developed over the course of the show, as Gobo can now simply request a horn from Doozer or Gorg friends, unimaginable at the show's outset. In the Junior and Gunge scenes, Hunt is directing not just his colleagues but himself, having to see the scenes from both inside and out.

Hunt deftly handles what is arguably the most significant scene in the entire series: the moment Doc finally connects with the Fraggles. At the episode's climax, Gobo instinctually extends his hand to Doc in a sad moment—and though Doc has never before been able to see the Fraggles, suddenly he *sees* Gobo, in this moment of empathy. Gobo realizes that he hasn't always "seen" Doc, either. "You're not just a Silly Creature!" says Gobo, using the Fraggles' dismissive phrase for humans. "You're a *You*! Like me!" The scene comes off as a tender and nuanced illustration of the episode's refrain, a cornerstone of Hunt's spiritual beliefs: "We're all a part of everything, and everything is a part of us." One final horn in hand—from Doc, a souvenir of their connection—Gobo troops back to the Great Hall to blow the Honk of Honks, and everyone breaks into a rousing, catchy "Song of Songs."

Hunt singled out Mills to add mischief to the song, casting him as an Inkspot, a cute brown bean-shaped backup character with bulgy eyes. Hunt decided this little guy would belt out the low bass line, a great running gag. "I want you to be in as many shots as possible," he told Mills. "Upstage, as much as you can. Stay close to Jim, don't get into trouble, and don't do too much." Mills didn't quite heed this last bit of advice; as the song fades out, the Inkspot cheerily waves to the camera— much to Stevenson's chagrin. "Jocelyn was so pissed," Mills recalls. "She said, 'We don't break the fourth wall!'"

Hunt's colleagues noticed a heightened focus from Hunt while he was directing, a deeper sense of presence and calm. He wasn't in his usual boisterous performance mode; he was in serious work mode. He listened closely to everyone, grateful for suggestions, again as part of an atmosphere where a good idea could come from anywhere. He was well aware of how much his success was dependent on the cast and crew—and grateful to them. "I could not have done that at all without all the help that I had from all of you," he told everyone a few weeks later at the wrap party. "You had the perfect opportunity to make me look like a fool and see me fall flat on my face, but you decided against that." Overall, Hunt enjoyed the experience. "It [directing] was a lot of fun," he said. "It was a challenge, your brain went a little crazy, but you kept up with it."

Ultimately, Hunt's colleagues felt he did a good job: he translated the story well onto the screen, comfortably fielded the challenges of filming puppets, and stayed within the budget. "I thought he asked all the right questions and made all the right decisions," says Moss, who went on to a career in TV directing. But the definitive approval came from Henson. "I think we've found a new director," Henson said happily to Goelz over lunch that week. Ultimately, Hunt directing Henson shows the shift in dynamic between them—allowing Hunt to lay to rest any lingering doubts about his role in the company or in Henson's esteem.

Hunt would also direct the 1988 *Sesame Street* video *Sing-Along, Dance-Along, Do-Along*, another Stevenson script, as well as segments of the 1991 video *Elmo's Sing-Along Guessing Game*.

Art poignantly mirrors life in the last *Fraggle Rock* episode, "Change of Address," filmed in mid-May. Having finally come together, the characters—like those who created them—are preparing to part. Doc is moving to the desert. He encourages Gobo to come with him; Gobo consults the Trash Heap, who tells him, "You cannot leave the magic." When Gobo finds a Fraggle tunnel that leads him to Doc's *new* home, he realizes that this statement is not a command but a point of fact: you cannot leave the magic, because it is always with you. "Magic be with you," the Fraggles sing.

"Until next time," Mirkin said reluctantly at the end of shooting. "That's a wrap."

Having wrapped the show, it was time for the wrap party. Cast and crew came together in a ballroom at the Four Seasons Hotel to toast their work, appreciate each other, and live inside the magic a little while longer. Hunt, of course, emceed the roughly two hours of speeches and performances. Again, as after *The Muppet Show*, Hunt knew that it could be overwhelming to bring together a work family and then leave seemingly abruptly. People needed closure—and he was there to bring it.

Hunt kept up a running banter as *Fraggle Rock* personnel addressed the crowd: Mirkin, Juhl, CBC programming director Jack Crane. "How come it's always *men* talking?" Hunt quipped as he introduced production executive Diana Birkenfield. As he adjusted the microphone for Prell, he said offhandedly, "I forgot you were one of the midgets." He even good-naturedly slighted himself. "Unlike some people standing here on the stage, he only talks when he has something to say!" he said when puppeteer Bob Stutt finished his juggling act. "Did I just insult myself? I figured I'd say it before you did."

As usual, even Henson was not immune to Hunt's teasing. "Should I read the list of bad things about Jim Henson now?" Hunt asked as he introduced the head of the company. "No, we'll let him say those things for himself!" Henson noted in his speech that his first time working in Canada had been at this same studio, shooting Rowlf the Dog in the Purina Dog Chow commercials. "That was 1961, I think," he said. "Some of us weren't born yet!" Hunt shouted offstage, to enormous laughter. And when Henson finished his short remarks, Hunt poked fun at his discomfort with public speaking: "Now that didn't hurt, did it?"

After all the speeches and performances were done, Hunt took the stage himself. He had prepared something special for his colleagues. He started off riffing about his earlier characters—*Sesame Street*'s Sully, *The Muppet Show*'s Beaker—but soon focused in on *Fraggle Rock*'s Junior Gorg. "Junior was the easiest character I've ever done because he's the little kid in all of us," Hunt said.

All I had to do was walk in there, and just feel and remember and trust the way I am as a human being. 'Cause that's what we all are. You have a tendency to lose it after you're about seven years old, that's the drag. But Junior keeps it, and he kept it through the whole time.

And all the troubles he had with the Fraggles and everything else, he was always chasing them and carrying on, but deep down inside he just wanted to have a good time and get to know who these creatures were. Whenever anything would go wrong with them, instead of giving up and blowing his brains out, or whatever he might do, he somehow persevered and said *Aw, forget it! I'll just get through that old thing!*

This is the part I want to give to you all. I want you to share in this. I want you to take the part of you that's Junior Gorg. Because when we leave here, we're going to have to go back into the real world. This can be a pain in the ass, to put it bluntly. And I think you realize that all those demons out there, all those demons of greed and jealousy and bitterness and all that—when you take that in on yourself, you only hurt yourself. No one else gets hurt, and it's not healthy for you. So you have to let the part of Junior Gorg that's in you, out. And remember that you're not going to let nothing bother you.

The audience gasped as Junior Gorg was led in. *"Hi, I'm Junior Gorg. What's your name?"* For one last time, Hunt and Mills reunited to perform Junior Gorg, Mills inside the suit and Hunt remotely performing the voice and facial features.

Hunt had come to Mills with the idea during the last few weeks of filming. Would he do a song as Junior at the wrap party? "I immediately said yes," says Mills. They rehearsed once in the sound studio at Eastman with musical director Don Gillis on piano; Hunt sang the lines while Mills worked out the movements. "That's probably the only time I ever rehearsed anything with him!" Mills laughs.

Accompanied by Gillis on piano, Hunt as Junior sang one of his favorite songs, "Not While I'm Around" from Stephen Sondheim's *Sweeney Todd.* The song is an anthem of protection: "Nothing's gonna harm you, not while I'm around." The song exhorts the listener to keep their integrity, to see through the fakers and treasure what's real. The listener may feel alone in the scary world, Hunt told his audience, but Junior/Hunt/ the spirit of *Fraggle Rock* would always be there to keep them safe.

Hunt concluded with a gentle exhortation: *"Remember, I'll be with you, all the time. Hehehehehe."*

When Mills took off the heavy Gorg head, his own face streaked with tears, the entire room was on its feet, applauding. "There he is, Rob Mills, underneath it all," Hunt said proudly. "Junior Gorg. Thank you." And in a magnanimous gesture, Hunt said, "Rob and I would especially like to express our appreciation to the new Junior Gorg, Frank Meschkuleit, for allowing us to get back together." The applause and cheers went on and on and on—and many people in the audience wiped away tears. "That was a really sweet moment and I'm glad I got to do it," Mills says. "Closure. Richard and I didn't make a big deal out of it but we knew it was special."

Mills wasn't the only member of the *Fraggle* personnel to find closure in the performance. "Oh, Richard, that was so great," writer Sugith

Varughese gushed to Hunt at the party afterward. Hunt looked him straight in the eye. "That was for you," he said.

Varughese felt connected to Junior Gorg, having written seven episodes featuring the character. In early seasons, Varughese had resented that Hunt would come crashing into the studio and improvise with his scripts after he had labored over every syllable. Hunt didn't tinker with Juhl's scripts to the same extent, Varughese observed. But over the course of the show, Varughese noticed Hunt treating him with increasing respect. "We had to earn his respect over time," says Varughese. "By the end he loved the character and what we had given him to do. He became a different person, as far as I was concerned." This interaction at the wrap party epitomized how their dynamic had changed. "I still get choked up thinking about that," says Varughese.

The wrap party ended with the five major Fraggles singing "Magic Be with You" from the last *Fraggle Rock* episode, with Nelson, Goelz, Whitmire, Mullen, and Prell emerging from behind a curtain to perform openly for the whole audience, and the lyrics projected onto a screen for everyone to sing along. The *Fraggle* folks sang to remind themselves and each other that they truly couldn't leave the magic—in this case, the magic of a work environment where people felt free to stretch and grow, to work harmoniously together and genuinely connect with each other.

"So that brings to a close, our last wrap party, our last show," Hunt concluded. "Just as dreadful as the ones before. It doesn't get any better. I know that. We all know that. All of us felt very, very deeply. There's never been a crew that's been closer to us, both professionally and personally, than this crew. It's like leaving home. It's a tough thing for a lot of the people in the Muppets. We love you very much and you will always be a part of our lives."

A voice shouted from the audience: "And Richard, we love you!"

Hunt later characterized *Fraggle Rock*, even more so than *The Muppet Show*, as his most lasting work: "It's an amazing show because it holds up better than anything else we've ever done." The show met its goal of being truly international, airing in nearly one hundred countries in over ten different languages, across Europe, Africa, Australia, Asia, and the Middle East. Despite its international audience, however, Hunt felt the show had not received sufficient attention in America. "*Fraggle Rock* is still a show no one has seen," he said disappointedly in 1991. "It's only been on cable, HBO, which was very limited. Then on TNT [Turner Network Television] now, which is broader, but still, cable-related. I don't think people have ever really seen this show."

Yet in the long run, Hunt's hunch about the show's longevity would prove correct: *Fraggle Rock* would become a beloved cult favorite in America and beyond, in wide syndication throughout the 1990s and most of the early 2000s and 2010s, with a popular, celebrity-studded, full-season reboot, *Back to The Rock*, on streaming service Apple TV+ in 2022. Whether he trusted it or not, Hunt was building a legacy, a body of work that would, like Mudwell the Mudbunny's singing, keep his memory alive.

"That's the magic of Muppets," Hunt said. "It's not just a couple of people wiggling dolls and doing funny voices and telling jokes and stuff. The reason they work so well is because *they're so real*. And because there is *so much truth in it*. It sounds so corny . . . If you're not embarrassed, or ashamed, you buy right into it, because you realize, my god, I've got a second chance here."

Hunt and other *Sesame Street* performers, with musician Ray Charles, film the anniversary special *20 and Still Counting,* 1988. Performers, left to right: Hunt, Jerry Nelson, Kevin Clash, David Rudman, Noel MacNeal, Rick Lyon, and Martin P. Robinson.

CHAPTER 15

Resilience

S UMMER 1986 lay in front of Hunt, open with possibility but also suffused with loss. *Fraggle Rock* was over, sooner than expected. He
was still rebuilding the Truro house. He was still carrying the sea-green
stone in his pocket to remind himself of Nelson, a literal touchstone.
What to do with himself?

Hunt and his Closter friend Ernie Capeci flew to Italy in June, on a
trip that seemed oddly doomed from the start. They boarded an eerily
empty plane, as most Americans were afraid to fly overseas given the
recent U.S. bombing of Libya. The flight attendants had little to do, as
they practically outnumbered the passengers, so Hunt befriended them
by sharing the cocaine stashed in his carry-on. He spent most of the
ride in the back of the plane, sending the attendants into gales of laughter, his manic patter amped up even more than usual.

Though Hunt and Capeci had planned to fly to Rome, the travel
agent had mistakenly booked them to Milan's Malpensa airport; in retrospect, Capeci sees the name (which translates to "bad thoughts") as
an ominous sign. Hunt sent Capeci to stand in a different customs line,
telling him he looked "like a terrorist" with his scraggly hair. Capeci
watched, heart racing, as the drug-sniffing dogs got a whiff of Hunt's
carry-on, the customs officials arrested him, and he was led away.

Hunt and Capeci had flown in on the Friday of a long weekend, with
the courts closed for the feast of the patron saint of Rome, so Hunt spent

three days in a bare-bones Italian jail. Though Capeci was able to visit him, Hunt found the whole experience unnerving, especially as he didn't know the language. Hunt later joked about his confusion when people kept telling him he needed an "avocado"; certainly they didn't mean the fruit. Eventually he figured out that they were saying he needed an "avvocato": a lawyer. Yes, that would help.

When Hunt finally appeared before a judge, he was charged a hefty fine—and promptly kicked out of the country. More suspicious than the drugs, the Italian officials were concerned that Hunt was carrying a second passport: Bird's. Hunt's plan for the trip had been to retrace the steps of his previous trip with Bird, to revisit the places they had enjoyed together, while carrying Bird's passport close to his heart in his inside jacket pocket, much as he carried the small green stone. Capeci surmises that the aborted trip might have been for the best, forcing Hunt to start the painful process of letting go.

Once Hunt was released from jail, he and Capeci stayed with Louise Gold in London, then friends in Paris, before parting ways; Capeci went back to Italy, and Hunt went to visit his friend Jesper Haynes in Sweden. By the time he got to Stockholm, he saw the humor in the incident, which he laughingly recounted over glasses of Dom Perignon. "He almost enjoyed the spectacle of it," says Haynes. By now, Hunt had mastered the art of turning a painful experience into a funny story.

He did much the same with another strange disappointment that arose around this time. Hunt found out that he had been born out of wedlock; his parents hadn't married until he was in high school. "I'm a bastard!" he joked to his friends. Still, his distress sometimes showed through. Brian Meehl recalls this discovery as "the one time I remember seeing Richard really upset about something. He was really hurt by it."

Hunt felt particularly betrayed by his sister Kate, who had kept the secret for nearly two decades. "How could you not tell me?" he asked her. Kate had found out shortly after the wedding, when she came upon a dried rose wrapped in an off-white stocking in her mother's makeup case. "Oh, you can't tell anybody," her mother had said when she asked about it. "Your father and I just got married." Jane and Richard Bradshaw had married at the suggestion of a therapist; if anything, their fracturing relationship had only worsened once they tied the knot.

Hunt took the news hard because family was everything to him. "It really did mean something to him, that his parents weren't married when he was born," says Stuart Fischer. "Richard wanted a real, ordained, legal relationship between his mother and father, and he wanted a real relationship in his life." In Hunt's mind, the two things were connected. Not only had he lost Nelson, the love of his life, but his family of origin was even more fragile than he had thought.

Hunt's work, and his work families, remained a productive and comforting respite. Back at *Sesame Street* in the fall, Hunt played a couple of characters that enabled him to bring two of his great passions onto the screen: opera and partying.

When head writer Norman Stiles, writer Mark Saltzman, and songwriter Christopher Cerf came up with the idea of Placido Flamingo—a bright pink bird who sings opera, modeled after famed tenor Placido Domingo—they knew immediately who would perform him. "Once we said it, we knew it would be Richard, because he was clearly the person who would play this over the top," says Stiles.

Though a parodic role, Hunt sings beautifully as the avian Placido, using humor to bring opera to a mainstream audience. Placido Flamingo often headlines at the Nestopolitan Opera House, a satire of Hunt's beloved Metropolitan Opera House, singing memorable arias such as the bilingual "Dentist of Seville," the riotously accident-plagued "Peligro" ("Danger"), and the priceless "Up and Down Opera" with Ernie. Some days Hunt would run straight from filming Placido to watching his real-life counterpart. "It'd be getting around 5 o'clock, and he'd be champing at the bit to get in the taxi and get up there to see opera," says Kevin Clash. "We'd be messing up on the script and he'd be ready to kill us." Clash and David Rudman once came outside to find Hunt sitting on the sidewalk, having sprained his ankle running for a cab. "We ran to help him, and he pushed us away and got in a taxi and went up to the opera. That's how much he loved it."

And Leo the Party Monster, who appeared from 1986 to 1987, allowed Hunt to express (and exaggerate) his love of partying. The bearish Muppet has a shock of pink hair, wears a pink-sequined vest and bow tie, and carries an ever-present radio (since parties need music). As his name suggests, Leo the Party Monster is largely a one-note character: he loves to party—and, indeed, feels sad when the party is over. Leo's parties attract a motley crew of Muppets and *Sesame* humans; as at Hunt's parties, everyone is welcome.

One notable Leo sketch seems almost like a dramatization of the era's real-life debates. The sketch was written by Mark Saltzman, who decades later would provoke great controversy by mentioning that he had modeled some Bert and Ernie sketches after his own dynamic with his life partner Arnie, implying that the longtime roommates might be gay.

Leo stands at a row of pay phones hosting a talk show called "Party Line." The topic is—what else—partying! The first caller (Robinson), practically hyperventilating with excitement ("Hello? Hello? Am I on?"), has obviously partied too much. Even Leo can see this, chiding him, "Where's your head at, buddy?" The second caller (Bonora) admits that partying has its downsides, but still prefers even the worst party to no party at all. But the third caller (Robinson again, in a pinched, nasal voice) changes the tone of the discussion. He believes that partying "has gotten out of hand. . . . I don't like partying, and I don't like people who like partying," he says unkindly, hanging up on Leo.

Then no one calls. Leo's spirits sink. "Gee, maybe partying is all finished," he says sadly. "Maybe the day of the party is over. Maybe the party monster has gone the way of the dinosaur." His disappointment is surprisingly touching, especially considering Hunt's real-life grief and the last decade's changes in the gay community. Has the era of festivity come to an end? Is the reveler indeed extinct?

But then the phone rings again. "You gotta come over," says Duke (Clash). "We got a crowd over here . . . This is a parrtay!" Leo drops the phone in his excitement, showering himself with confetti. He struts off camera, singing to himself, "I like a good time, I like to party." And so the revelry continues.

The *Fraggle Rock* spirit—and the Christmas spirit—was alive that fall, as Hunt and many of his *Fraggle* colleagues were back in Toronto filming *The Christmas Toy*, with a script by *Fraggle* writer Laura Phillips. The TV special told the story of toys that came to life, a full decade before Disney's feature film *Toy Story* had a hit with the same concept.

Hunt played Belmont, a rocking horse with an Eeyore temperament. The special aired on ABC on December 6, 1986, to warm reviews.

Around this time, Hunt's doctor Robert Friedman confirmed the suspicions Hunt had harbored since Bird fell ill: he was indeed HIV-positive. Hunt told only a few close people for now, and he felt fine. Still, the news spurred him to prioritize traveling. He had places that he wanted to see, and little sense of how much longer he would have the energy to go see them. Hunt called Rudman out of the blue one day and said, "Hey, what are you doing for a couple of weeks in April? Wanna go to Peru with me?"

"He was on a spiritual mission," Rudman says. "I just thought, 'When am I ever going to do anything like that?'"

When Hunt and Rudman went to Machu Picchu in April 1987, the majestic Incan site wasn't today's sought-after destination. The violent guerilla group Shining Path and Peru's strong military presence made for tense, warlike conditions throughout much of the country. Landing in Lima, the friends felt intimidated by the omnipresent men bearing machine guns, standing on street corners and cruising slowly by atop trucks. At night they heard gunshots outside the hotel. While they waited in the Lima airport for their flight to Cusco, the police suddenly tear-gassed the crowd, and everyone made a mad dash outside. No explanation came until they were sitting dazedly out on the runway: someone had called in a bomb threat, and this was how the military emptied out the airport.

Hunt and Rudman were relieved to spend a few quieter days in Cusco, acclimating to the formidable altitude of the Andes. Once they had adapted, the friends hiked for three days on a guided ten-person tour along the Inca Trail, the famous (and famously tough) pilgrimage route to Machu Picchu. The local guides, in addition to leading the way, carried gear, set up camp, and prepared meals, enabling the visitors to focus on their surroundings. Hunt, healthy and strong, enjoyed the challenging hike, which ascended steeply at one point to nearly 14,000 feet. Rudman recalls some "scary moments" when the guides led the group along a narrow ledge beside a vertiginous drop, and the hikers had to watch their footing carefully.

But the demanding trek just sweetened their arrival at the ancient site. Machu Picchu, often called the "lost city" in the clouds, is a massive Incan citadel built in the 1400s, an elaborate and intricate network of stone ruins, a breathtaking archeological wonder even five centuries later. "When you're in Machu Picchu, there's something in the air, the vibe of the place—you feel it," says Rudman. Hunt, on his own private mission, left the group for a few hours to wander around by himself and take in the sacred energy.

Hunt and Rudman stayed overnight at the Machu Picchu Sanctuary Lodge, the only lodging on the grounds of the ruins. At the time, rooms cost $25 a night; a luxury hotel built on the same site in the late 1990s now charges over a thousand—a sign of how the famous destination has changed, and an indicator of Hunt's prescience in visiting.

Hunt traveled vigorously over the next few years. He took a big group of family and friends to Hawaii; organized a family skiing trip at Robert Redford's Sundance resort in Utah; and, happily, took his whole family to Italy, where he finally had a calm, enjoyable trip where no one got sick and no one got arrested, visiting Rome, Venice, and Tuscany in turn and stopping to scatter Bird's ashes in a Venice canal.

But for all his travels, Hunt was grateful to return to his house on Cape Cod in summer 1987. He had rebuilt the house essentially from scratch, bringing in an off-Cape crew to copy the original 1892 house down to the baseboards, at a cost of tens of thousands of dollars, largely covered by insurance. Hunt was careful to rebuild in keeping with the original historical materials and design. "The house was exactly the same way it was before, only better," says Corn Hill caretaker Paul LaFrance. "He was very proud of that."

Once again fit for guests, the Truro house generally burst at the seams with family and friends—even people Hunt was furious with. Hunt and his old high school friend Glenn Mure had long had a competitive "frenemy" aspect to their friendship. Around this time, they had a falling out. Still, Mure stayed at the Truro house for two weeks, deliberately trying to get a rise out of Hunt by doing things like putting out cigarettes on the expensively rebuilt exterior. When the visit ended, the friends were no longer on speaking terms.

Hunt was likely on the Cape for the long holiday weekend when he realized another one of his longtime dreams: on July 3, he appeared in a sitcom pilot, *Puppetman*, on CBS. By this point, Hunt had appeared on television many times, but always hidden underneath a puppet. Now he was *acting* (though playing a puppeteer); it wasn't just his work that would appear on TV, but his *face*.

Puppetman, in some respects, was a Muppet project. Henson had dreamed up the concept, imagining a behind-the-scenes look at an all-ages magazine show like those he had worked on in the 1950s, replete with backstage antics and flirtations, showcasing puppetry and letting viewers in on what happened outside the frame. And when *Puppetman* filmed in April 1987, the sitcom had a number of Muppet connections. Hunt acted in it, as did *Muppet Show* first season head writer Jack Burns. The show featured dragon puppets, including a full-body dragon costume, made by the Muppet workshop and designed by Ron Mueck (who would later design the puppets for *The Ghost of Faffner Hall*).

Yet as with the Muppets' failed stint on *Saturday Night Live*, the pilot for *Puppetman* suffered from being put in the hands of writers who had little experience writing for puppets. Sitcom veterans Mark Reisman and Jeremy Stevens turned the intriguing, behind-the-scenes puppetry conceit into an extraneous gimmick. Rather than the adult magazine show Henson had imagined, *Puppetman* dramatized a saccharine children's show, *Dragon Time*. Hunt played Del Zivic, the second male lead (his lot since high school), the edgy snarker who keeps things interesting. While casting agents had considered the manic Jim Carrey for the lead of Gary, instead they chose the genial Fred Newman, best known for using his mouth to produce special effects such as pops, clicks, and whistles (or as he called them, "mouth sounds"), another needless gimmick. What's more, the tone of the show didn't have the "affectionate anarchy" viewers might have expected from a Muppet-related production. The characters mostly sniped at each other; some of the jokes were openly offensive and most of them just fell flat.

Except for the puppets, *Puppetman* seemed like a hundred other short-lived 1980s sitcoms. All of Hunt's mugging and sharp line delivery couldn't save it, let alone Newman's mouth sounds. The show just didn't work; Hunt knew it, and the network knew it too. The pilot aired in the Thursday evening CBS Summer Playhouse series; though viewers were exhorted to call in and vote for their favorite pilots to be picked up, once a show aired in the doomed slot, the verdict was already in.

Still, Hunt couldn't get the concept out of his head, convinced it still had plenty of potential. Shortly after *Puppetman* aired, he came to Meehl with an idea. "We can write a better version of this," he said. Hunt was a performer, he had been a director—why not try his hand at being a writer?

Over lunch on Manhattan's Upper West Side, Hunt and Meehl pitched their idea to Henson. "Richard and I asked Jim if he would mind if we took the idea of a sitcom about puppeteers and came up with a totally different sitcom for Richard to appear in," Meehl recalls. "Jim basically said, 'Yeah, go ahead.'"

The pair came up with a rough script in just a few months, titling it *Read My Lips*, then revised it on and off for another year and a half, appreciating the excuse to hang out. They fell into a writing routine at Meehl's Murray Hill apartment, with Meehl at the typewriter and Hunt taking catnaps on the couch. "He'd wake up, spew out an idea, or say, 'So what have you written?'" Meehl recalls. "Or he'd go to the bathroom and floss his teeth. We complemented each other as writing partners very well." By 1989 Hunt and Meehl had a pilot draft, now titled *They're Only Human*, which they shot on their own dime.

Hunt and Meehl's pilot is genuinely funny, capitalizing smartly on the behind-the-scenes puppetry conceit. Hunt plays Kyle, a puppeteer at an ad agency. He and a nonpuppeteering colleague, Vicki (played by Broadway actor Catherine Cox), need another puppeteer for a new campaign, but who? Enter Jerry Nelson as Vicki's ex-husband, Davis, a Shakespearean actor with lofty ambition—even if he has to lure audiences into his theater by promising them free sandwiches. Watching Nelson in the role is especially delightful knowing his ambivalence about puppetry and his lifelong ambition to be taken seriously as an actor. Davis is outraged to find out that the new gig involves puppets. "Puppets!" he says in disgust. "I'm an actor, not a dolly wiggler!"

Hunt and Nelson's long-honed comic pairing shines in the show's vaudevillian patter. Art imitates real life as Kyle teaches Davis the basics of puppeteering. "You don't close the mouth on the sound, you open it.

It's called lip-synch." The characters often talk through their puppets, who have personalities in their own right: Hunt's character Kyle puppeteers the friendly, spaniel-like dog Mutt, while Nelson's character Davis puppeteers the macho bulldog Dutch, replete with red leather collar. In an extra show of talent, Nelson pretends to puppeteer badly, moving Dutch's mouth out of sync with his speech, until he miraculously gets the hang of it and has the bulldog recite Hamlet. The script abounds with real-life details: When Davis's head appears in the shot, they have to do another take; and, naturally, Hunt's character Kyle talks right up until the cameras are rolling. As usual, Hunt isn't afraid to make fun of himself. "What have you been doing for the last fifteen years?" Davis asks Kyle, who laughingly answers through his puppet: "Birthday parties."

Meehl and Hunt pitched the pilot to CBS producer Jeff Sagansky in February 1990, unfortunately to no avail. Still, the *Puppetman* remake wasn't Hunt's only attempt to write himself a prime-time vehicle. "Richard was often thinking about ways of moving on from puppets," Louise Gold recalls. Hunt called her up late one night excited about an idea for a sitcom starring the two of them, based on his experiences in England. She would play the "starchy" English woman who worked in a bar, and he would play "the loud cliché American" who wins her over. Hunt's friend Stuart Fischer remembers Hunt writing an entire script based on this idea to pitch to NBC president Brandon Tartikoff. "I read it, and I said, it's not funny. He got very mad. I actually gave the script to my mother. She said to me, 'Tell Richard that when he goes to Brandon Tartikoff, he should have two copies of his script.' I said, 'Why?' And she said, 'Because Brandon Tartikoff's going to throw this out the window.'" When Hunt heard the story, he quipped, "That's funnier than anything I wrote."

Hunt was growing in many ways during this period, exemplified by his traveling to new countries and trying his hand at being a writer. He was also becoming increasingly open about his sexuality, his love for Bird, and his health issues. He was no doubt influenced by how many Americans were mobilizing in response to the AIDS epidemic, keeping tabs on these developments through his ever-present newspaper. Over a half-million people turned out for October's weeklong Lesbian and

Gay March on Washington, which featured a march, a rally, and a mass civil disobedience action at the Supreme Court, in which over 800 people were arrested, to protest the recent Bowers vs. Hardwick decision upholding state sodomy laws. Nascent New York–based activist group ACT-UP (AIDS Coalition To Unleash Power) made a strong presence at the various actions, spawning chapters across the country. The gathering also featured the unveiling of the NAMES Project AIDS memorial quilt, a striking visual representation of the virus's impact: the quilt's nearly 2,000 panels covered more ground than a football field.

Hunt participated in the movement in ways that were more his style. He took Fischer to the first AIDS benefit at Carnegie Hall on November 8, paying a thousand dollars a ticket, with funds going to the Gay Men's Health Crisis (a New York–based nonprofit serving the needs of people with AIDS). Leonard Bernstein and James Levine shared conducting duties, with a superstar cast that included tenor Luciano Pavarotti, groundbreaking soprano Leontyne Price, violinist Yo-Yo Ma, and diva Marilyn Horne. The audience, too, was peopled with stars, from Paul Newman (whose wife Joanne Woodward co-chaired the event) to Paul Simon, and even Danielle Mitterrand, wife of the French president. "One could have made an evening's entertainment out of the audience alone," reported the *New York Times*.

Like many of his peers, Hunt felt more and more that he had little to lose and everything to gain by dropping any pretenses about his private life, drawing closer to his loved ones by being more present and authentic. And while he was always the consummate entertainer, the animated center of a crowded room, friends report him quieting down in these years, listening more, seeming calmer.

Yet even as Hunt adapted to the changes in his life, he did a Muppet shoot that felt like old times: *A Muppet Family Christmas*. The hourlong TV special brings together characters from the three main Muppet worlds—*The Muppet Show*, *Sesame Street*, and *Fraggle Rock*—and, therefore, brought together nearly the whole Muppet tribe to make it, the largest gathering of the troupe since the Muppets' thirtieth anniversary special two years earlier. Indeed, the Toronto shoot seemed almost like a Christmas reunion, mirroring the gathering onscreen.

This moment was a "golden time" for the troupe, recalls Whitmire, where "everything felt warm and comfortable and uncomplicated." While the special required a lot of hard work, particularly the large group caroling scenes, the Muppet veterans were accustomed to the job. "We all knew the deal, and could get the machine up and running, and enjoy each other at the same time," says Prell, who characterizes the shoot as a "mutual appreciation retreat." The performers valued the opportunity to show their gratitude, to celebrate each others' contributions to their shared body of work.

And yet, for all this joy, Hunt didn't always exhibit his usual vigorous energy. "Something seems wrong here," Terry Angus recalls noticing. "He doesn't want to do characters. Seems to just want to sit out on things." Hunt asked Angus to stand in for him as Gladys the Cow when the bovine diva made her entrance and sang in the big caroling medley. Hunt also had to be urged to perform a Janice close-up, rather than passing off the puppet. He did show more enjoyment playing the Snowman, a Fred Astaire–type character who sings and dances with Fozzie. Impressively, when the duo is heckled by Statler and Waldorf, Hunt voices two out of the four characters in the scene.

Writer Jerry Juhl peppered *A Muppet Family Christmas* with his trademark character-based humor, taking pleasure in bringing together the different Muppet worlds. Fellow trash aficionados Oscar the Grouch and Rizzo the Rat become fast friends, as do mutually id-centered characters Animal and Cookie Monster. Juhl seemed to especially delight in writing for Bert and Ernie, putting Bert in drag for a Christmas pageant, shoehorning an alphabet lesson into their conversation ("Where we come from, this is small talk"), and giving Ernie a hilarious moment of single-or-plural pronoun confusion regarding the Two-Headed Monster ("He said he'd never been in a play before . . . I mean they said it . . . um . . . both of him said it").

A Muppet Family Christmas is truly touching, a thank-you among the troupe but also to the viewers, with obscure character appearances (Fozzie's mom!) and a homey feel. Muppet critic Danny Horn calls the special a "victory lap" for the Muppets, a richly deserved assessment. Hunt was pleased with how the special turned out. "Have you seen the last Christmas show we did?" he asked an interviewer a few years later. "It's marvelous."

A Muppet Family Christmas aired December 16 on ABC to high ratings and appreciative reviews. The following week, Henson threw his annual Christmas party at the East 69th Street Muppet townhouse, and Hunt threw his own party at his West End Avenue apartment on the same night, by now an annual tradition. While the lavish company parties were fun, they were also work, requiring the performers to be "on," to talk to the right people and make connections for themselves and for the company. Once you had done your duty, however, you could cross the park and blow off steam at Hunt's. "That was the real intimate party," says Arciero. "That was where you just went and had fun with Richard."

So much was changing, people were dispersing, the clock was ticking—but Hunt would try to enjoy each moment to the fullest, surrounded by his loved ones, as he had always done.

PART V

Hunt with his Wild Impresario character on the set of *The Ghost of Faffner Hall*, 1988.

CHAPTER 16

Moving On

HUNT AND DAVID RUDMAN were crouched behind a prop onstage at the Chicago Theater one late night in January 1988, miked and ready to perform Placido Flamingo for a full house, when they ran into a technical snag. The puppeteers squatted uncomfortably, conscious of the rising murmurs from the increasingly restless audience. Filming for the PBS special *A Grand Night: The Performing Arts Salute Public Television* had begun at 7:30 P.M. and would drag on until nearly two in the morning; even a veritable Who's Who of public television luminaries couldn't keep these people in their seats. Almost to himself, Hunt muttered, "I gotta keep this audience entertained."

"He didn't put the puppet up—he got up," Rudman recalls. "He stood up, came out, and started doing a stand-up act." Hunt delivered a full five minutes of "hilarious" material, delighting the crowd. "They were cracking up. They were shouting out, talking back, and he was interacting with them, and it was so funny."

When Hunt rejoined Rudman, the younger puppeteer asked, aghast, "How could you just do that?" Hunt grinned and said, "Are you kidding me? I was holding back. That was nothing."

Even as many things were changing, some things didn't change.

On the surface, Hunt was up to his same playful larks. He brought a new puppeteer—a slim blond, his usual type—to Henson's masked ball in March at the Waldorf-Astoria, circulating with him and talking him up to everyone from Andy Warhol to Kitty Carlisle Hart. But at the costume awards Hunt and his "friend" gleefully revealed the prank, as the mystery man tore off his wig and mask to reveal himself as Steve Whitmire—a brilliant hoax even for this crowd of tricksters.

Henson and Hunt represented the Muppets for the British royals on April 24 at the Children's Variety Performance, with Kermit performing "Being Green" and Statler and Waldorf right at home heckling from a side box at the Victoria Palace Theater. At the curtain call, they stood grinning in black tie (even Kermit wore a tiny tuxedo) alongside Princess Margaret and entertainers ranging from girl-pop trio Bananarama to a Shakespeare ensemble, and even a live elephant. Yet Henson and Hunt may have felt as old as the men they played, thinking back to their Royal Variety Performance a decade earlier: a starry-eyed troupe finding their way up together, amped up about meeting the queen, with Louise Gold making mischief in a monster costume. This appearance was a great honor—but seemed more like an honor of what had been, an ending, rather than the salad days' giddily open-ended sense of what might be.

Fortunately, Hunt would find—and create—that kind of playful, productive atmosphere on his next and last television series, *The Ghost of Faffner Hall*.

By now, Henson Associates was far bigger than just Henson himself, with creative teams on both coasts and in multiple countries developing projects under the company's aegis. So when Henson came to *Fraggle Rock* writer Jocelyn Stevenson with the idea of a children's show about music, he helped her secure funding and coordinate personnel— but then stepped back and left the show in her hands, trusting her to express the vision in her own terms.

The Ghost of Faffner Hall's multinational deal resembled *Fraggle Rock*'s: American cable channel Home Box Office provided U.S. distribution, and the Tyne Tees channel in northern England supplied facilities and crew. But while the show's fundraising took after *Fraggle Rock*, its format was closer to *The Muppet Show*: a running sitcom-like plotline provided plenty of amusing antics, conflict, and character development, while guest segments added a variety show format in an admirable swath of musical genres. The conceit was that the titular music conservatory, Faffner Hall, was at risk, and by metaphorical extension so was music itself. The show combined Muppet chaos with an underlying classiness, at times truly moving.

The Ghost of Faffner Hall kicked off with a big meeting in New York of Muppet people and international music experts. Ron Mueck (who had done the *Puppetman* dragons) was brought on as puppet designer; Pete Coogan as production manager; Stevenson, Patrick Barlow, and David Angus as writers; Stevenson as producer—and as Stevenson's right-hand production consultant, her old friend Richard Hunt.

Hunt's talents were especially suited to the show, with its democratic "anyone can make music" curriculum and striking roster of stars. "Richard was part of the whole DNA of the production," says Stevenson, who as a first-time producer relied heavily on Hunt's input and experience. Hunt wore a number of hats on the production, serving as both production consultant and puppet captain. He welcomed the musical guests, organized the performers, trained the locals, translated for crew and directors who were unfamiliar with puppet shorthand and technique, advised everyone, and as usual kept up spirits on set, even when filming ran overtime.

Hunt brought the fun to the Tyne Tees studio in Newcastle upon Tyne, and to the guest segments filmed all over the world, as they shot a full season of thirteen episodes throughout the second half of 1988. "It was a very happy cast and crew and Richard was central to that happiness," recalls puppeteer Mak Wilson.

In addition to his backstage duties, Hunt performed one of the five main characters, the delightfully dotty music enthusiast Wild Impresario, sort of an older and more self-assured version of *Sesame Street*'s Don Music. Hunt was elated to work alongside his impish old pal Louise Gold, who played the hall's titular ghost, Fughetta Faffner. "With both Richard and Louise on the project we had two powerful forces of nature on set," says Wilson, who played music-hating antagonist Farkas Faffner. Happy to play along were newlyweds Mike Quinn and Karen Prell as two young, eager musicians, and a few locals in supporting parts and as assistants.

Hunt's gregarious charm made him a perfect liaison to the musical guests, equally at ease with punk violinist Nigel Kennedy as with ebullient jazz master Dizzy Gillespie. He saved the day when *Faffner Hall*'s first major guest, folk legend Joni Mitchell, showed up four hours late for her London shoot, by which point the crew was furious and the schedule was very tight. "Don't worry, don't worry," Hunt reassured Coogan. "We're going to make this work." Hunt guided Mitchell through their segment, in which she and Hunt's Wild Impresario character ride in a convertible to her song "Night Ride Home." "It was amazing," says Coogan. "Richard took over. Literally she arrived, costume, makeup, on the set, shot it, done. Within a half hour of her coming over, we finished it." The seamless rapport carried over to a lively group dinner afterward. Hunt also brought in his famous brother-in-law, musician James Taylor, for a mirthful segment with the Wild Impresario.

The atmosphere on set was a typical Muppet workplace, silly yet prolific. New people sometimes misconstrued the playfulness as a lack of seriousness about the work. Director Tony Kysh, for example, was appalled at how things got done—until he realized that they did, indeed, get done. Old friends Stevenson and Hunt collaborated harmoniously—with one notable exception, the only one in their two decades of working together. "We had an absolutely blazing fight," says Stevenson. "He didn't agree with something I was doing, and he yelled at me in front of everyone." But this rare, uncharacteristic behavior was easily remedied. "I took him aside and I said, 'Don't ever do that again.'" Hunt heard her and heeded.

The *Faffner Hall* folks were such a tight-knit group that they spent most of their off-hours together. Hunt stayed at the Gosforth Park Hotel, a luxury hotel reminiscent of Toronto's Four Seasons. Wilson, a local, proudly showed the Americans around northern England, enjoying Hunt's "stunned" reaction to the Newcastle natives, or Geordies, who wore T-shirts and short kilts on a freezing winter night. Wilson organized a group trip to Langley Castle, a fourteenth-century Norman fortress turned upscale guesthouse, driving out along the picturesque, snow-covered moors. Hunt regaled them with funny stories as they ate a sumptuous meal, then played charades in front of a giant log fireplace set into the ancient stone wall. "In the end, after tea was served, we were all so relaxed we didn't want to leave," says Wilson. Another night they ended up singing for all the guests in a Mexican restaurant.

"Luckily it was good singing, especially with Richard and Louise there, so they didn't mind."

Hunt's friends noticed that he seemed to fatigue more easily than in the past—though he was still the loudest in any crowd. He was particularly solicitous of Wilson, recently diagnosed with Chronic Fatigue Syndrome; the two usually tired out and left outings around the same time. Hunt was open about his HIV status and his occasional need to rest or to gulp down a handful of pills, but in a very low-key way. Stevenson worried about Hunt's health, but more so about his devil-may-care attitude. "He would take holidays where he and Louise would take off in the car, and I would think, 'Oh God, please drive safely.'"

Though Hunt made little fuss about his illness, he made little pretense as well. He spoke frankly in a conversation with Gold and longtime Muppet director Peter Harris. An out gay man and no stranger to the epidemic, Harris initially tried to brush off the topic: "Oh, you'll be all right, you'll be fine." But Hunt was unyielding: "No, I'm going to die. I will die." Gold recalls how resigned Hunt seemed in that conversation: "Richard feeling he was going to die, and thinking that was how it had to be. Not looking for a cure, or looking for hope." Yet Hunt's stoicism sometimes gave way, especially in England, which never quite felt like home, despite his vast network of local friends who welcomed him into their homes and families. He showed up late one night, unusually disconsolate, at the west London apartment of his former roommate Gillian Lynne; she was out, but her husband Peter Land gladly comforted his old friend: "He wept in my arms—and then he snuck off into the night."

When *Faffner Hall* filmed the occasional segment in his hometown, Hunt delighted in playing the guide. He insisted that Quinn and Prell take his "famous" New York City tour. You couldn't just passively sit inside the car; you had to hang half out of the sunroof, the wind whipping your hair as the landmarks scrolled by: the Brooklyn Bridge, the World Trade Center, Central Park. Hunt demanded that friends do things his way, naturally the best way. "It wasn't an option not to," recalls Quinn.

Even as Hunt filmed *Faffner Hall* in Newcastle and all over the world, he was hard at work at *Sesame Street*—which was approaching an important milestone: twenty years on the air. Hunt's old resentment of *Sesame*

Street had largely fallen away. This freed up his work and brought back the old playfulness—not that it was ever really gone.

For many years on *Sesame Street*, for example, Hunt had performed Forgetful Jones half-heartedly. He had never quite unlocked the absent-minded cowboy he inherited from Earl, though he played off the character's memory lapses with good-hearted sincerity. "Richard didn't really like Forgetful Jones," says Kevin Clash. "He didn't know how to get the humor out of him being so naive and stupid." This all changed when Hunt and Henson filmed a performance that soon became canon: Kermit the Frog directing Forgetful Jones in the song "Oklahoma," from the musical of the same name.

"All you have to sing is Ohhhhklahoma," Kermit instructs Forgetful. The music plays, the horses and cows act out their complicated choreography, and Forgetful appears: "Aaaaaklahoma!" Take after take ("Eeeee-klahoma," "Iiiii-klahoma"), the absent-minded cowboy gets it wrong; Kermit grows more and more annoyed, until his temper finally explodes. The other puppeteers were wracked with laughter, says Clash, who performed one of the horses. "The timing of Richard and Jim—I mean, we peed on ourselves [laughing]. I was in tears. I could hardly see the monitor. And that's when he said, 'You know, this character *is* funny.'"

Forgetful's blank-slate naivete enabled Hunt to push the comedic envelope. "Richard was a master at doing stuff that was suggestive," says Martin Robinson. "It's easy to be blatant with a puppet: 'Ahahaha, Elmo just said *fuck*.' But Richard could do it in a way that we'd go, 'No. . . . Yeah.'"

One day Forgetful was helping the human character Gordon, played by noted Black actor Roscoe Orman, get some paint off his nose. "Did I get it all?" Gordon asked. Instead of saying yes, as the script decreed, Hunt had Forgetful recoil in shock. "Your face is still covered in paint!" he exclaimed. "You're scarred for life!" From a different person, the joke could have easily come off as racist and distasteful. "I could imagine, without a lot of effort, someone else trying to do that, and failing," says Orman. "But Richard's spirit was so open and without any sense of bias, that for *him* to do that, it's funny."

Sesame Street had changed a lot since Hunt's early days. The new generation now performed the bulk of the segments, with the shining exception of stalwart Caroll Spinney. Clash's giggly Elmo was on the ascent while the average viewer age was on the decline. But when Hunt came onto the set, it was like nothing had changed: his booming voice announcing his arrival, his personal greeting for each individual, his penchant to entertain everyone even when the cameras were off. He continued to influence the next generation, catching the eye of a visiting young performer while ad-libbing with a butler puppet. "Richard had the puppet's hands behind his back and he was very funny, but the stuff he was saying off camera was even funnier, he was cracking the crew up," says Joey Mazzarino, who would join up shortly and stay for fifteen years, emulating Hunt with his playful improvising. "I just said, 'I want to be that guy!'" And so the legacy would endure.

To celebrate *Sesame Street*'s milestone, in fall 1988 Hunt and his colleagues filmed an anniversary special, *Sesame Street: 20 and Still Counting*—and Hunt got to check a major item off his wish list. Hunt's avian opera singer Placido Flamingo sang a duet with the famed tenor on whom the character was based, Placido *Domingo*, a thrill for the longtime opera fan. The two Placidos sing *Sesame* composer Joe Raposo's lovely "Look Through the Window." Though Hunt's character is meant to be parodic, the duet is truly beautiful, with Hunt delivering a dead-on rendition of Domingo's gilded tenor. "Richard was nervous, but he held his own," recalls Larry Mirkin. "Placido Domingo really enjoyed doing it too." Hunt would later mention the moment as a highlight of his career, calling it "fun." The special is poignant in hindsight, the last major *Sesame* hurrah for a number of artists, including Hunt, Henson, actor Northern Calloway, and Raposo, to whom it is dedicated. The special snagged an Emmy nomination for "Outstanding Special Event."

Fall 1988 was a season of anniversaries, commemorating time's passage with an increasing consciousness. While *Sesame Street* turned twenty, Hunt's mother turned sixty, an event which Hunt marked in November with a huge surprise birthday party on a barge in the East River. He staged the whole event, hoping to elicit genuine surprise from a woman who, like him, was always on, always performing. He told Jane the party was for *Sesame* director Jon Stone, and asked her to perform, an impressive gig with over one hundred guests. He instructed Jane's partner Arthur Miller to make her late for the party, so Miller pretended not to know how to get from the Upper West Side over to Brooklyn Heights, as Jane grew increasingly agitated. "You've lived in New York your whole life and you don't know where the Brooklyn Bridge is!" she railed at him. She was rattled, as planned, when she finally arrived, supposedly an hour late. Hunt met his mother outside, escorting her to a front-row seat beside him. The performances had already started; Stuart Fischer was onstage in a spotlight singing "Don't Tell Mama" from *Cabaret*, a little too on the nose: "Hush up, don't tell Mama. Shush up, don't tell Mama." Jane squinted at the audience in the dim light. She could swear a woman a few rows back looked like a childhood friend from Ohio, but what would she be doing at a party for Jon Stone?

The instant Fischer finished his song, the house lights came up blazing. The audience members stood up, one by one, as Hunt had instructed them: Jane's family and friends from the last sixty years, from Marietta and the Bronx and Closter and Elmwood and Manhattan, like an episode of *This Is Your Life*. Hunt watched proudly, wearing a great big "gotcha" grin, as the understanding lit up Jane's face and she joyfully sprang from her seat. "I got up and danced and I said, 'This party is for *me!*'"

Hunt looked out for his whole family. Youngest sister Rachel's experience with the medical industry had inspired her to pursue a career as a Child Life practitioner, helping children and their families cope with illness and treatment. She was applying for scholarships when Hunt said, "Don't be ridiculous. Scholarships are for people who can't afford to pay for college. I can afford it." So Hunt gave his sister what she calls "the greatest gift ever": a college education.

Drawing his loved ones close, Hunt reconciled with his old Closter friend Glenn Mure—even if he had to be tricked into it. The friends hadn't spoken since their falling out. "They hated each other's guts," says mutual friend Fischer, who couldn't stand to see them fighting any longer. Fischer invited both men to his apartment for dinner, making sure Mure arrived first. When the buzzer rang, Fischer hurried over to the stereo and put on the triumphal scene from *Aida*, Mure looking at him quizzically. "Richard walked in, and bing! The two of them started talking as if nothing had happened."

The reunion came just in time. In early February 1989, Mure collapsed onstage in Paris during a State Department tour of "You're a

Good Man, Charlie Brown." He couldn't afford to fly home, so Hunt paid the fare. In a sense, Hunt and Mure had switched places over the years. Hunt had been envious of Mure at Yale, watching him rehearse *The Fantasticks*, sleeping on the floor of his dorm room, cadging his leftovers in the dining hall. But now Hunt was the more successful performer, taking care of his old friend. This didn't surprise Hunt, who had been raised to see people as inherently equal; privilege and fortune were merely the luck of the draw, and he knew it could just as easily have been him in Mure's shoes.

Glenn Mure died in Manhattan of AIDS-related complications on February 26, 1989, just thirty-eight years old. Then on March 27, Hunt's high school choreographer Gerald "Buddy" Teijelo also died of AIDS-related complications, at the age of fifty-nine. The loss was piling up, and the clock seemed to be ticking even more loudly.

Hunt took refuge in Truro as the weather warmed, especially grateful for the house since it had been rebuilt. Losing Teijelo reminded him to appreciate his friendship with his high school music teacher, Gail Poch, whom he invited up to the Cape. He was direct and low-key about having to look after his health. "If I need to, I'm going to go lie down and take a nap, and that's the way it is, don't worry about it," he told Poch. But Hunt wasn't too tired to enjoy his brand-new car, a mint condition 1960s sea-green Cadillac convertible with fins, so big it seemed an entire block long. "He was like a kid with a new toy," says Poch. When they took the car on its inaugural run to Provincetown for dinner, he insisted on having the top down despite the evening's chill and fog—it would be more fun that way.

Hunt also mustered the energy for a bit of "Baseball Glasnost": in August he flew to Detroit, Moscow, and Leningrad to film Beaker and Scooter segments for a documentary called "To Russia with Baseball: A Muppet Report." No other Muppet performers were involved in the film, in which Beaker and Scooter gave sportscaster commentary on a landmark tour of exhibition baseball games between a team of fourteen-year-old American All-Stars and Soviet teenagers. Though producer Okean Films pitched the film widely throughout the next couple of years, the project was never finished.

The *Faffner Hall* cast had a reunion of sorts in September at Pete and Jane Coogan's wedding in the East Midlands, as their show premiered in England and the United States. When Coogan had invited Hunt to the wedding, Hunt had pretended to be busy: "Fuck off, I'm doing my hair that weekend." As usual, the more he liked you, the more he ribbed you and gave you a hard time. Hunt was glad to attend, as he was close with both Pete and Jane. Though he seemed a little tired at the celebration, a low-energy Hunt could still run circles around everyone else.

Hunt was so happy about the Coogans' marriage that he insisted they honeymoon in his Truro house, loaning them the house for ten days as well as organizing the fun, writing out a long list of recommended local restaurants and bars. "You're going to have a great time, and I'm going to tell you where to go," he said. When Coogan went to pay the bill at the first bar, the Diana Ross drag queen behind the counter refused to take his money. "Oh no, the drinks are on Richard," she said. Coogan's currency was no good again at a different restaurant a few days later, after a big meal and a bottle of wine. The experience repeated itself a half-dozen times. Hunt had made the rounds in advance and had all the establishments put the Coogans' meals on his tab. Unless they went somewhere off the list, Coogan recalls, "We simply could not buy a meal in Provincetown."

The newlyweds capped off their trip with a stay in Hunt's Manhattan apartment. As they prepared to fly back to the United Kingdom, they discussed how to repay Hunt's generosity. Noticing a vase of dried flowers in his room, they decided to throw them out and replace them with a fresh bouquet. But when Hunt came home and noticed the new flowers, he immediately became upset. "It transpired that that was the last bunch of flowers he'd had with Nelson," said Coogan. "We were like, *Oh shit*." But with a tear in his eye, Hunt thanked them, saying, "It's time for me to move on."

Coogan will never forget saying goodbye to Hunt at the airport, at the end of an idyllic honeymoon: "He gives Jane a big hug and a kiss, and I go to hug him, and he turns and walks away and gives me the finger under the arm. That was it! That was Richard."

The Ghost of Faffner Hall met a warm reception on both sides of the ocean, with all thirteen episodes airing through the fall. Audiences especially appreciated the show's musicality. "This one sings," said *People* magazine. Some critics felt the show needed more consistency in its tone, more balance between its educational and entertainment aspects, issues the show hoped to work out in a second season. Unfortunately, to much regret, *The Ghost of Faffner Hall* was not renewed.

Henson, too, faced disappointment, striking out with his new pet project *The Jim Henson Hour*, which for Hunt had been the road not taken. While Hunt had filmed *The Ghost of Faffner Hall* in Newcastle, segments of *The Jim Henson Hour* had filmed in his old stomping grounds of Toronto, with his close colleagues Nelson, Goelz, Whitmire, and Mills among those involved. The hourlong show, modeled after the wide-ranging anthology format of Walt Disney's long-standing Sunday evening series, had an ambitious, grab-bag design, ranging from quirky experiments in digital puppetry to macabre dramatizations of classic fairy tales.

This multifariousness may have impeded the show's success. Stevenson and Henson compared notes as their shows progressed. They both had difficulty securing guest stars at first, but Henson continued having trouble much further into production. "Why are you getting guests and we aren't?" Henson asked Stevenson. She answered him frankly: "Because our show is *about* something, Jim."

Stevenson's instincts proved right, as *The Jim Henson Hour* swiftly came and went in spring 1989. Audiences were unsure of what to expect from the NBC Friday night slot. It didn't help that the first episode was *Sesame Street: 20 and Still Counting*, leading viewers to assume that what they saw on NBC would be little different from what they saw on PBS. Certainly NBC didn't give the show a chance. Henson had advocated for the show to be moved to Sunday evenings, but when the network made the switch abruptly and without promotion for the fifth episode on Mother's Day weekend, audiences didn't follow—and NBC pulled the plug. Four more episodes aired over the summer, but some of *The Jim Henson Hour*'s best work, including the intriguing, behind-the-scenes "Secrets of the Muppets," didn't air until years later, or never aired at all.

Henson's disappointment motivated him to move forward with a controversial idea that had been quietly simmering for some time: selling the Muppets to the Walt Disney Company, making his own company a subsidiary and ceding his position as top boss. Suddenly everything seemed up in the air. Hunt worried that the Muppets as he knew them were ending. And they were—but not in the way that he thought.

The core Muppet troupe, New York, 1989. Clockwise from left: Dave Goelz, Hunt, Steve Whitmire, Jerry Nelson, Jim Henson, and Frank Oz.

CHAPTER 17

Saying Goodbye

A T HIS TWENTIETH HIGH SCHOOL reunion in March 1990—a big
Richard Hunt party—Hunt used his Muppet characters to act out
the stages of life. "I had something to tell these kids I grew up with," he
said later. "I played our lives. And I did it through these puppets."

To represent life's final stage, Hunt put on Statler, one of the two old
men from the *Muppet Show* balcony. He bore a striking resemblance to
the aged character with his own receding hairline and bushy gray
eyebrows.

"Where's the other guy?" Statler asked—meaning Waldorf, played
by Henson.

"I think he died," Hunt replied.

"Oh," said Statler. "He forgot to say goodbye!"

1990 opened with Hunt and his Muppet colleagues filming and recording a number of projects for the Walt Disney Company—a good-faith
gesture toward the merger of the two enterprises.

"The Disney deal," as everyone called it, was underway. Ironically,
Henson had considered buying the Walt Disney Company in 1984; now
the shoe was on the other foot, and Disney wanted to buy *Henson* (and
his company). Henson met with Disney chief executive Michael Eisner
on May 29, 1989, just after *The Jim Henson Hour* got canceled, and shook
hands on a possible deal. On August 25, at 12:30 in the morning after hours
of haggling, Henson and the company signed a tentative, nonbinding

agreement-in-principle: in exchange for $150 million in Disney stock, Henson would sell the Walt Disney Company the copyrights to the Muppet characters (except the *Sesame Street* characters and possibly some others); Henson would also essentially sell *himself* to the company for fifteen years, and they would own any creative output on his part.

Henson wanted to sell the Muppets to Disney because he wanted to be creative. He wanted to be surprised again. He wanted to try new things. This is the man who quit doing *The Muppet Show* at the height of its popularity when he could have easily kept it going at least another five years, because he felt he had done all that he could with the medium. Yes, he was in charge of this huge company, juggling offices in New York and England—but, at heart, he was an artist. With this deal, the buck wouldn't always stop with him; and he wouldn't always have to go chasing the buck. He could spend less time in the world of the board-room and more time in the world of the imagination. Henson was also excited by the potential of doing Muppet projects in the Disney theme parks, such as rides and immersive experiences; he always enjoyed experimenting with new forms.

What's more, Disney looked promising for the Muppets' legacy. The company excelled at keeping characters in the public eye long after their performers had passed on; Mickey Mouse, for example, while initially vocalized by Walt Disney himself, was still going strong over two decades after Disney's death. Hunt later surmised that maintaining his legacy was one of Henson's main motivations for the deal: "He wanted the characters to live on," said Hunt. "He said to me he thought there was more integrity in the Disney company to keep characters as they are, which I don't agree with. And I think he learned that but didn't want to learn it at the same time."

Despite the handshake and the tentative agreement-in-principle, plenty of specifics needed to be ironed out before the Disney deal could be completed—many of which had important ramifications for Hunt and his fellow Muppet company members. Would Jim Henson Productions be a wholly independent company, or wholly subordinate to Disney, or something in between? What would that look like?

And how would the transition be handled? Would the company be downsized and people laid off? Undoubtedly it would be a marked switch to go from answering to Henson, who had likely handpicked you and appreciated the full picture of your quirks and assets, to reporting to a faceless corporation. It seemed unlikely that Disney would treat the Henson employees—especially old hands like Hunt—with the same attention, trust, and respect they received from Henson himself.

Especially important for Hunt was the question of how the deal would affect the performers. Disney didn't seem to understand the medium of puppetry; they seemed to think of it like animation, as if it entailed merely doing voices rather than physically embodying the puppet, requiring skills that took years of training to master.

Disney also seemed to disregard the special relationship between the performers and their characters, perceiving Hunt and his colleagues as largely replaceable. Would Henson even get to select and train his puppeteers? Performer Pam Arciero articulates the worst-case scenario in many people's minds: "They were going to put a Muppet in every single theme park all over the world, and just hire someone to do the voice. That's not who we are." With a half-dozen interchangeable Scooters around the globe, would Hunt's individual stamp on the character retain any value? Even Henson worried about losing the rights to Kermit, his Muppet alter ego. What if someone else's Kermit spoke or behaved in a way that contradicted Henson's long-honed, carefully constructed persona? It seemed clear to many performers that Disney had far less interest in the quality of the puppetry than in the Muppet brand's potential to make money. "We all hated the Disney deal," says Arciero. "Because we didn't know what it was going to bring." Hunt, too, was opposed to the deal, complaining about it with his fellow performers.

But even as the deal was being determined, and despite the performers' opposition, the Muppets got down to work on Disney-related projects. Starting in January 1990, Hunt, Henson, Oz, Goelz, Whitmire, Rudman, Mullen, and a dozen others—with Nelson notably absent—filmed two separate movies for a Walt Disney World theme park attraction called Muppet*Vision 3-D: a main 3-D movie and a non-3-D preshow. Already Henson was gleefully tinkering with the technology afforded by the potential deal. Both movies were written by Bill Prady, who later co-created the sitcom *The Big Bang Theory*.

Though heralding changes in the Muppets, the preshow was filmed on intimate, familiar ground: the Henson carriage house on Manhattan's Upper East Side. In a cute conceit, the thirteen-minute film portrays the characters setting up for the main 3-D movie. Hunt's Scooter is in charge backstage, a nice nod to real life, though sounding worrisomely nasal, indicative of Hunt's increasing respiratory challenges.

The preshow amusingly plays with technology in that it uses three television sets: sometimes they're treated like one big screen, with characters moving back and forth between them; sometimes they're treated like three identical screens, with mirrored identical action; and sometimes the concept gets shaken up for a laugh, such as when three identical Gonzos dance to "Tea for Two" with flowerpots on their heads, and one Gonzo's flowerpot crashes to the ground. (Who better to perform this than Goelz, with his experience playing *Fraggle Rock*'s multiple Sidebottoms?) Directed by David Gumpel, the preshow reflects its era in Whitmire's increased role: the ubiquitous cuteness of Bean Bunny, as well as Rizzo the Rat's fun gag of pretending to be Mickey Mouse.

Hunt and his colleagues mostly shot the main 3-D movie on Stage 3 at Disney Studios in Burbank, California. Distressingly suggestive of how the Disney deal might go, the Disney lawyers haggled fiercely with Henson over his $1.2 million budget for the film, most of which he needed to pay the performers, as well as over his own director's salary.

The 3-D movie—actually not much longer than the preshow—would be shown in a reproduction of the theater from *The Muppet Show*, featuring an animatronic Statler and Waldorf sitting in a side balcony, voiced by Henson and Hunt. These mechanically controlled animatronic Muppets seemed to embody (or at least enable) the Disney perception of puppeteers as mere voice actors, in this case without even a puppeteer needed to physically manipulate the characters. Still, Statler and Waldorf interact with the onscreen characters in a way that is wonderfully reminiscent of their role on *The Muppet Show*.

Onscreen, the characters act in keeping with their established personas: Kermit is in charge, showing viewers around the studio, promising they won't do any "cheap 3-D tricks"; Fozzie, of course, does every cheap 3-D trick in the book; Miss Piggy acts the diva and sings a ballad; Sam the Eagle blusters through a patriotic number; and the adorable Bean Bunny, again in an increased role, pesters everyone as he tries to help.

Hunt's one fully puppeteered character here—both physically and vocally—is Beaker, who, characteristically, is injured in the name of science. Hunt also plays Sweetums, who in a neat gimmick appears both onscreen and in the audience at the same time. However, Hunt only contributes the character's voice; when Sweetums strolls across the screen, playing with a paddleball that seems to bounce out at the audience, it's John Henson inside the heavy, full-body costume. (John Henson began physically playing Sweetums around 1987, possibly hinting at Hunt's health woes, but also of Hunt's rise in the company: he was no longer an apprentice, needing to be willing to do anything.) Meanwhile, another performer in a walkaround costume plays Sweetums ambling around the theater, shining a flashlight at the audience and lip-synching prerecorded lines. At one point the audience Sweetums has some dialogue with Statler and Waldorf, with Hunt doing both voices.

The 3-D movie ends with a fun metajoke from the animatronic old men in the balcony: Waldorf asks Statler if they have time to go to the bathroom before the next screening; Statler says they can't, because they're bolted to the seats—which they are.

In the off-hours in Los Angeles, Hunt often hung out at Henson's house in Malibu, high on the bluffs overlooking the Pacific Ocean. As usual, Hunt was a pied piper trailed by a group of kids, including producer Martin Baker's twelve- and nine-year-olds, taking them all to play on the beach. "Someone would say, 'Where are the kids?'" Baker recalls. "You'd say, 'Oh, they've gone off with Richard,' and you didn't worry! He was Uncle Richard."

In a further show of good faith toward the Disney deal, Hunt and his colleagues—the full Original Five, plus Whitmire—also recorded vocals for two live shows to be staged in the theme parks. Again, this project fueled the performers' fears that their puppetry would be undervalued by Disney, as these vocals would be lip-synched by minimum-wage park employees wearing full-sized walkaround suits. The live shows featured Kermit, Piggy, Fozzie, Gonzo, Bean Bunny, and the members of the Electric Mayhem; Hunt's only character was Janice. She served as emcee in "The Muppets on Location: Days of Swine and Roses," introducing the band members as well as the autograph break, in addition to singing the Beatles' "Ob-La-Di, Ob-La-Da." And Janice memorably closed out the other live show, a stage revue called "Here Come the Muppets," with a familiar joke: as the audience left, the Muppets could be heard talking backstage—until Janice awkwardly realized that she was still audible, making this the *third* time she does this gag.

Increasingly aware of the clock ticking, Hunt had some more things he wanted to wrap up. He wanted to give the people he had grown up with some thoughts on life, and to try to connect with them while he still had the chance.

Twenty years after graduating from Northern Valley Regional High School, Hunt still ran into his classmates from time to time. He had first met Barbara McDonald in the fifth grade, when she slapped him for making fun of her as they waited in line to go in after recess. And he'd never forget falling onto a fencepost during a kickball game at her thirteenth birthday party; they had to break up the party to rush him to the hospital. But in early 1990, the two were in a place to really connect. "It was a time of confusion and loss and change," says McDonald. Her parents had just died, within two months of each other; she had sold her Manhattan graphic design business and moved back to Closter to care for them. Now she was closing up their home, tying up loose ends, and finding herself with a surfeit of free time. People were encouraging her to organize a belated twentieth high school reunion, but she couldn't be bothered—until Hunt asked her to do it.

When the two spoke about the possibility of organizing a reunion, Hunt stressed how important it was to him. "He told me his lover died in his arms from AIDS," says McDonald. She volunteered as a buddy with Gay Men's Health Crisis, helping people with AIDS do the ordinary tasks that had become insurmountable with illness: buying groceries, preparing meals, paying bills. She didn't need him to spell out why this reunion needed to happen *now*.

Hunt convinced McDonald to spearhead the event, paying her long distance bills as she spent six weeks tracking down and calling up all 300 of their classmates all over the country. Hunt also subsidized the reunion, never forgetting his hard-luck roots. "I don't want money to be a reason why people can't come," he told McDonald. "Tell me how much I have to pay to make the tickets $20 for everyone." Yet for all his contributions, Hunt was nervous about the gathering, confessing over a drink with McDonald and fellow organizer Jerry Raymond that he felt distant from their classmates. "He started talking about how he didn't think people really liked him," says McDonald, who nearly spit out her drink in surprise. "I said, 'That is just not true. You were really loved.' He was shocked."

Over two-thirds of the Northern Valley class of 1969 turned up on the evening of March 17, 1990, for their twentieth reunion at the Florentine Gardens, a brick Georgian-style manor in River Vale, New Jersey, not far from Closter. But this wasn't just any reunion—this was a Richard Hunt party, and it was his job to make sure everyone had a good time.

Characteristically, Hunt played host, kicking off the gathering with an introductory speech. He encouraged everyone to move freely through the three rooms, stopping as they pleased at the multiple bars and buffet tables, enjoying the music, looking forward to the meal to be served at 9:30 P.M. He exhorted everyone to be friendly, even to people they didn't know. He also admitted his own fears about the event. "How many people got cold feet?" he asked, raising his own hand. "Everybody. Everybody was terrified. No reason to be. This is one of these light, entertaining evenings. So enjoy yourselves! At some point, just turn and say hello to the person next to you. Let them know that you remember they're alive." He paused and added, "Those of you that are still assholes, please, keep it to yourself." This got a big laugh.

Hunt and his classmates circulated, ate and drank, and caught up with each other. And indeed, encouraged by Hunt, people did try to go out of their way to speak to people they didn't necessarily already know, or know well.

A Hunt party would not be complete without entertainment, of course, so at one point Hunt got up before the assembled guests and took the mic. He looked healthy in his shirt and tie, but compared to his usual self his energy seemed lower, his voice nasal, his hair increasingly white, especially around the temples.

Hunt began by claiming that his performance wasn't his idea. "Barbara said, 'Come on, Richard, you gotta show everybody what you do.' I said, 'No, I don't. I went through eighth grade already, I don't need that again. I know what these people are like.'" Though clearly a joke, the remark showed that he had never forgotten the tough time his classmates had given him in middle school. This was his chance to lay some of those demons to rest, to show his peers what he had made of himself.

"So, I thought I'd let you know, first of all, who I do, so we get this over once and for all. I am not Big Bird. I am not Miss Piggy. I am not Fozzie Bear. I am not Gonzo. Well then, who the hell are you?" Hunt ran through his Sesame Street characters, speaking in each of their voices in turn: Forgetful Jones, Placido Flamingo, Gladys the Cow, Don Music, the Two-Headed Monster, *Fraggle Rock*'s little rat Gunge and his local origins—"He talks like dis, like some of us from New Jersey, all's you gotta do."

But then Hunt's performance turned more solemn, more reflective of their experiences. Hunt used his main Muppet characters to act out the phases of life.

"I want to talk about the four stages of us," said Hunt. He put on a Scooter puppet and spoke through his young alter ego: *"I'm the first stage."* Hunt used Scooter to run through a rapid-fire comedy routine, name-dropping their teachers at Tenakill Elementary, the Village School, and Northern Valley, racing through imitations of bantering English teacher Vincent Fondacaro, outré film teacher Rodney Sheratsky ("Film is *film*"), strict disciplinarian Anthony Colantoni, the comedic senior assembly. "Then what happened?" Hunt asked. "We got out of high school. And we were on our way someplace else."

To represent the second stage, Hunt put on the dog puppet from *Puppetman*, speaking in his Leo the Party Monster voice. "Oh boy oh boy! College! Sex, drugs, and rock and roll. Yeah, it was a fun four years. Very informative. Very educational. I didn't learn a thing!" (Though Hunt didn't go to college, he certainly followed high school with a parallel apprentice period.)

But then Hunt put down the puppet, wearing a serious face and speaking in his own voice. "It was the real world. We'd been promised this thing by our parents, the American Dream. Remember that? Honey, all you have to do is go to college, and then you'll have a big house in New Jersey. Right! And two big cars, and vacations, and so much money you won't know what to do with it, and plenty of time. And the kids, kids are nothing, they're just around when you want them around. This is the American dream! As we have all seen for the last twenty years, we've just been having the time of our lives."

Hunt used Beaker to represent the third stage, shrieking and squeaking in Beaker's frantic, high-pitched gibberish. "Now Beaker, settle down. Aren't you having the time of your life? [Beaker gibberish] You owe money? [Beaker gibberish] You can't afford to buy a house? The kids are on you every minute of the day? [Beaker gibberish] What do you want to do when that happens? [Beaker plunges his head down into his shirt.] That doesn't do you much good, does it? Well, let me tell you, there are good times and there are bad times. It gets better though. Yeah, it does. Yeah, I promise."

Hunt addressed the audience directly. "It's been tough in the last few years. Jerry Raymond and Barbara McDonald and I organized this reunion. Jerry's wife's mother just died this morning. And this brings it back to us once again. Probably we've all lost parents, or friends, or lovers, even children maybe. That's a tough thing for us to go through, but we do go through it. And we have a responsibility to keep living our lives."

Hunt segued into a passionate performance of "Move On" from Stephen Sondheim's *Sunday in the Park with George*. The song is a perfect choice for a reunion, for taking a moment to look back on the last twenty years: "I chose and my world was shaken/So what?/The choice may have been mistaken/The choosing was not." Hunt gestured to the whole room as he sang, "We always belong together. We will always belong together." His voice sounded a bit shaky, but he put his whole heart into the song, receiving huge applause from his classmates.

To represent life's final stage, Hunt put on Statler, one of the two old men from the *Muppet Show* balcony. Hunt had the puppet take a verse as he sang "Try to Remember" from the long-running show *The Fantasticks*, again a perfect song for the occasion, about getting through hard times by visualizing the happier times in your past.

"What a life, huh?" Hunt asked the audience at the end of his performance. "We sure had a good one. We had a funny life. Not over yet. Thank you."

After dinner was served, McDonald found Hunt eating alone in a small private room. "I said, 'What are you doing in here?' He said, 'Come in here, I want to talk to you.' That was when he told me that he had AIDS. I said, 'I know, Richard.' He said, 'Why didn't you say anything?' I said, 'I wanted to wait for it to come from you.'"

Hunt's quiet hibernation made a striking contrast with his extroverted public self. "It was an interesting dichotomy," McDonald mused. "Here he is in front of everybody, doing his shtick, and the next thing you know he's hiding in a side room all by himself eating." Ultimately, McDonald feels that Hunt got what he wanted out of the reunion: "It was closure for him."

The closure from his high school reunion was just the beginning of a spiritual change in Hunt. A few years after his lover Nelson Bird's death, he had convinced himself that he had moved on. "But in reality I was clinging to him," he said. "I had this stone that was a connection between the two of us and I carried it in this pocket for four years. I literally was clinging to him through this object. Whenever I was sad or anxious or afraid or whatever, I would hold the stone."

Around the time of his reunion, he went to a somatic Native American therapist, an uncharacteristic move, and had an epiphany that shifted his whole thinking: "What happened was, I said, 'Can I keep this green stone?' He said, 'What's the problem?' I actually started crying and said, 'My mind won't let my heart do what it knows is right.' I said, 'Nelson brought me to life and I'm afraid,' because I haven't had another relationship since. I was clinging to Nelson desperately in this stone and I had to let go of it."

Just articulating the sentiment, and having it heard, snapped Hunt into a different mindset. "It was like getting hit with a wave and then the water receding. And so I made a shift with Nelson which was so important." Hunt gave the stone to a friend to hold onto for him.

Hunt's "shift" on Bird, in turn, led to other changes in perspective. "It got me into this understanding of myself as a human being and as part of this existence and this universe. I found myself in this place of enlightenment which we all possess, but we can't get to, because we usually try too hard." Hunt felt calmer than ever before, building on the peacefulness that had begun from the moment he met Bird nearly a decade earlier. "Here all of a sudden Richard, this crazy off-the-wall, never-shuts-up, never-sits-down person was extremely calm," he said. "People would say, 'What's wrong with you?' 'Nothing. We are all one.' I mean, make a joke about it. But whenever I was in any of these places within myself I felt it was important to share it."

Hunt was having trouble holding onto his newfound calm in late March amid the cheery cacophony of the Disney World theme park in Orlando, Florida, filming *The Muppets at Walt Disney World*. The NBC special immersed the Muppet characters in the Disney milieu, and served as the biggest promotion yet for the upcoming merger.

A high school friend had given Hunt two books by American Buddhist author Stephen Levine, which he had thrown into his Florida luggage. "He's written two books that are particularly important to me: *Healing into Life and Death*, about how we as a society have always been very much afraid of death instead of realizing it's there, babe." Hunt was also reading *A Gradual Awakening*, the best-selling introduction to meditation and to learning to be more present in everyday life. "I'd start to read it and it'd say exactly what I had just gone through. So it was an interesting supportive thing."

But Disney World was hardly the place for this kind of spiritual thinking. "I started going nuts. Orlando was going to kill me. *Oh, God, I'm going to lose this*—because I'd had this incredible shift and it was too important to let go. I said, I should be able to do this in a garbage dump, but it's just too much." Thankfully, after a couple of weeks Hunt spent a free weekend with friends who lived an hour away on the ocean, where the nature and downtime brought him back to himself.

Around 9 A.M. on the morning of April 9, Hunt was back at the studio, drinking tea and reading his usual newspaper, when he saw an obituary that took his breath away. "Ryan White had finally died," said Hunt. "The boy with AIDS. He was an amazing kid." White, a hemophiliac, had contracted AIDS at age thirteen from a blood transfusion, and was subsequently ostracized and banned from attending school by his hometown of Kokomo, Indiana. The genial, all-American boy went on to become a household name, with a TV movie made about him and prominent supporters including Elton John, who was at his bedside when he died on April 8 at age eighteen.

Hunt was reading the obituary when Henson approached his table with a bun and a cup of coffee. "Hi, Richard," said Henson. "Mind if I share your table?"

"Sure," Hunt replied. "I'm reading about Ryan White, isn't he an amazing kid?"

"Anything, uh, new happening in your life?" Henson asked.

At first Hunt hesitated, his mind racing as he considered whether to truly answer the question. Henson was central to any production, with everyone asking him questions and demanding his attention. "I went, *Oh, my God, I can't start this conversation; there's gonna be people coming in here at any time. It's something you can't just tell in pieces.* This was all split-second. I said, *I can't talk to him about this.* I said, *No, it's too important, this has to do with him too.* I said, *Yes!* And I just focused myself. It created this invisible wall around us." Occasionally people would approach their table, see the two men deep in conversation, and turn away on their own. "Nobody bothered us."

Hunt was able to tell Henson about his spiritual shift and, presumably, his illness. "I went through this thing and he listened intently to the experience, because it is a shared experience, this being able to let go and move on. It's so much that philosophy of searching and pursuing your dreams. That 'going back there someday.'" Hunt is referencing the *Muppet Movie* song "I'm Going to Go Back There Someday," which he seemed to interpret as returning from whence we came.

For the rest of his life, Hunt treasured this moment of mutual attention and connection. "In retrospect, I realized that my going through it, my pulling him in on it—I think that was part of the gift we gave each other. Knowing that, no, something important enough is worth grabbing and holding onto the other person for that moment."

Hunt's talk with Henson wasn't his only important conversation in Orlando. Whitmire found out that Hunt was HIV-positive, though he had heard murmurs about it since *Fraggle Rock*. "I probably heard it officially during the filming of the Disney World special," Whitmire recalls. "I think that's when he told us all." Around this time, Hunt also shared his diagnosis with his friend Mark Zeszotek, a Muppet workshop builder and designer who wrangled puppets for the special. Zeszotek had some news for him: he was HIV-positive too. The epidemic truly was everywhere.

Poignantly, *The Muppets at Walt Disney World* was the last major hurrah for the Original Five of Henson, Oz, Nelson, Hunt, and Goelz—as well as for the expansion thereof that Hunt called the Original Eight, with the addition of Whitmire, Clash, and Rudman. They were joined by Camille Bonora and a half-dozen other performers playing smaller roles and assisting. Familiar faces Diana Birkenfield and Martin Baker produced, veteran Muppet writer Jerry Juhl penned the script, and *Muppet Show* director Peter Harris was at the helm. It would be the end of an era.

Despite being a flagrant hour-long ad for Disney World, the special makes good use of the potential humor in the concept of letting the Muppet characters loose in the park. Juhl brings his usual entertaining attention to character detail, such as Gonzo forgoing the park's more mainstream attractions in order to serenade his chicken gal pal Camilla in its extensive laundry facilities. Juhl also nicely utilizes Nelson's characters, bringing back Fozzie's mother Emily Bear after her beloved presence in *A Muppet Family Christmas*, and writing sweet scenes between Kermit and his nephew Robin. The costume crew outdid themselves for the Electric Mayhem, who play "Rockin' All Around the World" as they tour Epcot Center's World Showcase, wearing everything from German lederhosen to fur-lined Inuit parkas to Mexican sombreros, plus an exquisite tiny kimono for Janice. (Clash's cool humanoid Clifford does a great job in his one appearance with the band.) And it wouldn't be a Muppet special without Kermit singing "The Rainbow Connection," this time with charming child star Raven-Symoné.

Hunt's characters are especially true to form, and true to *him*: when the Muppets meet Kermit's frog relatives (since Disney World is located near the swamp), Scooter is the one to try to learn everybody's names, as well as to say of Bean Bunny, "The rest of us got sick of being cute so we hired him to do it." (Again, Hunt's illness is audible in his voice.) The unfortunate Beaker gets a bucket stuck on his head for most of the special. And Statler and Waldorf don't like Disney World because it's so perfect that there's nothing for them to complain about. They appear in a cable car, singing the vaudeville standard "Who's Your Lady Friend" to a clearly tickled elderly woman, changing the lyrics to suit the occasion: "Who's the girl I saw you with at Epcot?"

In what could be read as an ironic metaphor for the controversial Disney deal, the Muppet characters don't pay the entrance fee for the park, so a security guard played by Charles Grodin tries to throw them out. But the Muppets' hides are saved when Kermit turns out to know Mickey Mouse, taking everyone in to meet him in a nice combination of puppetry and animation.

Yet even there, the two alter egos don't quite see eye to eye. When Robin says Walt Disney World is "like a dream come true," Mickey replies, "You know what we say: 'When you wish upon a star, your dreams come true.'"

Kermit chimes in, "Well actually, what *we* say is, 'Someday you'll find it, the rainbow connection, the lovers, the dreamers and me.'"

"Uh oh, they're starting to argue philosophy," quips Nelson's groovy bassist Floyd Pepper. Given the contentiousness of the Disney deal, the joke is funny in more ways than one.

The Muppets at Walt Disney World aired on May 6 on NBC as an episode of Disney's Sunday night prime time anthology series, *The Magical World of Disney*. Ten days later, Hunt's world turned upside down when Jim Henson unexpectedly died.

Hunt emcees Henson's memorial service, May 21, 1990.

CHAPTER 18

Sage

HUNT CAME HOME from the doctor on May 15, 1990, in a funk, his mind occupied by his health. He'd had a bad cough for a few months, which Dr. Bobby Friedman had thought might be asthma, but now, after an unsettling X-ray, seemed to herald something worse. "Something showed up [on the X-ray] and he didn't know what it was," Hunt recounted. "And I went home, I thought, 'Oh my god, what is this all about?'"

Hunt's worried distraction was interrupted by the phone. "It was Frank [Oz]; he said, 'Jim's died, come to the hospital.'"

Hunt and his colleagues had actually kidded about Henson's health the day before, because it was the first time they had ever known him to miss a day of work. Henson had stayed home after a few days of feeling under the weather, figuring he had a cold or mild flu. "We were joking around, we said, 'He's either really sick, or he's finally getting smart and staying away from all this stuff,'" Hunt said. They, too, thought it was just a bad cold and maybe a fever—nothing serious.

Hunt hung up the phone and raced across town to New York Hospital. He walked into Henson's room in the Intensive Care Unit to discover that Henson wasn't technically deceased, as Oz had said—but that the man they had known was gone. Diagnosed at the hospital with severe pneumonia and renal failure, Henson had slipped into unconsciousness around 7 A.M. By the time Hunt arrived, Henson was breathing only with the help of a breathing tube, his body starting to shut down. "I walked in—I'm so used to this stuff—I looked across the room and he was attached to a lot of stuff," said Hunt. "I knew. I deal with these things on a very cosmic level." Still, Hunt's priority was to support Henson's loved ones. "I told the family, don't give up. Don't, 'til it's over."

Hunt was one of many of Henson's family members and colleagues who gathered at the hospital over the course of the day, including Henson's wife Jane; his daughters Cheryl, Lisa, and Heather; his son John (his son Brian, working in England, was frantically trying to make it back to the States); Oz; Nelson; Whitmire; Mullen; and others. While they waited around in the hallway outside Henson's room, Hunt told Mullen that he was HIV-positive. "I got my diagnosis," he said. For her, it was a harrowing piece of news on an already harrowing day.

Jim Henson died of Group A streptococcal pneumonia at 1:21 A.M. on May 16, 1990; he was only fifty-three years old. Hunt was stunned. While he had certainly seen his share of death over the past decade, he had expected to precede his mentor out of this world. "Richard was just shaking his head when Jim died, because he was convinced he was going to go first," says Brian Meehl. "He was thrown by that."

After Henson's death, there were more surprises. Henson's attorneys from the law firm of Kleinberg, Kaplan, Wolff & Cohen gave the Henson children an envelope containing two letters from their father. He had written them on a quick, idyllic weekend in the south of France in March 1986, just before *Fraggle Rock* shot its last dozen episodes. In the midst of this beautiful moment in life, Henson had decided to prepare for his death.

In his letters, Henson outlined the "nice, friendly little service" he envisioned for his memorial, with his Muppet colleagues and friends speaking and singing, as well as a religious figure reading some classic texts "to remind us how this"—meaning death—"is all part of what is meant to be." Henson wanted a joyful celebration rather than a dour, somber service, with attendees in brightly colored clothes rather than the traditional black. Indeed, he wanted to go out with a bang—or, rather, with a trumpet blast, requesting that a Dixieland band conclude the service with a "rousing" rendition of "When the Saints Go Marching In." The letters were somewhat vague on exact particulars—who would say what, who would sing what, etc.—but Henson did specify whom he wanted at the podium: "It would be nice if Richard Hunt, if he's still around, would talk and emcee the thing."

It is hard not to look askance at that little clause, "if he's still around." Did Henson already suspect that Hunt was ill? When Henson wrote the letter, the two had not yet talked about Hunt's illness, nor had Hunt officially received his diagnosis. Perhaps Henson simply didn't expect the letter to be used so soon, as his death was so unexpected.

To Hunt, Henson's request felt like the ultimate redemption, quashing any lingering doubts over whether Henson appreciated him. Hunt had sometimes played a contrary role in the company, pushing back against decisions he disagreed with, such as when he demanded a pay raise for Mike Quinn during *The Dark Crystal*. "All those years I'd talk to him and say, 'Well, you can't do this or that or yaddada.' He'd go, 'Richard, please, I'm trying.' A lot of times he'd just walk away from me. I'd go, *dammit*, doesn't he know, arrgh—my youthful exuberance carrying on." So when Henson stipulated that Hunt should emcee the service, it felt like a huge affirmation. "To have Jim request this made me realize how much he respected me, and how many times when I could see him say, 'Richard, shut up,' that he was listening to me. I thought, 'Oh my God, he was listening all the time!'"

Nearly a quarter century earlier, Hunt had skipped his father's funeral, choosing instead to cast his lot with the Muppets. Now he was saying goodbye to another father figure, one who had expressed his thanks and approval even from beyond the grave, a kind of resolution he had never gotten with his own dad.

Hunt mused that the spiritual shift he had made just a couple of months before Henson's death—letting go of Bird, accepting death as a natural process—put him in the right frame of mind to emcee the memorial. "In retrospect it appears very strongly to me that I had gone through a very important change in my life, in order to be able to open my heart so honestly and speak for Jim's heart," Hunt said. "Because it is something you can't make up. It has to be true. You have to open up and expose yourself completely."

Henson picked Hunt to speak for him after his death, because hadn't Hunt been doing that all along? Hunt was the social ambassador of the

Muppets, their gregarious best foot forward, whether leading tours at *The Muppet Show*, holding auditions, training performers, welcoming guest stars, or intermediating with the crew. And now Hunt was in his usual role of emcee, bearing up himself (and everyone else) by putting on a show. He was standing in for Henson, as he often did at a wrap party—except now Henson wasn't there. Indeed, this was the ultimate wrap party, commemorating the end of an era.

Henson's colleagues had just five days to put together the memorial, organized by longtime Muppet producer Martin Baker. At first they weren't sure what it would look like, arguing amongst themselves, unmoored without their captain. But once they realized it would be a show, everything fell into place.

Over five thousand people packed the Cathedral of St. John the Divine on Manhattan's Upper West Side on May 21 at noon, with a line out the door even on a gray and rainy day. The service was open to the public, ensuring that every seat was taken, with people filling the pews and sitting in the aisles and on the floor in the back. Many in the audience—children and adults alike—clutched dolls of Henson's beloved characters such as Kermit and Ernie.

The audience watched as the Dirty Dozen Brass Band processed in playing a dirge, followed by the Reverend Canon Michael C. Kuhn, other religious figures, and the church choir in their red-and-white robes; then the performers and major Henson company figures walked up the aisle in pairs, with Hunt and Mullen bringing up the rear.

After the opening choral anthem and prayer, Hunt took the podium, looking noticeably skinnier than he had just two months earlier, his hairline having receded and his hair almost completely white.

"Welcome all," Hunt said. "We are here today to grieve the death and celebrate the life of Jim Henson. He requested that this be a happy occasion, and therefore asked that people could avoid wearing black. It seems that's happened quite well. This is my Jim Henson shirt." Hunt motioned to his dark green patterned shirt, far livelier than his usual stripes or solids. "I bought this the day I was going to look just like him. But someone else decided to look even more like him." Hunt pointed to Steve Whitmire in his electric green suit, to great laughter. "Kermit green. If you can find that at Barney's, I'll be surprised."

Hunt read some words from fans of *Sesame Street*, who appreciated its almost magical powers to mesmerize even the most difficult baby-sitting charges; to teach kindness, leadership, and character; and to inspire the imagination. "After seeing pigs and frogs that could speak and dance," said one fan, "I remember thinking *anything* was possible."

And while millions of children all over the world were watching *Sesame Street*, Hunt continued, their adult counterparts were equally entranced by *The Muppet Show*. "All over the world, people changed their dinner hour according to when it was shown in their local station," said Hunt. "Pubs in England would shift their opening hours. In the Eastern Bloc of Europe, when *The Muppet Show* was on, the streets of Czechoslovakia and Yugoslavia were empty. The one place they could escape to from the hard times they were having then was through the magic of Jim and his friends." Even far-flung Indonesia appreciated the Muppets. A friend of Hunt's had been visiting a tiny village in Sumatra on the day that Henson died. "They have one TV in their village," Hunt said. "And as Jim was leaving us, all the adults and all the children of this village sat around watching *The Muppet Show* and laughing at what Jim had left them."

Hunt wrapped up his introduction by ceding the stage to more of Henson's loved ones. Some speakers, such as Frank Oz and Henson's agent Bernie Brillstein, left the podium in tears. Writer Jerry Juhl took another playful dig at Whitmire's outfit. Duncan Kenworthy, wearing a somber gray suit, spoke of Henson's connection to England, and indeed to the entire world. (Kenworthy was the ideal person to point that out, as he had overseen many international co-productions of Henson projects, including *Sesame Street* and *Fraggle Rock*.) *Sesame Street* showrunner Jon Stone poignantly appreciated Henson's extended Muppet family. Allelu Kurton, of the international puppeteer organization UNIMA, praised Henson's generosity toward his fellow puppeteers. Puppet designer Michael Frith recounted a tale of a rough workday on *The Dark Crystal*. "Why is this so hard?" performer Kathy Mullen—Frith's wife—asked Henson, who replied calmly, "Because if it wasn't, everybody would be doing it."

Jerry Nelson read a wonderful beatnik-type poem in Floyd Pepper's voice, "Fearless Leader," praising Henson's "whim of steel." (Hunt later said the poem was "a very important piece, and very much Jerry Nelson.")

By now, Nelson, Hunt, and the others had largely resolved their initial resistance to puppeteering. "I started out to be a folksinger, maybe an actor," said Nelson as he introduced his poem. "Jim gave me a chance to be all those things and many, many more."

The Muppet troupe delivered some of their most heartrending musical performances during the two-and-a-half-hour service. Caroll Spinney, as Big Bird, sang "Being Green" with all the honest grief of a six-year-old, audibly stifling tears. Louise Gold dueted with Nelson on "When the River Meets the Sea," from *Emmet Otter's Jug-Band Christmas*, and gave a stunning solo rendition of "Bring Him Home" from Broadway musical *Les Misérables*. And actor Harry Belafonte sang "Turn the World Around," which he had performed memorably on *The Muppet Show*.

As Henson had stipulated, the Reverend Canon Kuhn and Bishop Paul Moore read some religious passages from Hinduism, Buddhism, and Christianity. Moore preached for about fifteen minutes, exhorting the mourners to "embrace" each other—which they did, touchingly, with hugs all around.

The Henson family took the podium next to last. Henson's wife Jane spoke extemporaneously, looking both forward and back: introducing and praising Henson's children, who would carry forward his genes and his spirit, but also sweetly enumerating the deceased colleagues whom Henson would now be able to "work with" again. Cheryl Henson read a piece her father had written about his spiritual beliefs, and Brian Henson read from the letters his father had left after his death. "Please watch out for each other, and love and forgive everybody," he concluded. "It's a good life, enjoy it."

Finally, Hunt delivered the closing eulogy, memorializing Henson and providing a window into his own recent revelations and philosophy.

"Family, that's the key word," he began. "I think we've all realized that. Today, starting with Jim, he believed in Jane. Through their love, they were able to bring us five more beautiful human beings who learned to believe in themselves." Characteristically, Hunt portrayed Henson as a full human, fears and all. "Jim had doubts of his own," Hunt said. "Sometimes he'd go, 'Hmmm.'" Hunt made a scared face.

"'What do we do now?'" Hunt praised *Muppet Show* producer David Lazer for standing by Henson through the years. "He made Jim remind himself to believe in himself. Because it takes an enormous amount of belief, every single day of our lives."

Hunt tried to comfort the audience. By now he was almost inured to losing loved ones, if such a thing is possible. He knew the drill of grief, and had come to a certain acceptance of death as part of the natural process of life.

"I wish there was some way to get rid of this pain that we're all feeling," he said. "This enormous sadness. But, there are no words. There's nothing any of us can tell each other, except to be there, to support, to love, to have someone to hug. And it takes time. Sometimes lots of time, each unto his own. But there is solace, and there is joy, to know that Jim has returned home for a little while, and that all of us are 'going to go back there someday.'" Again, Hunt seemed to interpret the *Muppet Movie* song as meaning to return from whence we came.

"The spirit of Jim was here before, during, and remains after his stay," Hunt continued. "Hopefully that part of him that we each keep will help remind us to stop rushing, stop trying to control things, instead to experience the wonder that God has given us, through this vastness, this divinity, this oneness, this being, that we all share, with all living things. With the animals, most especially for me the singing birds. There's nothing I like better than to stop for a moment, turn off a car, walk out into the woods, and just sit and listen to those guys sing. Not bad.

"The flowers. The irises. The lilacs," he continued. "And the peonies—my favorite flower. Go and smell the richness of their aroma, their fragrance. The earth—we can feel it under us. We have this thing called gravity that pulls us to the earth, and here we are feeling this enormous planet support all of us, and help sustain us. The sun, the warmth of the sun, the light as it shines through a piece of colored glass. The stars, that we look up in wonder and say, 'Is that where we're going?'

"And most especially, the smile and the laughter of the children. If perchance somewhere down the line you see a child, who when you speak to him or ask him a question, he says, 'Mmm, possibly. Maybe. Hmmm,' watch out, because there's more magic to come." Hunt voiced the child in the same Henson voice he had used at the beginning of the eulogy, implying that Henson's spirit lives on in all who come after him.

Hunt's conclusion was the strongest part of his speech, the clearest encapsulation of his hard-earned beliefs. Though speaking of Henson, Hunt's words easily applied to himself as well, the way he lived his own life.

> Jim did not cling to the past [Hunt said]. He did not worry about the future—that would work itself out—and he did not live for the moment. Instead, he lived *in* the moment. Because that's all we really have.
>
> It's important that we all stop giving ourselves such a hard time. We've got to remind ourselves, and push ourselves, to let go. Not much we can do except to be, and in being, become aware. See what's going on around you all the time, and allow it to happen. All the sadness, all the joy.
>
> And that's why Jim's last words are most important: Please watch out for each other. Love everyone. And *forgive* everyone—including yourself. Forgive your anger. Forgive your guilt. Your shame. Your sadness. Embrace and open up your love, your joy, your truth, and most especially your heart. Let us all have mercy on each and every one of us, and every day, we will open up, like a cocoon, and turn into beautiful butterflies, and live this moment—and the next, and the next, and the next.

Hunt's eulogy impressed his friends, showing them his transcendental side. "I remember coming away from that memorial thinking Richard should have been a preacher," says Muppet designer Richard Termine. "He had this insight. There was a spirituality about him." Closter friend Geni Sackson refers to this part of Hunt's life as the "sage stage": "When he had AIDS, and he saw the end, and his hair turned white, then he was a sage. Then he offered his musings."

Hunt segued from his eulogy to reminiscing about the "relaxed atmosphere" of recording vocal tracks in the studio, which Henson especially enjoyed, a nice parlay to singing some of Henson's favorite songs. Hunt, Oz, Nelson, Goelz, Whitmire, and Clash launched into a lively medley. Though not puppeteering, they moved seamlessly from character to character, voice to voice: everything from chickens clucking "Baby Face" to Hunt's Scooter and Oz's Fozzie dueting brightly on

"Simon Smith and His Dancing Bear"; to Clash warbling "Lydia, the Tattooed Lady"; to the whole gang caroling "It's in Every One of Us"; to Goelz's Gonzo singing, fittingly, "I'm Going to Go Back There Some-day." They wound up with the American standard "You Are My Sun-shine," the only song in the medley *not* a Muppet hit, all six voices melding in gorgeous harmonies.

Then Hunt put on Scooter and began to sing on his own. "If just one person believes in you . . ."

The song "Just One Person," from *Snoopy! The Musical*, became a Muppet tune when Broadway diva Bernadette Peters sang it on *The Muppet Show* to cheer up Nelson's tiny frog Robin. The song perfectly captures the spirit of the Muppets: You may be different, you may be weird, the world may not know what to do with you. But all you need to do is find *one* person who believes in you. And then that faith may gain momentum, create a snowball effect.

One by one, the performers joined the song: first Hunt as Scooter; then Nelson as Gobo Fraggle ("Making it two whole people who believe in you"); then Whitmire as Wembley Fraggle ("Three whole people"); Clash as Elmo ("And if three whole people, why not four?"); and then the whole Muppet troupe ("And if four whole people, why not more? And more? And more?"), Oz, Goelz, Gold, Spinney, Mullen, Prell, Quinn, Brill, Arciero, Robinson, Bonora, and Rudman, bringing together char-acters from *The Muppet Show*, *Sesame Street*, *Fraggle Rock*, and even the short-lived *Little Muppet Monsters*, sixteen performers in all.

Again, the song parallels the Muppets themselves. Henson may have doubted himself sometimes, as Hunt said, but he believed in the people he hired, and created an atmosphere of trust in which they believed in each other and worked amicably together, combining their unique talents and skills, creating something bigger than themselves. The performance brought down the house, the cathedral echoing with applause as the pup-peteers hugged each other close.

After the closing blessing, the Dirty Dozen Brass Band led the pro-cession out to a merry rendition of "When the Saints Go Marching In," as Henson had requested. The audience clapped and shimmied and sang along. Hunt delivered his usual antics: clapping a little kid's hands together in time to the music; clowning around, mugging, waving at people; then marching out, head up and eyes bright, clapping and singing—lifting the mood as always.

A few days after the memorial, Hunt and his colleagues flew down to Walt Disney World for the opening of the live show "Here Come the Muppets." The park reminded Hunt of performing with Henson in *The Muppets at Walt Disney World*—and triggered a sad realization. "The last thing Jim and I did with Statler and Waldorf, that was nice. We're in this cable car, singing some song and flirting with everybody. And when we went back down there after he died, the cable car passed me, and for the first time I realized that Statler wouldn't [be here] anymore."

Hunt gave another eulogy at Henson's memorial service at London's St. Paul's Cathedral on July 2, with about 2,000 people in attendance. In many ways, the two services were quite similar: everyone wore bright colors, as instructed; Jane and Cheryl Henson spoke, and Brian Henson read from his father's letters; Kenworthy and Oz gave tributes; Spinney as Big Bird sang "Being Green"; Hunt, Oz, Goelz, and Whitmire did a medley of Henson's favorite songs; and the service wound up with a grand finale of "Just One Person." Jocelyn Stevenson and Lord Lew Grade, bright additions to the London service, delivered thoughtful testimonials. St. Paul's was artfully strewn with foliage to reflect Henson's love of Hampstead Heath, a gesture that surely resonated with Hunt.

Compounding Hunt's sense of loss was the context of all the other losses he had endured over the last decade. "I've lost seven of my best friends in the last eight years," he told an interviewer shortly after Henson's death. "Jim makes number eight. That's the hardest thing to get a grip on, why is there any of this stuff? Why this century? Maybe it's because we needed to see the bottom in order to come up to the top."

Hunt and Stuart Fischer had box seats for opening night at the Metropolitan Opera in September 1990, seeing Placido Domingo in *La Boheme*. At the end of the performance, as the young character Mimi dies of consumption in her lover Rodolfo's arms, Fischer glanced over at Hunt. Was he thinking of Bird dying in his arms? Was he thinking of all the loved ones he had lost? Hunt stared fixedly at the stage, totally engrossed, not seeming to notice the tears trickling from his eyes.

Henson's death accelerated *Sesame Street*'s already shifting puppeteer dynamic. When the show began filming season twenty-two in fall 1990, Spinney and Nelson remained invaluable mainstays—but now the next generation stepped up to join them as senior hands. Clash, for example, had recently won a daytime Emmy for Outstanding Performer in a Children's Series. "Richard Hunt jokingly said I owed him half an Emmy for tossing Elmo my way," says Clash. The torch had been passed. Meanwhile, a bevy of fresh hires took *their* places as newbies and assistants.

As the show unveiled a bunch of new characters, giving the next generation more to do, Hunt performed some of his old characters for the last time. Placido Flamingo—opera star Placido Domingo's avian namesake—organized an animal opera; sang the lovely "Music Can Have Feelings" about expressing one's emotions through music; and held his own in a duet with renowned diva Wilhelmenia Fernandez, his final appearance. Hunt's disgruntled pianist Don Music banged his head on the keys for the last time, and his absent-minded cowboy Forgetful Jones made his final failed recall. Forgetful was supposed to duet with Natalie Cole on her aptly titled "Unforgettable," but the segment was rescheduled due to conflicts, then canceled entirely due to Hunt's illness.

Sesame Street's new puppeteer dynamic seemed clear that fall when Hunt filmed the show's first sing-along home video, *Billy Bunny's Animal Songs*. Clash both served as puppet captain and played the title character, sort of *Sesame*'s version of Bean Bunny, a young curious rabbit who hops around singing with different groups of animals. Hunt played a rapping bear in a trio with Rudman and Nelson, and had a fun duet with Nelson as a pair of raccoons. They were joined by Mullen and a half-dozen *Sesame* performers, including Brill as a sexy porcupine. Though the video contained framing scenes with Whitmire performing Kermit, they were shot months later. The video utilized some of the same personnel as the 3-D movie and preshow, such as writer Bill Prady (with Jim Lewis) and director David Gumpel. *Billy Bunny's Animal*

Songs didn't come out until 1993, making it Hunt's last work to be released.

In the 1990s, as Barney gave the show a run for its ratings, the atmosphere would shift on *Sesame Street*. The show would move to a new studio, hire new directors and producers, focus more on its preschool audience. The salad days of *Sesame Street* would give way to a new sensibility, with Clash's giggly Elmo as its ubiquitous symbol; one might call this new era the "Elmonopoly." Times would change, and the show would change along with them.

Fittingly, the last major project Hunt filmed with the Muppets was a tribute to their "fearless leader." A few days after wrapping *Billy Bunny's Animal Songs*, Hunt was at the Henson carriage house filming the hour-long special *The Muppets Celebrate Jim Henson*. He and sixteen colleagues spent November 10 reading through the script and recording the vocal tracks, then devoted three jam-packed, fifteen-hour days to filming. "Hard shoot," recalls Arciero. "It was all of us together, trying to figure out how to honor Jim and do a show that people outside of us understood." In a way, the special takes Henson's real-life memorial services and translates them to a wider and more general audience.

Indeed, *The Muppets Celebrate Jim Henson* bears many similarities to Henson's memorials. The Muppet characters, many of them stand-ins for their performers, try to put together a performance honoring Henson—but they struggle to do it without Kermit, Henson's alter ego. Oz and others give tributes to Henson, interspersed with striking montages of his work (put together by David Gumpel, who would later do the same for Hunt). Harry Belafonte sings "Turn the World Around," as he did at St. John the Divine; and as with the real-life memorials, Martin Baker produced. Fozzie Bear even hires a Dixieland band (of pigs, because this is the Muppets)—a sweet nod to Henson's wishes.

As usual, writer Jerry Juhl (with Bill Prady) captures some wonderful character moments. When Carol Burnett says the Muppets are like a family, Gonzo and Robin bicker in a familial way over whether or not that's true. And it's a testament to the strength of the various Muppet alter egos (Hunt's Scooter, Nelson's Robin, Goelz's Gonzo, Oz's Fozzie, Clash's Clifford) that their reactions to reading "real letters from Jim's fans" (again, as at the memorial) are so touching. When the Muppets realize through these letters that Henson has *died*, and a panicky Fozzie declares that they should cancel the performance, Robin talks him out of it—by leading the Muppets in "Just One Person."

While Robin begins, Hunt's Scooter is the second character to join in—in Hunt's last official performance as Scooter. Appropriately, the last time Hunt performed his alter ego was in a tribute to his mentor, and to the power of the whole troupe that Henson brought together. Again, dozens of characters join in one by one, a wide representation from *The Muppet Show*, *Sesame Street*, and *Fraggle Rock*. As with many of the Muppets' large group scenes, anyone that could wiggle a puppet was roped into doing so, including Kenworthy and Muppet writer Craig Shemin as Statler and Waldorf, respectively.

In answer to the audience's unspoken question, at the very end of the special Kermit comes in and watches them sing, almost like Henson watching from beyond. Yet when Kermit speaks to praise their performance, in Whitmire's first attempt at the character, he sounds jarringly unlike his predecessor. "Here's Steve taking over Kermit, and we're trying to figure out how to make that all believable, and it's just not, for any of us," Arciero recalls. "Even Steve." Kermit assures the audience that the troupe will be back with more projects, "because that's the way the boss would want it." Henson's death wouldn't mean the end of the Muppets; Henson had made sure of that. The special aired on CBS on November 21, the day before Thanksgiving.

Hunt showed up for the Henson family after Henson's death, a sympathetic family friend. On November 5, he presided over Brian Henson's wedding to fashion designer Ellis Flyte on Tortola in the Virgin Islands. Just as at Jerry and Jan Nelson's wedding, Hunt was in full-on Reverend Richard Hunt mode. As the crowd stood around waiting for the ceremony to start, performer Bill Baretta recalls, "A booming voice rose at the back of the crowd which began to part like the Red Sea, as Richard's traveling preacher's sermon made its way toward the bride and groom." Hunt made "an indelible impression" on Baretta, no shrinking wallflower himself. "I'll never forget the power of his energy, smile, and humor. The only other person I've personally witnessed such magnetism in was when I met Prince." Once at the front of the crowd, Hunt "did the whole ceremony," recalls Brian Henson, though a local officiant technically presided. "It was hilarious, of course. And loud."

Hunt also supported the Henson children as they struggled with the future of the Henson company. Since Henson had never signed an official deal with Disney, his death threw the whole merger into question. His children tried to continue the negotiations. "We were of the opinion, my dad was selling the company to Disney, so we tried to do it because it was what my dad was doing," says Brian Henson. Though Hunt had never been afraid to stand up to or contradict Henson, and though he had been vocally opposed to the Disney deal, the Henson children never heard a peep from him in that department. "I don't remember Richard almost ever talking about the business," says Brian Henson. "Other performers had strong opinions, but Richard was not one of those voices. He was extremely respectful of not inserting himself in complicated situations like that." Perhaps Hunt's opposition had mellowed; more likely, he felt it was a higher priority to be there for Henson's kids.

Henson Associates and the Walt Disney Company officially stopped negotiating the merger on December 13. This cast doubt over the collaborative projects already underway. The live show "Here Come the Muppets," which had opened shortly after Henson's death, ran until September 1991; the second live show, "The Muppets on Location," opened two weeks later and ran for three years as an oddly bare-bones production staged on a loading dock. The 3-D movie and attraction fared better, opening in Walt Disney World in May 1991 and still running over thirty years later (and running in the Disney California Adventure Park from 2001 to 2014). The Henson children, led by Brian and Lisa, controlled the family company for a decade before selling it to the German media company EM.TV in 2000; three years later they bought it back at a loss.

In 2004, at long last, the Walt Disney Company purchased the Muppets for $75 million, buying the rights to the Muppet name and the majority of the television shows, movies, and characters, including Kermit the Frog (with the exception of the *Sesame Street* and *Fraggle Rock* characters). It took fifteen years, but the Disney deal was finally completed.

"I think Jim made this deal because something sensed inside him that he was tying things up," said Hunt. "I think they had to drag this out a long time and nitpick it and try to get as much as they could out of it, while Jim remained this honest—I mean, never signed a contract with them. Who else in the world would do that, would have that sense of honesty and trust. It was protected by his soul. But that fits right into the personality of the person and the unbelievableness of it all."

By early 1991, Hunt's health was starting to limit his activities. He was spending more time resting at home, much of it in front of the television—and found himself watching *Sesame Street* with new eyes. Two decades earlier, he had been captivated by the brand-new show, so much so that he had called up Henson Associates and launched his entire career. Now he was appreciating Henson's work all over again. "They seemed to be showing a lot of Jim's work, lots of Ernie and Bert and Kermit the reporter stuff. So I saw a lot of things I hadn't seen in quite a while," he told an interviewer a year after Henson's death. One day Hunt was watching one of Henson's characters and had to remind himself, "No, he's not here anymore."

"On a very personal level, I had an interesting reaction," he said of the experience. "I realized that I still have not dealt with Jim's death, because I've lost so many of my friends. I feel very sad, but accepting in a strange way. I think it's a protective device I have. So I don't think I've even resolved it yet. And this is a year this week."

Much as he had used his Muppet characters to act out the stages of life for his high school classmates, Hunt used them in shows for HIV-positive people, through the Community Research Initiative on AIDS (CRIA). "Jim was very good about letting me use puppets for something like that," he said. "He was very much in support of anything he could do, while the rest of the country slept."

Hunt liked to sing "No One Is Alone" from the Stephen Sondheim musical *Into the Woods*, a fractured fairy tale. The song comes when an angry (female) giant is loose in the town, wreaking havoc and destruction. "She's so big she's stepping on people, people are losing their husbands and wives, and it really is a parable to a certain degree on the AIDS epidemic," Hunt said. "But it could be any loss."

"No One Is Alone" portrays the characters feeling isolated and dis-connected. Yet the song brings them together—ironically through their shared experience of loss. "This beautiful lyric about how 'Some-times people leave you halfway through the wood,' halfway through your life," Hunt said. "And while it will grieve you, 'no one leaves for good. You are not alone. No one is alone.' It's a beautiful thing."

Hunt had an idea to build on this by bringing in Statler and Waldorf. "I did this comic bit and I pulled Statler out," he said. "He's making all these jokes: 'Shoot the piano player! Please!' Laughing and saying 'Ha! Ha! Ha!'" But in the melee, Waldorf disappears from view. Like the characters in the song, Statler finds himself alone. "I go, 'Waldorf, I always thought he'd be there and now he's gone.' Exquisite moment. Which I guess touches on my whole reaction. I always thought he'd be there."

Hunt watches the sunset over Cape Cod Bay at his house in Truro, undated.

CHAPTER 19

A Whole New Adventure

IN AUGUST 1991, Hunt spent his fortieth birthday weekend holed up at his Truro cottage—despite the impending presence of Hurricane Bob, headed straight for the Cape. The cottage residents, with their houses precipitously high on the dunes over the bay, were urged to evacuate to the local high school. Hunt had no desire to evacuate—but he also had no desire to stay holed up in the house. He climbed out the second-floor bathroom window and sat on the porch roof, hugging his knees, leaning against the house's weathered gray shingles, gazing far out over the water, watching the storm come in. It may have been risky, but at this point, he had bigger fears looming.

Still, he had some comfort, having gotten back the small sea-green stone from the person who had been holding it for him. "I was ready again to take it back, 'cause it was my friend," Hunt told an interviewer. "It helped."

To celebrate his fortieth birthday, Hunt threw himself a "Going Away Party," as he called it. He held the party on Saturday, September 7, renting a meeting room at St. John the Divine and filling it with over one hundred of his dear ones: his family, his fellow performers, most of Henson Associates, his friends, his Junior Gorg co-performer Rob Mills all the way from Toronto, even his high school choral teacher Gail Poch. "I'm throwing this party because I didn't think I'd make it to my own fortieth birthday party," he told the crowd.

The gathering began at 5 P.M. with mingling, eating, and drinking, a typical Hunt party. But at 6:30 Hunt took to the stage for a show that seemed different from what his friends were used to. First he served as emcee as his mother and siblings performed—but then he took to the stage alone, for over an hour of singing and cracking jokes and preaching, despite being visibly depleted. He had rested for weeks in order to save up the energy for the performance.

Hunt went through some of the routine he had done at his high school reunion, putting on puppets to talk through the stages of life—only now, he was talking about his own life. To some of the people in the room, it was the first time he talked openly about loving and losing Nelson Bird. Even those who had known Bird had rarely heard Hunt speak about his personal life so frankly, and certainly not in front of a crowd. Hunt also used his platform to voice some doubts about the direction the Muppets were taking, some decisions he might have made differently at the company. He spoke largely extemporaneously, without notes, from the heart. "He was doing shtick," recalls Mills. "'This is gonna go on for a long time, folks! I've got the stage, I'm not getting off.'"

Hunt also performed a number of songs cabaret-style, including Sondheim's "No One Is Alone," accompanied by a friend on piano. He seemed to many in the audience to be speaking through the songs he had chosen. "There was something very open, the lyrics of those songs and what they said," says Richard Termine. "It was like saying this is my life, this is who I am, this is what I believe in. It was remarkable. And painful. I'll never forget it." Hunt's old friend Stuart Fischer found the performance painful for other reasons, characterizing it as a "sorry spectacle," saddened by watching Hunt struggle to sing songs which had once come easily. Other friends were also struck by Hunt's health woes—and by his triumphant ability to entertain despite them. "I realized there wasn't that much of him left compared to what I had known in high school," Poch recalls. "But he was still able to have everyone on the floor with laughter."

Hunt shared his philosophy and beliefs, all tinged with his unique personality and sense of humor. "He was pure Richie, which was completely unbridled," recalls Oz, who sees the performance as a "remembering ceremony," a chance for Hunt to memorialize himself while he was still around. Others in the audience saw it that way as well. "When

I look back on it, it was about Richard having the last word," says Whit-mire. "'This is what I want you to remember. Not what you're going to say when I'm gone.'" In a sense, the party was Hunt's way of saying goodbye—on his own terms.

The party ran on until 11 P.M., with most everyone conscious of the importance of the moment, lingering and reluctant to leave.

Despite his waning health, in early fall Hunt filmed a few last *Sesame Street* appearances for season twenty-three. Fittingly, three of these appearances were in a pair with his old friend and colleague Jerry Nelson. The dramatic Gladys the Cow argues with Nelson's gruff Herry Monster over who gets to introduce the show, not realizing that Susan and Gordon have already done so. And Biff and Sully play piano for Bob in a reshoot of a 1982 segment, with Hunt's puppeteering style notice-ably more restrained than the original, especially the character's double-take reactions. Finally, Hunt sounds painfully hoarse in his last Two-Headed Monster segment, in which the two monsters take turns surprising each other, then charmingly team up to surprise the viewer. "He performed until he absolutely could not hold the puppet up," says Arciero. Hunt would be credited as a performer on the show through season thirty-one in the year 2000, a telling indicator of how much the show needed him as well as how much his colleagues honored him.

Hunt was increasingly in and out of the hospital throughout the fall. In a sweet turn of events, he had put his sister Rachel through college to become a Child Life practitioner, helping children and their families cope with illness—and her subsequent expertise in health care enabled her to be a great help to him. This connection brought them closer than ever before.

Despite his health woes, Hunt was still the perpetual performer. His friend Barbara McDonald, who had organized the high school reunion, was talking quietly with him in the hospital one day when a group of his friends came in—and Hunt's entire demeanor changed. "All of a sud-den he's sitting up in bed, even though he feels rotten. Even when he was really sick, if he had a crowd around him, he would hold court."

And even when he was asleep, his loved ones suspected he was still part of things, still paying attention. "I watched him pretend to sleep, in a room full of people," says his mother's partner Arthur Miller. "But he was listening." Miller likened this to Hunt as a young kid in the elevator in the Bronx, fascinated by his fellow passengers. "He was listening to everything; he didn't miss a thing."

By early December, Hunt was quite ill with Kaposi's sarcoma and other opportunistic infections, starting to lose his vision, largely confined to the apartment. But on December 6, Oz and Nelson showed up at Hunt's apartment, helped him bathe, shave, and dress, assisted him into a wheelchair, and took him in a cab over to the Muppet mansion—for a surprise party! The low-key 7 P.M. potluck brought together about thirty-five of Hunt's family and colleagues. "He was in bad shape, but he got up for the occasion, and he really appreciated it," says Oz.

Hunt especially treasured the half-hour reel of his work put together by David Gumpel (who had put together the montages for *The Muppets Celebrate Jim Henson*) and Dave Goelz. The reel delightfully mimicked MTV—only this was RTV, Richard Hunt Television. Goelz voiced the host, a punk humanoid Muppet created for the occasion, clad in a tiny leather jacket, yellow leopard-print shirt, and sunglasses. "Welcome to Richard Hunt TV, in your face, twenty-four hours a day!" Goelz's VJ gleefully exclaimed. The puckish character popped up to introduce each clip.

Hunt's loved ones were blown away by his incredible talent, skill, and versatility showcased by the reel. Many of the clips paid tribute to Hunt's work with Henson and Nelson, such as *The Muppet Show* segments of Scooter meeting Kermit; Scooter and Floyd singing "Mr. Bassman"; Sweetums and Robin singing "Two Lost Souls"; and, touchingly, Statler and Waldorf singing "It Was a Very Good Year." The reel also highlighted Hunt's musicality, featuring Miss Piggy in her breakout moment, making a play for Kermit as the Muppet Show Glee Club sings "Temptation"; Beaker passionately singing "Feelings"; and Janice singing "Rockin' Robin," as well as her famous adlib from *The Great Muppet Caper* ("Look mother, it's my life, okay, so if I want to live on a beach and walk around naked . . .").

The partnerships were front and center again in the *Sesame Street* clips: Forgetful Jones provoking Kermit to lose his temper as he blows take after take of "Oklahoma"; the Two-Headed Monster trying to buy shoes; even Hunt right-handing with Henson as Ernie, making the character wave at the camera. The reel also featured one of Hunt's proudest career moments, dueting with opera star Placido Domingo as the singer's avian counterpart Placido Flamingo, singing "Look Through the Window" in *Sesame Street*'s twentieth anniversary special. Another proud moment came when Hunt spoke directly to the camera about directing an episode of *Fraggle Rock*. The *Fraggle Rock* clips further emphasized his acting and singing skills, as Junior Gorg renounced the crown; little rat Gunge sang "Gonna Party! (Saturday Night)"; and Hunt's powerful punk one-off, the Mean Genie, hypnotized the Fraggles as he sang "Do You Want It." The clips even included some original footage of Hunt and Goelz clowning around on *The Christmas Toy* set, as well as a slo-mo version of Hunt fainting in the John Landis movie *Trading Places*.

The room was quiet when the reel ended, everyone struck by what they had just seen. "We were all flabbergasted," says Goelz. "When we saw the sheer volume and range of Richard's work, it really sank into us what a huge talent he had. And what an enormous loss we were facing." Most crucially, Hunt got to witness his value to the troupe. "That was important, for him to realize what he's given," says Oz.

When Oz had first brought up the idea of the party to Martin Baker, the producer had objected. "I was really against it, because it sounded not quite the right thing to do," Baker recalls. "Was I wrong!" Ultimately, Baker characterizes the evening as "very warm, loving and emotional—really lovely."

And Hunt being Hunt, he cracked jokes on even this most somber of occasions. His mother Jane brought the first paycheck Hunt had ever received from Henson, which he had kept as a souvenir and never deposited. "That's the last time I ever did that!" he shouted. Recalls Pete Coogan, "He was weakened, but he hadn't lost his spirit."

As people left the party, they kneeled down in front of Hunt's wheelchair to say goodbye. "He looked like he was giving blessings," Jan Nelson recalls. And perhaps, in his own way, he was.

Hunt was aware that he had little time left. When his friend Jesper Haynes left New York in December for his annual stint in Sweden,

Hunt's goodbye had a certain air of finality. "He knew at that time it was a matter of weeks," says Haynes.

Jocelyn Stevenson, on a visit to New York, called to ask if she could come and see him; Hunt nixed the visit, but the two had a long, intimate phone conversation. "We were able to tell each other how much we loved each other, how much we'd been a part of each other's lives, and to say goodbye." Stevenson especially appreciated how "matter-of-fact" Hunt was about the situation. "I remember thinking, 'Wow, what a gift. Thank you. Let's not pretend it's not happening. It is happening.' It summed up his real connection with his own humanity, and consequently with everybody else's."

By contrast, however, Duncan Kenworthy came to visit Hunt around the same time, and was frustrated that Hunt carefully steered the conversation away from his health. "You wanted him to say, 'I'm dying, and I just want you to know x, y, and z.' But he could never say that." Kenworthy surmises that Hunt intended this as a kindness, "to save you from the details of what was coming to him."

And when childhood Elmwood friend Nancy Persons heard that Hunt was dying and called to talk to him, she was struck by how present he was to *her* life, rather than focusing on his own. When she mentioned that she had recently had a hysterectomy, Hunt said kindly, "Oh, that must have been so hard. I'm so sorry." Persons was awed by his sensitivity. "Here he was empathizing with me, when my intention was to empathize with him, and he beat me to it. Blew me away."

Oz was a frequent visitor to Hunt's bedside. "The one thing that sticks in me is when he was so ill, and I was sitting there by his bed, holding his hand as he was going in and out of consciousness, and he said to me, 'I didn't think it was going to be this hard,' meaning that he didn't think it was going to be that hard to die," says Oz. "That seared itself into my heart and brain."

Hunt organized a Christmas dinner at his apartment, just a half-dozen people including his mother, her partner Arthur Miller, and Stuart Fischer. Hunt ordered a full dinner and vintage champagne, but stayed in bed while the others ate without him. Brian Meehl came by and sat beside Hunt's bed and read him Dylan Thomas's "A Child's Christmas in Wales," which the Hunts always read on Christmas.

After the holiday, Hunt went into the hospice at Cabrini hospital—where Bird had died, a fact he was sure to have noticed.

Hunt was rarely alone in the hospice, his family and friends keeping a close vigil at his bedside, talking with him or just sitting with him in silence. Old friend Geni Sackson and others took turns reading aloud from one of Hunt's favorite books, Ray Bradbury's *Dandelion Wine*, an unusually nostalgic work from the science fiction author, a thin fictionalization of an idyllic childhood summer.

When Fischer, Hunt's opera buddy, came to visit him in the hospice, Hunt asked him out of the blue, "What opera would you want to see again?" Hunt said he would want to see *The Flying Dutchman*—which struck Fischer as an odd choice as Hunt didn't like Wagner. The title character, a sea captain, is cursed to remain at sea unless he can find a woman who will be faithful to him. "At the end he does find a woman true to him until death, and they're reunited in death," Fischer explains. "It showed me that Richard needed someone. He was looking for that and it didn't work out."

Hunt's favorite flower was the peony; the family had a peony bush outside their Closter home which bloomed beautifully every spring. "When he was doing the *Muppet Show* in England, he'd know that it was about time for them to bloom, so he called Kate every day," remembers his mother. "He'd say, 'Are they blooming yet?' 'No, not yet.' 'Okay.' Finally one day she said, 'All right, now they're coming out.' So he went right to Jim, and he said, 'I gotta leave now, I gotta go see the peonies.'"

When Pam Arciero visited Hunt in the hospice, he said to her, "You know, I told everybody, I don't want to die before the peonies bloom. I want to be here for the peonies." Arciero glanced over and noticed a huge bouquet of peonies in his room. "Fucking Steve sent me this bouquet of peonies," Hunt said. "Now what am I gonna do?" Even on his deathbed, Hunt could find a way to make a joke.

Hunt approached even death with his trademark fearlessness. "A very strong basic philosophy, if you can get there, is to believe and allow that anything is possible," Hunt said late in life. "It's like life after death. Maybe there is nothing; I mean, you die and that's that. Well, that may be. But why *make* yourself there? Why not take the excitement and the calm one gets from realizing, Gee—maybe there's a whole new adventure? Wouldn't that be great? Yes it would. So don't deny yourself that."

Hunt spoke frankly about death and its place in the vast scheme of things in his oration at Henson's London memorial service. "The circle is the form of nature," he said.

> All things move in cycles. Seasons. Day and night. Life and death. Light moves into darkness, returning to light. Energy moves in cycles. The orbiting of the planets. The electrons orbiting around the nucleus of an atom.
>
> But in our lives, we fight our circle. We try to construct a beginning, a middle, and an end. And if we just stopped. If we stopped giving ourselves such a hard time. Stopped! Stopped pushing. Stopped clinging. Stopped desiring. And allow this beautiful vastness. Realizing that each and every moment is a perfect circle in which there is room for everything. Room for love. Room for anger. Room for joy. And room for sorrow.
>
> We don't know where we're going. But it doesn't matter. We never become lost because—there's nowhere to go. We are constantly arriving home, in the next moment. Trust the process. Let go lightly. Pass on gently.

Rachel and Adam Hunt were lying beside their brother in the wee hours of Tuesday, January 7, 1992, when Rachel noticed a change in him. "I had been with people who had died so many times I knew that's what was going on," Rachel says. She nudged Adam awake. Together, Rachel and Adam watched over their brother as he passed away.

Hunt's sister Lyn found a thin silver lining in that the manner of his death at least allowed his dear ones some closure. "Like giving birth, where you love somebody into this world, when you know somebody is going to die, you get to love them out of this world," she says. "I appreciated that."

Hunt's friend Rob Gardner, a *Sesame Street* production assistant, found himself awake at three in the morning. "There's a voice, tells me to get out of bed, turn on the TV," he recalls. "I turn on the TV, it's a Rob Lowe movie. So I'm watching this, I have no idea what this is, and suddenly there's Richard Hunt, as the bellhop. I'm like, 'This is bizarre.'

I go back to sleep. The next day, I find out he's passed away." Gardner has no doubt what happened. "He woke me up, to say goodbye."

The news of Hunt's death stopped production the next morning at *Sesame Street*. Termine came in to find everyone at a standstill: the producers in the control room, the crew on set, the performers huddled in the Muppet lounge, everyone stunned and needing a breather to take in the news. "It was devastating," says Arciero.

Despite Hunt having a short life, observed Coogan, he made the most of the time he had, and went out as he had lived, with curiosity and sagacity. "He was never bitter," says Coogan. "It was never 'Why me?' or anything. He felt that he'd lived a good life. He was somebody who'd enjoyed the ride. There was no mistaking it."

As per his wishes, Hunt's body was cremated. His ashes were scattered at the Hunt family house in Closter; his beloved house in Truro; and the Venice canal where he had scattered Bird's ashes.

Hunt in Truro, mid-1980s.

CHAPTER 20

Legacy

Hunt's sister Lyn Hunt Russell stood at the podium of the Cathedral of St. John the Divine on Sunday, February 2, 1992, looking out over the roughly 350 people who had gathered for Hunt's memorial service, where she was serving as emcee. "The hard part about doing this today, is that Richard always did this," she said wryly.

Hunt's memorial service had plenty of pomp and circumstance: it was held in the stately cathedral, with a grand processional entrance, elaborate prayers, the Cathedral Choir, the Inspirational Riverside Choir, and even South African acapella troupe Ladysmith Black Mambazo. However, the aspects of the service that most reflected Hunt were the poignant performances put on by his loved ones. They gave tributes, performed songs, and read passages that were particularly meaningful to him, all the while acutely conscious of his glaring absence.

The location itself was meaningful, the same place where Henson's and Bird's memorials had been held. People wore their coats in the chilly, high-ceilinged space, sitting in rows of chairs, centered around the pulpit on its raised chancel.

Jane Henson, consciously representing "a lot of people and a lot of work," remembered Hunt standing where she stood, emceeing the memorial service for her husband. "I'm grateful that Richard was with us to send his words out into this space, for Jim, at Jim's request," she said. And in another callback to Henson's memorial, Jerry Nelson invited the audience to join him on the Christmas carol "It's in Every One of

Us," which he, Hunt, and their colleagues had sung there as part of a medley.

Louise Gold delivered a moving rendition of one of Hunt's favorite songs, Stephen Sondheim's "No One Is Alone." Following Gold at the podium, Stuart Fischer connected their performances thematically. "This also says 'No one is alone,'" he said, introducing James Agee's "Knoxville: Summer 1915." Hunt and Bird had watched Fischer read the nostalgic passage at Fischer's birthday party in 1985; just a few weeks later, Hunt, alone, had watched him read it at Bird's memorial; now Fischer, the last man standing, was reading it for Hunt.

Geni Sackson read a similarly wistful excerpt from another of Hunt's favorite books, Ray Bradbury's *Dandelion Wine*, which friends had taken turns reading to him in the last week of his life.

Many spoke of Hunt's generosity. Fred Newman, Hunt's co-star in the CBS pilot *Puppetman*, told a story of having dinner with Hunt in a formal Orlando restaurant, which ended up in the usual fight over the check—but this time it was a literal fight, the two men on the floor physically tussling, the whole restaurant hushed and watching. Finally the "stone-faced" maître d' intervened: "Is there a problem?" Straight-faced, Hunt looked up innocently and said, "We're just fighting over the check." When Newman delivered the punchline, the cathedral burst into laughter.

Hunt's friend Bobby Taylor told a similar story. Taylor had met Hunt at his workplace, the Manhattan Center for Living, which supported people battling life-threatening illness. The two became quite close, speaking on the phone almost every day for Hunt's last two years, and meeting every week for dinner.

As with Newman—as with everyone—Hunt would never let Taylor pick up the check. The two argued about this until finally Taylor issued an ultimatum: "I'm not going to see you anymore unless you let me pick up the tab." The stalemate lasted about two weeks, until Hunt called Taylor and said that his psychotherapist had convinced him that he should let Taylor pay for dinner, so he was willing to try it—just this once.

But as usual, Hunt had the last laugh. "He took me to the cheapest place in all of Manhattan, and ordered like a bowl of soup and a Coke," Taylor recalled. "At that point, I just gave up, and realized that this is what it's going to be like."

Hunt's family contributed especially poignant performances. His youngest sister Rachel sang James Taylor's "Shed a Little Light." While the song is about Martin Luther King Jr., Rachel substituted Hunt's name in the lyrics, making the song about her brother. "Oh let us turn our thoughts today/to Richard Henry Hunt," Rachel sang. The lyrics nicely relate to Hunt and his outlook on life, urging listeners to "recognize that there are ties between us/All men and women living on the earth/Ties of hope and love/Sister and brotherhood." The song is also an apt declaration that Hunt and his legacy live on: "Though the body sleeps/The heart will never rest."

Hunt's sister Kate read a sweet journal entry she had written to her brother a few weeks before his passing. "You are the one person who has never given up on me," she said. Kate's teenage daughter Amanda Smith read a letter from her great-grandmother in West Virginia, Jane's mother Evelyn Hall, about how he gave her one of his Emmys, and how proud she was to have it. Lyn's young daughters also performed: Ruby Russell tearfully read a poem she had written, and Savannah Russell sang the Beatles' "Golden Slumbers" with her grandmother Jane, the two of them wearing matching red blazers. Clearly, the next generation of Hunts was keeping up the family tradition.

But Jane didn't merely perform with her granddaughter; she delivered a striking eulogy, contextualizing Hunt and his illness. "In case there's someone in this room visiting from another planet, I should tell you I'm Jane. I'm Richard's mother," she said, her eyes flashing with emotion. "I'm not here to speak of Richard's kindness, his humor, his generosity, his sensitivity, his joyous talent, his astonishing integrity. Or his good looks. Or his cussedness, because we all know about that."

Jane told a story of going to visit Hunt at the hospice in the last weeks of his life.

I walked into the room and it was dark with the last light of day coming through the window. I looked at Richard, who for once was not on the phone with one of you. He was sleeping. And I looked at what once had been a beautiful, robust, strong, vital, active man, and he had lost a lot of ground. I knew then, when he woke, I wouldn't be able to take him in my arms, and say, "Don't worry. You'll be well by Saturday." I was helpless.

When he died, I'd been through so many emotions. I found in the last weekend of his life, that something was coming up. It was anger. I was very angry. Now, Richard stood here in this spot a year and a half ago [at Henson's memorial], and said we had to forgive our anger, and our shame. He said a whole lot of very wonderful and inspiring things, but I'm going to hold onto my anger right now, just long enough to try to empower all of you to do what has to be done, yet.

I want an end to all the moralizing about AIDS. I don't want to hear any more about people deserving to get it, or not deserving because they didn't do anything wrong, or any of that business. No more moralizing. These people are sick, and dying.

I want an end to greed. When shareholders get together and say, "Shall we do some research on AIDS, well, is there enough money for that, no there's not, oh let's forget it." I want an end to that.

I want an end to ignorance. Children growing into their teens without being educated. The problems of teenagers are hard enough. I want the schools to teach them all about sex education and love. And I want all of you to find the courage to speak up, as Magic Johnson did to our president, and say, "Look, that's very nice of you to be on this commission, but I want you to look me in the eye and tell me that you want to help too."

Jane's fiery speech provoked nods of recognition from the audience. As one way to get involved, the program suggested that mourners make donations in Hunt's name to the Community Research Initiative on AIDS.

Yet the most touching performance by Hunt's family was the one they put on all together. Hunt's brother Adam started it off, introducing himself and thanking everyone for coming. Eyes on his lyric sheet, he sang shyly at first, and then full out: "If just one person believes in you, deep enough and strong enough, believes in you . . ." One by one, the members of the Hunt family joined in: Hunt's mother, his siblings, and his young nieces, all singing in unison on "Just One Person."

Hunt had led his Muppet colleagues in this song at Henson's memorial, yet in another sense it was just as perfect for his family to sing it to memorialize him. Hunt had believed in his family unwaveringly, even when they didn't necessarily believe in themselves, let alone each other; what's more, he believed in his family as a whole, a unit that added up to far more than the sum of its parts. Hunt had done everything he could to keep his family together; now he was gone, but had left them the consolation of each other.

Most importantly, over the course of his life, Hunt had learned to believe in *himself*. Dave Goelz brought this point home in a stunning eulogy.

Goelz started out describing a dream he had a few days after Hunt's death. Hunt's loved ones were in the cathedral, preparing for the memorial, when Goelz caught sight of Hunt—but it was the twenty-five-year-old Hunt, wearing one of his old striped polo shirts and his *Muppet Show* tour guide hat. "In this dream, he was fifteen years younger, but something was different," said Goelz. "Richard was carrying himself with a quiet strength, moving with grace, and taking time as he walked with people to his service. He was so much more than the Richard of *Muppet Show* days."

When the two men were about twenty feet apart, Hunt caught sight of Goelz. "We moved toward each other. We put our arms around each other's shoulders, and walked side by side. Even though we didn't speak, there was more contact than we'd ever had before, and we started to cry. Soon, we were weeping openly." Goelz woke suffused with sadness. "He had achieved such wonderful growth at such a terrible price. Where was the good in this?"

Goelz found the answer to his question in his own dream. "The answer was in the new qualities I had seen in Richard. Faced with the knowledge of his probable destiny, Richard made some courageous choices. He used the disease that was tearing him apart to become whole. As I watched his body deteriorate, I saw his spirit grow. Instead of running *from* the truth of his life, he ran towards it. Everyone wishes for this kind of growth. Very few have the courage to seek it, and fewer still achieve it."

Goelz remembered being impressed by Hunt's fortieth birthday party, at this same cathedral.

It was his statement of who he was. It was clear that he had changed. He had learned to see himself, and to love what he saw, and to let us see him. He had stopped judging others, because he had stopped judging himself. In place of judgment, there was compassion. Finally, he felt safe enough to really let himself be seen. At last, Richard loved Richard— like the rest of us did.

My dream ended before I could tell Richard the one thing I left unsaid, so I'll say it now: Thank you, Richard, for arriving before you left.

Goelz's speech resonated with Hunt's Closter friend Ernie Capeci, who had known Hunt since the teen-aged Hunt had babysat Capeci and his rowdy band of brothers. In a sense, the friends had grown up together, and watched each other grow up.

"Dave Goelz said a moving thing at Richard's service," says Capeci. "He said he thought that when Richard got sick, he had finally started to accept himself. I think that's true. I don't think it was just his sexuality. I think there's a certain basic self-loathing that takes a lot of time to get through, that's societal. Whatever you are. Richard finally had acceptance, in a way. He had been fighting himself for so many years."

As at Henson's memorial, a large group of Muppet performers delivered the grand finale. *Sesame Street* showrunner Jon Stone introduced them, reminiscing about Hunt's early days as an apprentice doing right hands, and praising Hunt's growth into "a patient and inspired teacher to the next generation of apprentices and right-handers." Stone also touched upon Hunt's widespread legacy. "Perhaps it's some consolation that over the last twenty years, Richard's genius and irreverence touched virtually every child in this country, and millions upon millions in other parts of the world," he said. "We are truly privileged to have known him."

About eighteen *Sesame Street* puppeteers came together to sing "Look Through the Window," the song that Hunt, as Muppet opera singer Placido Flamingo, had so proudly sung alongside real-life opera star Placido Domingo. The *Sesame* performers ranged from Hunt's longtime colleagues like Nelson, Spinney, and Gold, through the next generation he had mentored like Robinson, Arciero, and Rudman, to brand-new apprentices like Joey Mazzarino and Carmen Osbahr. The lyrics wonderfully reflected Hunt's fearlessness even as he embarked on a whole new adventure. "Look through the window, walk through the door," the song exhorts. Step into a new, wondrous, awe-inspiring place, where you can "open your heart to joy evermore." The *Sesame Street* performers puppeteered and sang, and the whole room sang along.

> Love and trust are just waiting in a place we all can share,
> Look through the window, walk through the door—
> We're THERE!

After the service, the family held a reception around the corner at St. John's Synod Hall. From there, people trickled down to Hunt's apartment, where Jane hosted a get-together. Hunt's Elmwood friend Nancy Persons came with their mutual friend Matt McCabe. Jane said they could take something to remember him by, like one of his shirts, so they went into his room to look. Under Hunt's bed, McCabe discovered a big package of firecrackers. "To me that's quintessential Richard," laughs Persons. "What other forty-year-old is stashing fireworks under his bed?" After the gathering, Persons and McCabe walked around the corner to Riverside Park and set off the firecrackers over the Hudson in memory of Hunt—a fitting tribute, the lights dazzling against the dark sky and shining again on the water, bright against the backdrop of New Jersey.

Hunt's legacy lives on through all those who loved him, through the audience that appreciates his work, through the performers he taught, and through the continuation of his characters. Aptly, his mentees are carrying his legacy forward.

David Rudman inherited the bulk of Hunt's characters on *Sesame Street*, including silent construction worker Sully and Hunt's half of the Two-Headed Monster. "It was so fun to be able to do those, and see what it was like to be Richard," says Rudman. Placido Flamingo was retired with Hunt, because who else could play him?

The fate of some of Hunt's other *Sesame Street* characters reflects some of the show's overall changes. Gladys the Cow, after disappearing for over a decade, was taken over by Jennifer Barnhart, a hopeful sign of increased female Muppet characters played by female puppeteers. Around the same time, Hunt's neurotic pianist Don Music was canned for fear that he was a bad example. "The character was abandoned because of complaints about his alarming tendencies toward self-inflicted pun-ishment," reported the book *Sesame Street Unpaved*. "Apparently, kids were imitating his head-banging at home." Promisingly, Don Music (played by the impish, Hunt-like Ryan Dillon) returned in 2019 for *Sesame Street*'s fiftieth anniversary special.

As for Hunt's major Muppet characters, Sweetums was played by John Henson and then Matt Vogel; Statler was played by Nelson, then Whit-mire, then Peter Linz, always alongside Goelz, who had taken over for Henson as Waldorf. Beaker was played by Whitmire and then Rudman, who also took over the role of Janice.

Hunt's young alter ego Scooter lay low for a while, was voiced by Hunt's brother Adam in 1999's feature film *Muppets from Space*, then dis-appeared for nearly another decade. "Scooter wasn't around for a long time, and then they decided they wanted to bring him back," says Rud-man. Who better to play the role than Rudman, who had not only taken over so many of Hunt's other roles, but had been mentored by Hunt since his days as a young, eager apprentice, just like Scooter, a character based on Hunt in his own early days. "I think about Richard all the time when I'm doing the characters," says Rudman. "It's honoring Richard. It's keeping his legacy alive."

Hunt's legacy also lives on, hopefully, through this book.

Afterword

THIS BOOK BEGAN, as well it should have, as a labor of love.

When I was a kid in the 1980s, in America's rust belt suburbia, the Muppets were everywhere—television, movies, books, records, toys. You could say they were part of the very fabric of my life. Actually, you *could* say that—I slept on Kermit-print sheets.

I rediscovered the Muppets about twenty years later. I was living in Brooklyn, trying to find my footing as an independent adult. Once or twice a week, my next-door neighbor Effie and I would eat dinner together, watch *The Muppet Show,* and laugh our heads off. In a frightening, unpredictable world, the Muppets were one of life's reliable joys. I adored the dynamic of "affectionate anarchy" (Frank Oz's phrase) among the characters; they treated each other with genuine good feeling, even as they blew each other up.

But now, unlike as a child, I noticed the vast amounts of effort and illusion that went into bringing these puppets so vividly to life. Who was behind this? I had heard of Jim Henson, but now I paid attention to the different voices and puppeteering styles, the unique characteristics each performer brought to the job.

One performer in particular grabbed my attention: Richard Hunt. He played most of my favorite characters, a broad range of personalities from young, eager Scooter to old, jaded Statler; groovy, laid-back Janice to squeaking, freaked-out Beaker; huge, gruff Sweetums to an early version of queenly Miss Piggy; and so many more. Yet various as they were, his characters had a certain sensibility, his own individual stamp.

When I found out that Hunt was only forty when he died in 1992, I assumed it was a typo. Everyone knows you can't believe everything you read on the internet. Not only had he been the secret weapon of *The Muppet Show*, he had worked on *Sesame Street*, *Fraggle Rock*, three major Muppet movies, a handful of short-lived shows, countless specials, and even a couple of non-Muppet films. No way had he crammed all that into forty years.

But it was true. Hunt died at forty in the AIDS epidemic, predeceased by many friends as well as the love of his life. Yet day after day, in the face of grief and tragedy, Hunt showed up to work and was reliably funny. Was he just that talented, that driven, that resilient, or what? Yes, yes, and yes.

I caught a glimpse of Hunt in Charles Kaiser's dishy history *The Gay Metropolis*: "What I remember is Richard calling me in the wee hours of the morning, inviting himself down with a quart of orange juice and pot," recalled "on-again, off-again" lover Charles Gibson, a *Sesame Street* production assistant. "We'd get high and we'd drink our orange juice. And we'd go to bed."

I sure hadn't seen *that* side of him on *Sesame Street*. Or had I? I loved the detail of the orange juice, like a kid on a happy sugar buzz. Who was this playful, exuberant character? Now I couldn't see the Muppets without wondering what I *wasn't* seeing. How were Hunt's characters so iconic, yet his character so invisible? Who *was* this guy?

I guess you could say I was on a *Hunt*.

I was fascinated by the way Hunt's life brought together two worlds which are seen as separate—and, in fact, deliberately kept apart. Puppetry is ghettoized as being only for children—a disservice to a brilliant, all-ages art form—and queer topics are thought of as strictly for adults. Hunt's life explodes these boundaries. I was shocked to realize that the era of "peak Muppets" was also the era of "peak AIDS," though we think of these phenomena as completely disconnected. My Generation X heart was hooked.

As I uncovered Hunt's story, I was touched by how he came to terms with his sexuality over the course of his life. Hunt's experience reflects similar journeys taken by other members of his generation and the country as a whole, as one's life often reflects one's times. Hunt graduated high school in 1969, the same year as the Stonewall Riots, considered the beginning of America's LGBTQ+ rights movement. At first he didn't identify with the gay community, which was just beginning to cohere. He and lover Duncan Kenworthy quarreled over being out, with Hunt wanting to hide their relationship. But even as he became more open, he didn't like terms like "gay" or "queer." When he talked about his sexuality, he'd call himself a "funny boy." He didn't let his sexuality define him, and he didn't let other people define it for him. Characteristically, he defined it for himself—as a joke.

In that sense, "funny boy" is the perfect term for Hunt. "Funny" is his livelihood, his stock in trade, his trickster spirit, his most disarming weapon. Funny is larger than life, outsized, loud, and free. Funny gets away with pushing the line, making them think, because it also makes them laugh. Funny enjoys itself, even when life is rough. This terminology is classic Hunt: *If anyone's going to make fun of this, it's me.*

And "boy" reminds us that Hunt died at forty, costing him decades of promise, from a preventable epidemic exacerbated by prejudice. "Boy" is not to imply he was anything less than a man; in many ways he grew up early, as the oldest brother of five siblings, and as a performer at such a young age, already aware of his vocation. But there was a Peter Pan youthful playfulness to him, even in his most despairing moments, that he likely would have retained even as a senior citizen.

Given Hunt's outsized, fearless personality, it seems fitting that writing his biography often shoved me out of my comfort zone. I spoke with nearly one hundred of Hunt's family members, lovers, colleagues, friends, and classmates, each of them giving me a little piece of his larger story. I traveled to nearly all of Hunt's beloved places, interviewing people all around Manhattan, New Jersey, Martha's Vineyard, Truro, and Toronto, even taking my first trip overseas to London to research the book. I fought over a lot of restaurant checks. Mark Hamill's dog Mabel fell asleep on my lap. I made Frank Oz laugh.

And as I worked on this book, I found Hunt's personality rubbing off on me. Instead of being wary of people, I was curious to get to know them. Instead of hiding at home with a book (or an episode of *The Muppet*

Show), this hermit started going out. Lo and behold, I fell in love with a woman who lived in New Jersey, just six miles over from Hunt's old hometown of Closter. Reader, I married her. (Jerry Nelson's widow Jan, who became a friend, says that Hunt was "Jersey matchmaking from heaven.") I even caught a couple of geographical errors in the manuscript that I would have missed had I not come to know the area.

Following your heart is risky. Life can be scary. But you only get the one—so make the most of it. Enjoy the adventure. If I learned anything from writing this book, from Richard Hunt—that's it.

ACKNOWLEDGMENTS

THANK YOU SO MUCH to everyone whose words are woven into this book. Please see the exhaustive list of interviewees at the beginning of the sources section. Hunt's generosity lives on in his loved ones. Telling his story was truly a collaborative effort.

Thanks also to those I interviewed who were not quoted: Christopher Bartlett; Warrick Brownlow-Pike; Danette DeSena; Bonnie Erickson; Dan Fishback; Judy Freudberg; Donald Grove; Manny Gutierrez; John Kennedy; Julia Nock; Arthur Novell; Davina Parmet; Steve Quester; Eric Rhein; Gordon Robertson; Mark Saltzman; Steve Saunders; Michael Schiavi; Rick Schiaffo; Hollis Smith; Robin Smith; John Tartaglia; Hugh Taylor; Isaac Taylor; Jane Taylor; Jeanne Taylor; Karen Valleau; and those who chose not to be named.

Thank you to the countless friends of Hunt who sent me wonderful stories.

Thank you to the invaluably generous Karen Falk and everyone at the Jim Henson Company Archives. The Muppet Wiki was also a vital resource.

Thank you to those who shared private archival footage, especially Victor DiNapoli, Dave Goelz, Brian Meehl, and Rick Schiaffo.

Thank you for photo help to Ed Christie; Karen Falk; Stuart Fischer; the Hunt family; Jan Nelson; Jerry Nelson; Carmen Osbahr; Tana Reiff; Richard Termine; the Jim Henson Company; and Sesame Workshop.

A special "My Hero" award to this book's unofficial art director, Victor DiNapoli.

Thank you to all the patrons who supported this project on Patreon: Meagan Barbeau; Lauren ("Lolly") Bonanno; Jonathan Brangwynne; Nat Browne; Micky C.; Joe Coughlin; Zachary DiMotta; Priscilla Dowden-White; Mike Duncan; Grace Elizabeth; Luke Elmer; Simon Finger; Shannon Foster; Shira Fuchs; Matthew Gaydos; K. George; Charlotte Gilmore; Luc Goodhart; Kim Gyorkos; Kevin Hansen; Rae Hargadon; Christopher Harris; Samuel Horton-Martin; Chris Jones; Hannah Knizacky; Jamie Lutes; Abigail M.; Shannon Marinko; Ava Mas; Grace McBrian; Lisa McCarty; Mo McGrath; Sophie McGrath; Laura Mercer; Ursa Monroe; Theo N.; Meredith Octopoda; Ben Ossenfort; Amy Pratt; Kerry Purvis; Jonathan Renteria-Elyea; Al Rhodes; Michal Richardson; Lily Ritner; Barbara Katz Rothman; Hugh Ryan; Brendan Sandham; Ken Schatz; Chad Shonk; Zachary Neil Snyder; Annie Van Newkirk; Gabbi Verducci; and Amanda X.

Thank you for help and encouragement along the way: Sarah Chinn; Denise Dubois; Chelsea Goodwin; Naomi Jaffe; Brian Jay Jones; Stephen Kent Jusick; Theodore "Ted" Kerr; Jeffrey Lewis (of Bluestockings Bookstore); Rusty Mae Moore; Sarah Schulman; and Barbara Smith. Thank you to Lucy Thane, my London savior; Aria Stewart, webmistress extraordinaire; and Query, who helped with the title.

Thanks to my dad Martin Stein, who repeatedly said he couldn't wait to see *Funny Boy* in the bookstore, but died before it came out.

Special thanks to Jane Hunt and Jerry Nelson, who were incredibly encouraging in the early stages of this project, in what would turn out to be the last years of their lives. Without them, this book would never have happened.

Special thanks to *Fraggle Rock* producer Lawrence Mirkin, a true mensch, who provided detailed feedback on the entire manuscript, as well as great encouragement. Special thanks also to Pam Arciero, Dave Goelz, and Jan Nelson.

An extra-special thanks to the entire Hunt family: Jane Hunt, Arthur Miller, Kate Hunt, Lyn Hunt Russell, Adam Hunt and Rachel Hunt, as well as the next generation. Hunt's spirit lives on in your family.

Thank you to Robert Guinsler and everyone at Sterling Lord Literistic, for helping this book find a home.

Thank you to my editor Nicole Solano and everyone at Rutgers University Press.

Thank you to Sherry Gerstein at Westchester Publishing Services.

Thanks to Lisa and Sam, chosen family.

And Andrée Cornelia—my one.

SOURCES

List of Interviewees

A biography of someone as sociable as Hunt necessitates a large cast of characters. Here's a handy guide to the nearly seventy people quoted in this book. Everyone is introduced by full name upon first use, and afterward by last name, with additional clarifications as needed.

People who were not Hunt's co-workers or classmates are labeled as friends; however, most of his colleagues and classmates were friends as well.

Acronyms

FR	*Fraggle Rock*
GOFH	*The Ghost of Faffner Hall*
HA	Henson Associates
NVRHS	Northern Valley Regional High School
SS	*Sesame Street*
TMS	*The Muppet Show*

Aldighieri, Merrill: HA colleague
Angus, Terry: FR performer
Arciero, Pam: SS performer
Bailey, Joe: TMS and SS writer
Baker, Martin: TMS floor manager; FR associate producer
Baretta, Bill: Muppet performer
Blaylock, Cheryl: SS designer/builder and performer
Capeci, Ernie: Closter friend
Christie, Ed: Muppet designer/builder

Coogan, Pete: FR production assistant; GOFH production manager
DiNapoli, Victor: SS art director and production designer
Earl, Michael: SS performer
Fischer, Stuart: NYC friend
Gardner, Rob: SS production assistant
Goelz, Dave: Original Five, FR and TMS performer
Gold, Louise: TMS performer
Hamill, Marilou: friend
Hamill, Mark: TMS guest star, friend
Haynes, Jesper: NYC friend
Henson, Brian: Muppet performer, Jim Henson's son
Hunt, Jane: Hunt's mother
Hunt, Kate: Hunt's older sister
Hunt, Lyn: Hunt's younger sister
Hunt, Rachel: Hunt's youngest sister
Kaiser, Charles: lover
Karwat, Kathy: HA colleague
Kenworthy, Duncan: lover; FR co-creator and producer
LaFrance, Paul: caretaker at Corn Hill Cottages
Land, Peter: England friend
MacNeal, Noel: SS performer
McDonald, Barbara: NVRHS classmate
Meehl, Brian: SS performer
Miller, Arthur: Jane Hunt's partner
Mills, Rob: FR performer
Minogue, Terry: NVRHS classmate
Mirkin, Lawrence: FR producer
Moss, Wayne: FR floor manager
Mullen, Kathy: TMS and FR performer
Nelson, Jan: Jerry Nelson's wife
Nelson, Jerry: Original Five, FR, TMS, and SS performer
Nettinga, Jon: NVRHS classmate
O'Connor, Sean: NVRHS classmate
Orman, Roscoe: SS actor, played Gordon
Oz, Frank: Original Five, FR, TMS, and SS performer
Pearce, Neil: England friend
Pearce, Sally: England friend
Persons, Nancy: Elmwood friend
Pfeiffer, Dale: NVRHS classmate
Phillips, Laura: FR writer
Poch, Gail: NVRHS music teacher

Prell, Karen: FR and GOFH performer
Quinn, Mike: GOFH performer
Reiff, Tana: NVRHS classmate
Robinson, Martin: SS performer
Rudman, David: SS performer
Sackson, Geni: NVRHS classmate
Schwartz, Andrew: NYC roommate
Singer, Dulcy: SS producer/executive producer
Spinney, Debi: wife of SS performer Caroll Spinney
Stevenson, Jocelyn: FR co-creator and writer; GOFH producer, creator, and writer
Stiles, Norman: SS head writer
Stoddart, Matt: NVRHS classmate
Taylor, Livingston: friend, brother-in-law
Termine, Richard: Muppet designer/builder
Tripician, Joe: HA colleague
Varughese, Sugith: FR writer
Wilson, Mak: GOFH performer

Notes

All quotes are from interviews with the author, unless otherwise specified. All Richard Hunt quotes are from his 1990 archival interview located in the Jim Henson Company Archives, again unless otherwise specified.

Prelude

2 **"Gus went nuts"**: Michael Davis, *Street Gang* (New York: Viking, 2008), 241.
2 **"My qualifications"**: "Muppet Show Press Kit Biography," undated, ca. 1976, Your Face!, rhuntfan.tripod.com/press.html.
2 **"I'd drop anything"**: "Muppet Show Press Kit Biography."
3 **"Henson Associates"**: Confirmed by Henson Archives.
3 **"I'm a puppeteer"**: Jane Hunt interview, November 7, 2009.

Chapter 1   Jersey Boy

7 **"He loved performing"**: Steve Swanson, "Show #57: Mother's Day," *The MuppetCast*, audio podcast, May 11, 2008.
8 **"The hottest ticket in television"**: Davis, *Street Gang*.
8 **"Wanted more than anything"**: Dave Barry, *Dave Barry Turns Fifty* (New York: Random House, 1998), 43.

11 **"I got the lead"**: Ron X. Gumucio, "Playhouse Focus of Armchair Lecture," *The Journal News*, February 14, 2006.

12 **"Successfully disguised to myself"**: James Agee, *A Death in the Family* (New York: McDowell, Obolensky), 1957.

Chapter 2   *Making a Career*

18 **"Choir geeks"**: Dale Pfeiffer interview, June 20, 2012.

23 **"Oh yeah, I was even back then"**: Nancy Persons interview, April 23, 2012.

25 **"Best tenor in the state"**: Northern Valley Regional High School, Demarest New Jersey, 1968 yearbook.

Chapter 3   *Apprentice*

30 **"He created an atmosphere"**: The Jim Henson Company Archives, "9/–/1970—'Fran Brill Starts with Muppets on Sesame Street,'" Henson.com, henson.com/jimsredbook/2014/09/9-1970/.

31 **"Affectionate anarchy"**: Rhiannon Corby, "Frank Oz on Miss Piggy's Secret Backstory and Jim Henson's Legacy," *The New Yorker Radio Hour,* audio podcast, April 6, 2018.

31 **"A means to an end"**: Judy Harris, interview with Jim Henson, September 21, 1982, users.bestweb.net/~foosie/henson.htm.

32 **"I never wanted"**: Kenneth Plume, "Interview with Frank Oz," IGN.com., February 10, 2000, ign.com/articles/2000/02/10/interview-with-frank-oz-part-1-of-4.

33 **"I'm from Oklahoma"**: This section draws on my interview with Nelson; Ryan Dosier, "Interview with Legendary Muppeteer Jerry Nelson," *The Muppet Mindset*, November 12, 2010, themuppetmindset.blogspot.com/2010/11/interview-with-legendarymuppeteer.html; Joe Hennes, "A Chat with Jerry Nelson," ToughPigs.com, December 8, 2009, toughpigs.com/a-chat-with-jerry-nelson-part-1/; and Kenneth Plume, "Still Counting: An Interview with Muppeteer Jerry Nelson," MuppetCentral.com, March 1, 1999, muppet-central.com/articles/interviews/nelson1.shtml.

34 **"When Christine was born"**: Jacqueline Gordon, *Give Me One Wish* (New York: Berkeley Books, 1988), 4.

35 **"Jerry and I can't believe it"**: Gordon, *Give Me One Wish*, 11.

36 **"After that first series of auditions"**: Harris interview.

37 **"Seriousness"**: Grant Bachiocco, "John Lovelady (Muppets, the Great Space Coaster)—Under the Puppet #28," SaturdayMorningMedia.com, audio podcast, 2019, saturdaymorningmedia.com/2019/05/utp-28/.

40 **"A hell of a lot"**: Richard Hunt, letter to Dale Pfeiffer, April 1970. Personal collection of Dale Pfeiffer.

Chapter 4   Sunny Days

45 **"We knew that young children"**: "Children and Television Lessons from Sesame Street," *The Gallup (NM) Independent*, June 10, 1974.

46 **Kids who watched it**: Renata Adler, "Cookie, Oscar, Grover, Herry, Ernie, and Company: The Invention of *Sesame Street*," *The New Yorker*, May 27, 1972, newyorker.com/magazine/1972/06/03/cookie-oscar-grover-herry-ernie-and -company.

47 **"Even those of us who believed"**: Ron Grossman, "Sesame Streetwise," *Chicago Tribune*, November 13, 1988, chicagotribune.com/news/ct-xpm-1988 -11-13-8802160186-story.html.

47 **"It was a blessing"**: Plume, "Interview with Frank Oz."

47 **"Jim would never teach"**: Plume, "Interview with Frank Oz."

50 **It was the third murder**: "Fear Rules on Campus of Temple U.; 3 Students Slain," *Gettysburg Times*, September 26, 1972.

53 **"The wonder boy"**: Charles Kaiser, *The Gay Metropolis* (New York: Harcourt Brace & Company, 1997), 311.

53 **"Yeah, I fuck guys"**: Stuart Fischer interview, December 22, 2009.

53 **"Funny boy"**: From numerous interviews, including those with Stuart Fischer and Ernie Capeci.

Chapter 5   Camaraderie

62 **"No more. Jim is their equal"**: Joe Hennes, "'Turn Back Time': The Muppets on the Cher Show," ToughPigs.com, April 29, 2015, toughpigs.com/cher-1/.

62 **"Adult Muppets who can stay up late"**: *The Tomorrow Show with Tom Snyder*, 1975.

62 **"Just six Muppet performers appeared on *Saturday Night Live*"**: Rhonda Hansome appeared as Vazh in the first episode, but was subsequently replaced by Brill.

63 **"We were very friendly"**: Plume, "Interview with Frank Oz."

64 **"Jane said, 'But that's not Muppets'"**: Plume, "Still Counting: An Interview with Muppeteer Jerry Nelson."

64 **"I felt the thing"**: Harris interview.

64 **"Eventually it was obvious"**: Plume, "Interview with Frank Oz."

65 **"I was already busy"**: Bernie Brillstein, interview with Archive of American Television, 2001, interviews.televisionacademy.com/interviews/bernie -brillstein.

66 **"I'm having a really good time!"**: Richard Hunt, letter to Duncan Kenworthy, January 1976. Personal collection of Duncan Kenworthy.

Chapter 6   *Affectionate Anarchy*

74   **"I want you to meet some people":** Jerry Nelson interview, February 13, 2010.

75   **"The bus passed the limousine":** Joe Bailey, *Memoirs of a Muppet Writer* (New York: Walnut Press, 2012).

75   **"It was a band of misfits":** Dave Goelz, interviewed by Adam Kreutinger, "Puppet Tears ep 64—Dave Goelz Talks Muppets and Mayhem," Puppettears .com, video podcast, December 23, 2000, www.puppettears.com/davegoelz.html.

76   **"Me not crazy?":** TMS, Lesley Ann Warren episode, 1979.

76   **"Scooter is very much me":** *Of Muppets and Men* documentary, directed by Harley Cokliss and Peter Berry, 1981.

77   **"I'm your new gofer":** TMS, Jim Nabors episode, 1976.

79   **"Muppet Glee Club":** TMS, Juliet Prowse episode, 1977.

80   **Piggy's karate chop:** TMS, Ruth Buzzi episode, 1976.

83   **"I, of course, being the biggest, hunkiest dude":** Canadian Broadcasting Corporation interview with Richard Hunt, 1979.

Chapter 7   *Muppetmania*

87   **"We can have some deep dish":** Bailey, *Memoirs of a Muppet Writer*, 118.

88   **"Parallel universe of neon and linoleum":** Bailey, *Memoirs of a Muppet Writer*, 119.

91   **"It's a California surfer girl":** CBC interview.

92   **"Let's start with Richard's number":** Christopher Finch. *Of Muppets and Men: The Making of The Muppet Show* (New York: Alfred A. Knopf, 1981), 135.

94   **"When we had Raquel Welch":** Harris interview.

94   **"He waved and winked":** Finch, *Of Muppets and Men*, 102.

95   **"Well, fer sure. It's Danielle, right?":** Finch, *Of Muppets and Men*, 147.

96   **"When you're spending about three days":** *Of Muppets and Men* documentary.

98   **"You're working in a confined space":** *Of Muppets and Men*, 152–153.

98   **"Come on, Richard":** *Of Muppets and Men* documentary.

99   **"It was hard to make that entertaining":** "Toughpigs Talks the Muppet Show with Dave Goelz," YouTube, February 24, 2001, https://www.youtube.com /watch?v=K7EPg8iFOGA.

99   **Beaker's troubles:** Cloned (TMS 514), shrunk (TMS 306), enlarged (*The Muppet Movie*, implied), electrocuted (TMS 222), abducted by a germ (TMS 307), superglued (TMS 304).

99   **"I love this guy":** Finch, *Of Muppets and Men*, 147.

101   **"Being on the road":** Bailey, *Memoirs of a Muppet Writer*, 215.

101   **"Let's go backstage":** Bailey, *Memoirs of a Muppet Writer*, 218.

104   **"You like to suck cock":** Kaiser, *The Gay Metropolis*, 311. Verified in Kaiser interview.

104   **"We're not going to talk about this":** Brian Henson interview, October 27, 2015.

Chapter 8 Millions of People Happy

111 **"Calisthenics" and "craftsmanship"**: Kenneth Plume, "Gonzo Puppe-teerism: An Interview with Dave Goelz," January 28, 2000, MuppetCentral .com.

113 **"We're taking the characters"**: "On the Road with the Muppets," *Variety*, August 20, 1978.

113 **"If you don't dig sore arms"**: *Circus*, March 20, 1979.

114 **"Do you see that guy"**: Jim Hemphill, "Making a Hammer Film as If It Was Directed by Scorsese: John Landis on Innocent Blood and Operating Muppets with Tim Burton," *Filmmaker*, October 3, 2017.

114 **"Things were getting ugly"**: Rob Lowe, *Stories I Only Tell My Friends* (New York: Henry Holt and Company), 2011.

115 **"Perhaps the most widely seen"**: John J. O'Connor, "TV WEEKEND; Teen-Ager Is Challenged by Ultragorgon," *The New York Times*, July 7, 1989.

115 **"The most popular television entertainment"**: John Skow, "Those Marvel-ous Muppets," *Time*, December 25, 1978.

116 **"Forget about what those people"**: Caroll Spinney, *The Wisdom of Big Bird* (New York: Villard, 2003), 95.

117 **"One of my top three"**: *Disney 23* (fan magazine), Winter 2011, 52.

118 **"We're doing what everybody else"**: *60 Minutes*, March 17, 1979.

119 **"We get to know"**: Roger Ebert, "The Muppet Movie," November 14, 1979, rogerebert.com/reviews/the-muppet-movie-1979.

120 **"He would make the time"**: Bachiocco, "John Lovelady (Muppets, the Great Space Coaster)."

120 **"It's a very good thing"**: *Of Muppets and Men*, directed by Cokliss and Berry.

121 **"What do you do"**: Jan Nelson interview, not dated.

121 **"By asking a group"**: Bailey, *Memoirs of a Muppet Writer*.

123 **"What are you doing?"**: Plume, "Still Counting: An Interview with Muppe-teer Jerry Nelson."

125 **"Lo and behold"**: *Being Elmo: A Puppeteer's Journey*, directed by Constance Marks (Constance Marks Productions, 2011).

Chapter 9 Endings and Beginnings

128 **"I wish there was footage"**: Dosier, "Interview with Legendary Muppeteer Jerry Nelson."

129 **"Jim loved performers"**: Plume, "Still Counting: An Interview with Muppe-teer Jerry Nelson."

130 **"When you start making more money"**: Martin Baker interview, January 17, 2014.

134 **"No festival has so far"**: Nancy Straub, "Once in a Lifetime: The 1980 World Puppetry Festival," *Puppetry International*, July 2014, lacquiparledesign.com /pofa/puppetry-journal/once-in-a-lifetime-the-1980-world-puppetry-festival -by-nancy-staub-full-article.

134 **"That would have been"**: Straub, "Once in a Lifetime."

138 **"Hi, Gumbelina"**: All quotes in this section from Gordon, *Give Me One Wish*, 192.

139 **"If I want to live on the beach"**: Leighanne Mazure, "Tribute," Your Face!, rhuntfan.tripod.com/mazure.html.

142 **"Lose their special quality"**: Roger Ebert, "The Great Muppet Caper," January 1, 1981, rogerebert.com/reviews/the-great-muppet-caper-1981.

143 **"Health nut"**: Merrill Aldergheri interview, February 27, 2011.

Chapter 10   Top of the World

147 **"You sparked spontaneous joy"**: The Jim Henson Company Archives, "12/31/1983—'To Pasadena for the Rose Bowl—Miss Piggy Float— Lisa, Heather, Brian,'" Henson.com, henson.com/jimsredbook/2012/12 /12311983.

149 **"Okay. You go down to the bodega"**: Pam Arciero interview, May 22, 2010.

149 **"Hey, guess who I saw this weekend?"**: Pam Arciero interview.

150 **"The first show that I personally didn't"**: Henson in AFI seminar, May 6, 1986, qtd. in Brian Jay Jones, *Jim Henson: The Biography* (New York: Ballantine Books, 2013), 340.

150 **"Fearless leader"**: Jerry Nelson referred to Henson as the troupe's "fearless leader" at his memorial service.

152 **"Impossible, enormous, grandiose"**: *Fraggle Rock Complete Series Collection*, DVD, HIT Entertainment, 2008.

152 **"The audience is the only one"**: *Fraggle Rock Complete Series Collection*.

153 **"He's kind of the cement"**: *Fraggle Rock Complete Series Collection*.

154 **"Yes, but you have to come over"**: *Fraggle Rock Complete Series Collection*.

155 **"When he was a little boy"**: *Down at Fraggle Rock*, documentary, produced by Diana Birkenfield and Dave Gumpel, 1987.

158 **"Oh man, that fucking blind puppet"**: Martin Robinson interview, May 22, 2010.

159 **"Without any narrative drive"**: Vincent Canby, "Screen: Henson's Crystal," *The New York Times*, December 17, 1982, nytimes.com/1982/12/17/movies /henson-s-crystal.html.

160 **"Oh, like I'm going to say *that*"**: Rob Mills interview, July 6, 2010.

161 **"Technical wizardry"**: "Secrets of the Muppets," *Jim Henson Hour* episode 110, directed by Peter Harris, 1992.

161 **"I'm doing this under duress"**: Rob Mills interview.

Chapter 11   Making Connections

165 **"You've got it"**: "Showbiz: Of Muppets and Puppets," Linda Pender, *Cincinnati Magazine*, December 1983.

166 **"When Jim and I had worked"**: Plume, "Interview with Frank Oz."

167 **"You. *Trading Places*."**: Stuart Fischer interview.

175 **"I hate this damn puppet"**: Martin Robinson interview.

176 **"Richard immediately had a character"**: *Fraggle Rock Complete Series Collection*.

178 **"All right, we're done"**: Martin Robinson interview.

178 **"Extraordinaire"**: Vincent Canby, "Film: Broadway Setting for 3D Muppet Romp," *New York Times*, July 13, 1984.

179 **"*Manhattan* was like a restatement"**: Plume, "Gonzo Puppeteerism."

Chapter 12   Changes

181 **"This was pretty unusual"**: Spinney, *The Wisdom of Big Bird*, 109.

182 **"Richard saved his energy"**: Davis, *Street Gang*, 285.

182 **"I'm done"**: Noel MacNeal interview, December 15, 2011.

182 **"He was always throwing characters"**: Steve Swanson, "Show #41: The Richard Hunt MuppetCast Tribute," *The MuppetCast*, audio podcast, January 20, 2008.

182 **"If he doesn't know"**: *Being Elmo*.

183 **"When the character"**: Swanson, "Show #41: The Richard Hunt MuppetCast Tribute."

184 **"He felt it was inappropriate"**: Jake Rossen, "Her Name Was Skeeter: The Mystery of the Missing Muppet," MentalFloss.com, February 17, 2016, mentalfloss.com/article/75596/her-name-was-skeeter-mystery-missing-muppet.

184 **"Well, I think it'll make sense"**: Larry Mirkin interview, January 14, 2017.

186 **"Two little scaredy-cats"**: *Fraggle Rock Complete Series Collection*, Season 3 Special Features.

186 **"Do you know how many people"**: *Fraggle Rock* wrap party, 1986. Private collection.

187 **"Richard Hunt gave me"**: *Fraggle Rock Complete Series Collection*.

188 **"That's how I ended up"**: Herbie Hancock, *Possibilities* (New York: Penguin Books, 2015), 262.

188 **"There must be another side"**: *Fraggle Rock Complete Series Collection*.

189 **"You know, we had a fight"**: Pam Arciero interview.

Chapter 13   Three Terrible Things

197 "CBC would have been": Plume, "Still Counting: An Interview with Muppeteer Jerry Nelson."

199 "The juxtapositioning": Scott Shaw, "Muppet Babies and Me," *MuppetZine* 3, Winter 1993.

199 "So they said": Joe Hennes, "Mokey Fraggle Speaks: The Kathy Mullen Interview," ToughPigs.com, August 13, 2013, toughpigs.com/kathy-mullen-1/.

200 "I know that you're not": Martin Robinson interview.

203 "It brought back all those years": Swanson, "Show #41: The Richard Hunt MuppetCast Tribute."

Chapter 14   Magic Be with You

211 "Directing is a lot different": *Down at Fraggle Rock* documentary.

212 "Cantus *is* Jim": *Fraggle Rock Complete Series Collection.*

213 "It was a lot of fun": *Down at Fraggle Rock* documentary.

214 "Until next time": *Fraggle Rock Complete Series Collection.*

214 "How come it's always *men* talking?": *Fraggle Rock* wrap party.

Chapter 15   Resilience

223 "It'd be getting around": Swanson, "Show #41: The Richard Hunt MuppetCast Tribute."

228 "Puppets! I'm an actor, not a dolly wiggler": *They're Only Human*, sitcom pilot. Private collection of Brian Meehl.

230 "One could have made": Bernard Holland, "Concert: 'Music for Life,' a Benefit," *The New York Times*, November 9, 1987.

231 "Golden time": Steve Whitmire, "A Muppet Family Christmas," Steve Whitmire.website, December 8, 2020, stevewhitmire.website/?p=5712.

231 "Victory lap": Danny Horn, "My Week with More Christmas, Part Four," ToughPigs.com, December 25, 2005, toughpigs.com/my-week-with-more-christmas-4/.

Chapter 16   Moving On

240 "Richard didn't really like": Swanson, "Show #41: The Richard Hunt MuppetCast Tribute."

241 "Richard had the puppet's hands": Joe Hennes, "A Chat with Joey Mazzarino," ToughPigs.com, February 23, 2009, toughpigs.com/a-chat-with-joey-mazzarino-part-1/.

244 **"This one sings"**: Alan Carter, "Picks and Pans Review: Jim Henson's *The Ghost of Faffner Hall*," *People*, September 11, 1989.

Chapter 17 Saying Goodbye

253 **"How many people got cold feet"**: Hunt at Northern Valley Regional High School Twentieth Reunion, 1990. Private collection of Rick Schiaffo.

258 **"I probably heard it officially"**: Kenneth Plume, "Ratting Out: An Interview with Muppeteer Steve Whitmire." MuppetCentral.com, July 19, 1999, muppetcentral.com/articles/interviews/whitmire1.shtml

Chapter 18 Sage

264 **"Nice, friendly little service"**: Jim Henson, open letter to "Children and Friends," March 2, 1986, Henson Family Properties. Quoted in Jones, *Jim Henson*.

266 **"Welcome all"**: Richard Hunt, "Jim Henson's Memorial Service," Youtube, uploaded by The Jim Henson Collection, May 19, 2015, youtube.com/watch?v =mEArJXD8YFY.

273 **"Richard Hunt jokingly said"**: Kevin Clash, *My Life as a Furry Red Monster* (New York: Broadway Books, 2006), 57.

Chapter 19 A Whole New Adventure

282 **"When I look back on it"**: Plume, "Ratting Out."

285 **"We were all flabbergasted"**: Dave Goelz, "Dave Goelz Remembers," Your Face!, rhuntfan.tripod.com/goelz.html.

286 **"The one thing that sticks in me"**: Swanson, "Show #41: The Richard Hunt MuppetCast Tribute."

288 **"The circle is the form of nature"**: Hunt at Henson's London memorial service, 1990. Jim Henson Company Archives.

Chapter 20 Legacy

All quotes and information in this chapter from Richard Hunt's memorial service, 1992. Jim Henson Company Archives.

297 **"The character was abandoned"**: David Borgenicht, *Sesame Street Unpaved* (New York: Hyperion Books, 1998).

Afterword

300 **"What I remember"**: Kaiser, *The Gay Metropolis*, 311.

ILLUSTRATION CREDITS

Chapter 1, page 6: Courtesy of the Hunt family.

Chapter 2, page 16: Courtesy of private owner.

Chapter 3, page 28: Courtesy of Stuart Fischer. Photo: Stuart Fischer.

Chapter 4, page 44: Courtesy of The Jim Henson Company and Sesame Workshop. All Rights Reserved. Ernie and Bert © 2023 Sesame Workshop®, Sesame Street®, and associated characters, trademarks, and design elements are owned and licensed by Sesame Workshop. All rights reserved.

Chapter 5, page 56: Courtesy of the Jerry Nelson estate. Photo: Jerry Nelson.

Chapter 6, page 72: Courtesy of Victor DiNapoli. Photo: Victor DiNapoli.

Chapter 7, page 86: Courtesy of *The Daily Express*, UK/Mirrorpix. Photo: Barry Gomer.

Chapter 8, page 110: Courtesy of Ed Christie. Photo: Ed Christie.

Chapter 9, page 126: Courtesy of the Jerry Nelson estate.

Chapter 10, page 146: Courtesy of private owner. Photos: Stephen Finnie.

Chapter 11, page 164: From *Trading Places*, John Landis, director.

Chapter 12, page 180: Courtesy of the Jerry Nelson estate.

Chapter 13, page 192: Courtesy of Victor DiNapoli. Photo: Victor DiNapoli.

Chapter 14, page 206: Courtesy of The Jim Henson Company. All Rights Reserved. © 2023 The Jim Henson Company. FRAGGLE ROCK mark & logo, characters, and elements are trademarks of The Jim Henson Company. All Rights Reserved.

Chapter 15, page 220: Courtesy of Carmen Osbahr. Photo: Carmen Osbahr.

Chapter 16, page 234: Courtesy of The Jim Henson Company. All Rights Reserved.

Chapter 17, page 246: Courtesy of The Jim Henson Company. All Rights Reserved. Photo: Richard Termine.

Chapter 18, page 262: Courtesy of The Jim Henson Company. All Rights Reserved.

Chapter 19, page 280: Courtesy of the Jerry Nelson estate. Photo: Jerry Nelson.

Chapter 20, page 290: Courtesy of Victor DiNapoli. Photo: Victor DiNapoli.

INDEX

ABOUT THE AUTHOR

JESSICA MAX STEIN has been a New York–based writer since the early 1990s. Her writing has been cited in the *New York Times,* received an Amy Award for young writers from *Poets and Writers* magazine, and won an Ippie for Best Editorial from the Independent Press Association, as well as being published widely. She is a former editor and current reporter at New York newspaper *The Indypendent,* and a former coeditor of the Jewish feminist journal *Bridges.* Her book proposal for *Funny Boy* was shortlisted by the Biographers International Organization for its 2016 Hazel Rowley Prize. She teaches writing and literature at Hunter College of the City University of New York (CUNY).